SHAPING AIR TRANSPORT IN ASIA PACIFIC

T0298746

Shaping Air Transport in Asia Pacific

TAE HOON OUM
The University of British Columbia
Vancouver, Canada

CHUNYAN YU
The University of British Columbia
Vancouver, Canada

Routledge
Taylor & Francis Group

LONDON AND NEW YORK

First published 2000 by Ashgate Publishing

Reissued 2019 by Routledge
2 Park Square, Milton Park, Abingdon, Oxon, OX14 4RN
52 Vanderbilt Avenue, New York, NY 10017

Routledge is an imprint of the Taylor & Francis Group, an informa business

Publisher's Note
The publisher has gone to great lengths to ensure the quality of this reprint but points out that some imperfections in the original copies may be apparent.

Disclaimer
The publisher has made every effort to trace copyright holders and welcomes correspondence from those they have been unable to contact.

A Library of Congress record exists under LC control number:

ISBN 13: 978-1-138-70476-3 (hbk)
ISBN 13: 978-1-138-70474-9 (pbk)
ISBN 13: 978-1-315-20257-0 (ebk)

Contents

List of Exhibits

About the Authors

Tae Hoon (Tae) Oum, MBA, PhD
Dr. Oum is UPS Foundation Professor of Management, Faculty of Commerce and Business Administration, The University of British Columbia, Vancouver, Canada. Prior to joining UBC in 1983, he taught at School of Business, Queen's University at Kingston, Canada. He was also a Visiting Professor at Osaka University, Korea Transport Institute, and Shanghai Jiaotong University. Towards the later stage of writing this book, Tae Oum was the Albert Winsemius Visiting Professor at Nanyang Business School, Nanyang Technological University, Singapore.

Dr.Oum specializes in policy analysis, demand modelling, cost and productivity analysis, globalization and competitiveness issues of transportation and telecommunications industry. He has published and edited over 20 books and several major conference proceedings, published over 100 papers in academic and business journals, have written numerous research reports for Canadian and foreign government agencies, major corporations, and the World Bank on the transportation and telecommunications policy and management topics. He has also advised many Canadian and other government agencies, major airlines, and telecommunications firms in North America, Asia and Europe.

He is the president of the Air Transport Research Group (ATRG) of the World Conference on Transport Research (WCTR) Society. He is an Editor of *Journal of Transport Economics and Policy*, and serves on the Editorial Boards of *Transport Policy, Journal of Air Transport Management, Journal of Air Transportation World Wide, Transportation Research E, Journal of Air Transport World Wide, International Journal of Maritime Economics*. He is also a member of International Advisory Group (IAG) of the Pacific Economic Co-operation Council (PECC).

Chunyan Yu, Msc (Business Administration), PhD
Dr. Yu is a post-doctoral research associate at the Faculty of Commerce and Business Administration, The University of British Columbia. She specializes in productivity and efficiency analysis, cost structures and other industrial organization issues, and public policy analysis involving transportation industries. She has published a number of papers in various international journals. She has conducted a number of applied econometric research projects on air and rail transportation industries including a report

to the Royal Commission on Passenger Transportation, Canada. She has written her PhD dissertation entitled, "Alternative Methods of Efficiency Measurement, and Applications to Transportation Industry" (University of British Colubmia, Vancouver, Canada: 1995).

Preface

During the 1980's and 1990's, strong economic growth led to rapid increase in the demand for air travel in Asia Pacific, sustaining annual growth rates in excess of 10 percent. There were wide expectations that the Asia Pacific would be the engine of growth for the world's travel industry well into the 21st century. It was predicted that the demand for air travel in Asia Pacific would grow by 7.4 percent per annum between 1995 and 2010, twice the rate that was forecasted for the rest of the world. Also, by the year 2014, over half of all air passenger movements would be associated with travel to, from and within the Asia Pacific. The prospects for the aviation sector in the Asia Pacific appeared to be excellent, and confident airlines and airports embarked on expansion plans. 'Growth' was the driving force setting the agenda for policy makers, and governments allowed the private sector to participate in aviation in a broad scope through privatization and formation of new airlines.

During this period, major institutional, regulatory, and structural changes occurred in the international air transport industry. The most significant change was the formation of open skies continental blocs in Europe and North America. Major carriers in Europe and the United States have made tremendous efforts to penetrate the Asia Pacific market through negotiations of open skies and/or 'liberal bilateral' agreements and formation of strategic alliances. These developments have made significant impact on the aviation industry and air carriers in the Asia Pacific, and led governments and airlines to face increasing competition in international airline markets. The major challenges that governments and airlines are facing include how to deal with the U.S. and European mega carriers' attempt to align with multiple partner airlines in Asia; how to maintain cost competitiveness relative to non-Asian carriers while dealing with the rapidly rising input prices, currency appreciation, etc.; how to deal with the rising consumer power and declining airline yields; and how to balance between the need for liberalization in order to develop hub airports and the historically perceived need to protect flag carriers. On top of these challenges, the recent economic crisis has led to the emergence of a host of new challenges: currency devaluation, and sharp fall in Asia's wealth and international purchasing power, etc. All these have resulted in the substantial decline in air travel and freight transport demand.

There are a number of books on the airline industry in Asia Pacific. They are mostly proceedings of theme oriented conferences, with articles examining various aspects of the air transport markets in the region. The main aim of this book is to provide a comprehensive assessment of the current markets and outlook for the industry in the Asia Pacific region. It also examines options for improvement and development of the regulatory system and industry structure which will draw on experiences from both within and outside the region. The short and long term effects of the current economic crisis on Asian airlines and air transport markets are also discussed. During the past few years, we exerted significant efforts to understand current problems and issues in the airline industry through consulting/advising major airlines and government agencies, interviewing airline executives, participating in industry and academic conferences, communicating with practitioners and researchers in the field, and through published materials and information, etc. Tae Oum and his colleagues have written numerous monographs, research reports and papers on the related topics. This book draws on many of these reports and papers, but covers a wider range of issues to appeal to a broader audience.

We hope to target this book to airline managers, government policy makers and regulators, academic and industry researchers, especially those with a special interest in the Asia Pacific. The book could also serve as a reference for graduate and undergraduate courses on air transport, transport in general, international regulations and organizations such as ICAO and IATA, consultants, and others who are interested in airlines or airline industry. The book could also be of interests to those who have business and trade interests in the Asia Pacific region since air transport is an integral part of the trade and economic development in the region.

We gratefully acknowledge that during the course of writing this book we benefited significantly from past and on-going studies that Tae Oum conducted with his colleagues, including Anthony Chin, Martin Dresner, David Gillen, Richard Harris, Paul Hooper, Jong Hur, Michael Z. F. Li, Hideki Murakami, Jong-Hun Park, Bill Waters, Anming Zhang, and Yimin Zhang. We are grateful to Nozomu Takahashi for his comments and suggestions on earlier version of this book. We also would like to express appreciation for the benefits we received from the discussions on Asia Pacific aviation issues with Namsik Cho, Chi-Ming Feng, Christopher Findlay, Il Soo Jun, Yoon Hyung Kim, Gun Young Lee, Tae Won Lee, Kyung Sup Lee, Young Hyeck Lee, Duk Woo Nam, Yun Keun Pang, Karmgit Singh, Hirotak Yamauchi, and Soo Gil Young, and to acknowledge the competent research assistance of Alex Chan, Kevin

Cheng, Joanne Ferreira, Anne Park, and Angelica Sparolin. The continuous financial supports by Social Science and Humanities Research Council (SSHRC) of Canada through research grants to Tae Oum are gratefully acknowledged.

The views expressed in this book are those of the authors and should not be ascribed to those persons or organizations whose assistance is acknowledged.

Tae Hoon Oum and Chunyan Yu
Vancouver, Canada

1 Introduction

The airline industry is vital for the Asia Pacific economies. An increasingly large portion of high value products and intra-regional and inter-continental trade and business rely on air transport services. The volume of international scheduled air passenger traffic in the Asia Pacific reached over 135 million passengers in 1995, and is expected to increase to nearly 400 million passengers by year 2010 (IATA, 1997). As a results of high economic growth, and as many countries relax control on foreign exchange spending and travel restriction, the Asia Pacific region has recorded the highest air traffic growth rates in the world during the last twenty years. Despite the recent economic crisis in Asia, the high economic growth and air traffic growth will resume within a few years.

The single European aviation market, which came into existence on April 1, 1997, has begun to shape the structure of European airlines and their networks as it brings major changes to the European air transport market. Also, the United States and Canada signed their open skies agreement in February 1995, and the U.S. and Mexico signed one of the most liberalized bilateral air service agreements in 1988. As a result of the essentially North American open skies arrangement, the North American continental airline networks are being formed, using the U.S. super-hubs as the basis for traffic collection and distribution. On the other hand, the air transport markets in the Asia Pacific region continue to be fragmented by national boundaries, thus limiting the airlines' options for network development in the region.

On inter-continental front, the U.S. has been promoting 'open skies' agreements with *individual* nations in Europe. After signing its first open skies agreement with the Netherlands in 1992, the U.S. had managed to strike similar 'open skies' arrangements with nine other European Union nations (Belgium, Luxembourg, Sweden, Norway, Denmark, Austria, Switzerland, Iceland, and Finland) by the end of 1995. In February of 1996, the U.S. also persuaded Germany on board, to sign an 'open skies' agreement. Although the U.S. government is mandated by law to promote competition in the international air transport markets, it is also an important strategic move to secure U.S. carriers' advantage in Europe, by indirectly disturbing the collective actions of the EU nations on international air transport matters. Having succeeded in Europe, the U.S. shifted its focus to

1

Asia in 1996 in pursuit of similar strategies towards Asian countries. The U.S. has already signed open skies agreements with Singapore, Brunei, Malaysia, New Zealand, Taiwan, Korea and Pakistan. In March 1998, Japan signed a substantially liberalized air treaty with the U.S. via which the 'incumbent' U.S. carriers (United, Northwest and FedEx) were reaffirmed their unlimited fifth freedom rights beyond Japan, which was stipulated in the 1952 U.S.-Japan Air Service Agreement while other U.S. carriers doubled their access to Japan. China has recently signed a somewhat liberalized agreement with the U.S. The U.S. strategy will help its carriers continue to play leading roles in the global air transport market.

Although the international airline markets have been substantially liberalized over the last fifteen years or so, it is impossible for a carrier to set up an efficient traffic collection/distribution system in a foreign territory or foreign continent. Therefore, from the early 1990s, most major carriers have been developing their global service networks via strategic alliances with major carriers in other continents that have fairly complete continental coverage. However, a foreign carrier, when seeking to expand its global network, would need to align with more than one Asia Pacific carriers to effectively cover the entire Asia Pacific region. This poses a strategic challenge to all Asian carriers because it is difficult for them to cooperate with other Asian carriers within a global alliance family while competing with each other in intra-Asian markets.

Thanks to the earlier deregulation and introduction of competition, during the last two decades the U.S. airlines have been able to set up efficient hub-and-spoke airline networks, improved operational efficiencies, and managed input prices effectively. As a result, they have become the most efficient carriers in the world (see Oum and Yu, 1998). European airlines have also been busy in setting up efficient service network, and improving operational efficiency.

On the other hand, the airlines based in the Asia Pacific region have relied heavily on their lower input prices to compete in the international market. Until the recent Asian economic crisis, these carriers have been losing fairly steadily their input price advantages vis-a-vis the U.S. and European carriers because of the rapid income growth, general inflation and exchange rate appreciation in those countries. Experts are unanimous that Asian economies will recover its high growth mode within a few years. When the high growth returns, however, the airlines in those countries are likely to face the similar problems they were facing prior to the economic crisis: rapid increase in input prices.

During the last decade or so, most of the Asia Pacific countries have reorganized their airline industries by deregulating or liberalizing their domestic markets, increasing the number of carriers in the market place, and privatizing national carriers. For example, Japan allowed All Nippon Airways (ANA) and some small carriers to enter the international markets to compete with Japan Airlines (JAL). In Korea, Asiana was allowed to enter both the domestic and international markets in competition with Korean Air. The Chinese government divided the Civil Aviation Administration of China (CAAC) into six trunk carriers, and allowed a large number of regional carriers to enter the market. Australia deregulated its domestic markets and privatized and merged the two national carriers (Australian and Qantas). The pluralization of air transport industry creates both consumer and carrier pressures for the liberalization of airline markets.

Most of the Asia Pacific countries have attempted to develop continental super-hubs within their respective territories. All of the new large scale airports such as Hong Kong International Airport (Chek Lap Kok), Seoul's Inchon, Shanghai's Pudong, Osaka's Kansai, Taipei's CKS airport, Singapore, Bangkok, and Kuala Lumpur, are attempting to become the super-hub of the region. This poses a considerable dilemma for the governments in Asia. Developing a regional super-hub airport in a country necessitates the government to liberalize its bilateral air treaties with as many countries as possible, and allow many foreign carriers to build mini-hubs at the airport. However, this means that the government will no longer be able to protect its own flag carriers from competition with aggressive foreign carriers.

These internal and external factors are likely to bring major changes to the Asia Pacific air transport industry, and the air transport policies of the governments. The main objectives of this book, therefore, are to examine the factors that make changes inevitable, to predict what is likely to happen as a result of such changes, and to suggest what can be done by both airline management and governments in order to improve anticipated outcomes. In the process, we will also examine what changes have occurred so far in the air transport industry in Asia as a result of the recent economic crisis in Asia, and what are the likely impacts of the economic crisis on air transport scenes in the long run. Throughout the book, Asia Pacific refers to the entire Asia and South Pacific. However, our focus will be on Northeast Asia, Southeast Asia, and South Pacific.

In order to accomplish the objectives, the rest of this book is organized as follows. Chapter 2 describes the current status and future prospects of the air transport markets in the Asia Pacific region. In this chapter, the past, present and future traffic growth in the Asia Pacific region are compared with those of the European and North American markets. Chapters 3 and 4 review the development of the airline industry and major carriers in selected countries in Northeast Asia, Southeast Asia, and South Pacific. Chapter 5 discusses the current regulatory approaches in

Asian countries and points out their major flaws.

Chapter 6 focuses on the issues and problems associated with liberalizing air transport markets in the Asia Pacific. It also provides a brief overview of international air services regulation, bilateral air treaties, and some liberalization initiatives including 'open skies' agreements by the United States and creation of a single European market. Chapter 6 also examines what the U.S. open skies initiatives mean to the Asia Pacific airlines and governments.

Chapter 7 discusses external and internal challenges that the Asia Pacific airlines and governments are currently confronting, including the process of global alliance network formation and diminishing input price advantages. It also discusses the approaches to liberalization of the Asia Pacific air transport markets.

Chapter 8 examines the current and future airport capacity issues and the logistic hub development efforts of the Asian governments. The short-run impacts and long run consequences of the recent economic crisis in Asia are examined in Chapter 9. Finally, Chapter 10 presents a short summary and conclusion.

2 Current Status and Future Prospects of Air Transport Market in Asia Pacific

In 1998, the Asia Pacific region accounted for 20.8 percent of the world's total air passenger volume, 21.8 percent of the world's total revenue passenger kilometres, and 31.5 percent of the world's total freight tonne-kilometres.[1] This chapter reviews the region's traffic growth over the last two decades, and discusses its growth potentials and its future importance in the world air transport market.

2.1 Past, Present and Future Traffic Growth

The Asia Pacific market has enjoyed the highest growth in commercial air traffic over the past two decades. Exhibit 2-1 shows that Asia Pacific airlines' international traffic experienced average growth of 12.1 percent per year over the 1991-1997 period. During the same period, traffic grew at an average of 11.6 percent per year for European airlines, and 5.7 percent for U.S. carriers (Boeing, 1998). In early 1997, IATA forecasted that Asia-Pacific passenger traffic would grow 7.4 percent per annum between 1995 and 2010, more than twice as high as the growth rate for the rest of the world (3.4 percent). In terms of volume, IATA expects that international scheduled passenger traffic in Asia-Pacific will grow from 112 million passengers in 1993 to 200 million in 2000, and further to 398 million by 2010 (see Exhibit 2-2). Two thirds of this will be travel within the region. Asia-Pacific's share of worldwide international scheduled traffic increased from 26.2 percent in 1985 to 36.2 percent in 1995 and was forecasted to reach 49.8 percent by 2010 (Exhibit 2-3). However, a successive wave of financial and economic turbulence since 1997 has significantly affected the current level of profitability and prospective growth for carriers based in the region. Consequently, IATA has revised its passenger forecast for the 1997-2002 period to reflect the impact of the economic crisis (IATA, 1998).[2] The revised estimates suggest a reduction in the 1997-2002 average growth rates for Asia-Pacific traffic, from 7.7 percent to 4.4 percent for passengers and 9 percent to 6.5 percent for cargo traffic.

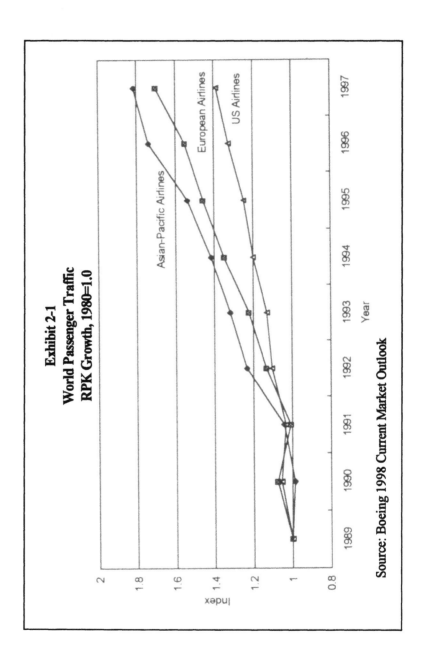

Exhibit 2-1
World Passenger Traffic
RPK Growth, 1980=1.0

Source: Boeing 1998 Current Market Outlook

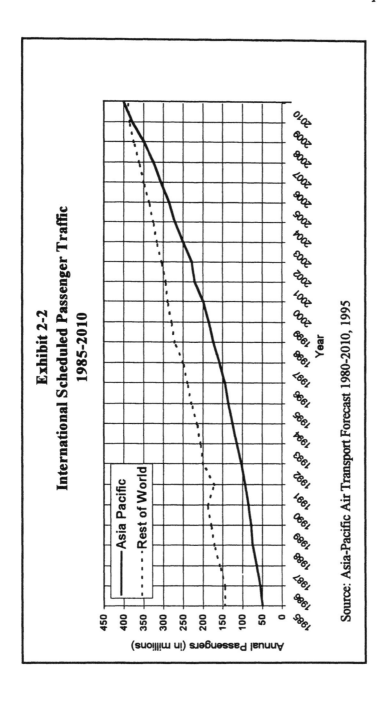

Exhibit 2-2
International Scheduled Passenger Traffic
1985-2010

Source: Asia-Pacific Air Transport Forecast 1980–2010, 1995

Exhibit 2-3
Asia-Pacific Share of Total World
International Scheduled Passengers

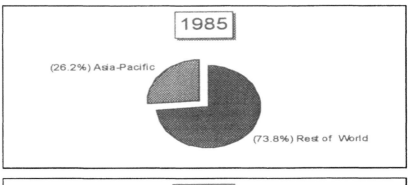

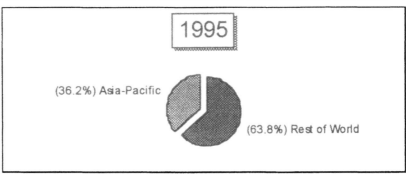

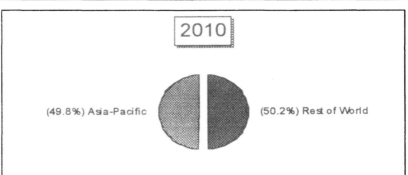

Source: Asia-Pacific Air Transport Forecast: 1980-2010. Geneva: IATA, 1997

According to early IATA forecast, Asia Pacific's economies will be similar in size to North America or Europe by 2010, and will account for one half of the world's international air travel. Normally, short-term economic downturns do not alter long term growth forecast in a significant way. However, the current Asian crisis has gone beyond a normal business cycle. The growth lost during the downturn is unlikely to be recovered fully, and forecasts for future growth are somewhat reduced. Asia's revised GDP forecast for 2018 is almost 16 percent lower than the forecasts before the crisis (Boeing, 1999). GDP growth accounts for two-thirds of air travel growth. Trends of increasing trade, lower airfares, and more flights explain the other third. Air travel growth is expected to exceed GDP growth. Accordingly, Boeing expects air traffic in the Asia Pacific region to grow faster than average despite their current economic difficulties. Within Asia Pacific, total air travel is expected to grow at an average rate of 8.0 percent per year in the next 10 years for China, 6.0 percent for Northeast Asia, and 6.4 percent for Southeast Asia (see Exhibit 2-4).[3] Further, as shown in Exhibit 2-5, Asia-Pacific's fast-growing economies are nearly twice as important in growth as they are in current volumes of air travel. For example, China accounted for 4.2 percent of the world's revenue passenger kilometers (RPK) in 1998, but will contribute to 8.1 percent of expected RPK growth over the next 10 years. Although some inaccuracies are bound to exist in forecasting demands, given the phase of economic growth and population size in the region, it is fairly certain that the Asia Pacific region will become the most important airline market in the world by 2010.

The reasons behind the rapid growth leading to 1997 include strong economic growth in the region and thus, increased personal disposable income; relaxation of travel restrictions (mainly in Korea and Taiwan); and air transport reform/liberalization (even though it is still in its early stages). Unfortunately, the economic boom came to an abrupt end in the middle of 1997 as the region headed to a dramatic economic downturn. In 1998, the effects of the Asian crisis on the real economy deepened significantly. Declining consumer confidence exaggerated the impact of the financial turmoil. Domestic and international traffic growth evaporated from Asia, and overall traffic fell by 7.6 percent (Boeing, 1999). Some regional flow volumes declined substantially. Southeast Asia traffic fell by 20 percent, airlines reacted by slashing capacity, moving airplanes to intercontinental routes where feasible, and selling or parking excess airplanes. With most regional economies in sharp recession, fare reductions had only limited ability to prop up load factors. Capacity reductions did not keep pace with traffic declines. Thus, airlines in the Asia Pacific region experienced the

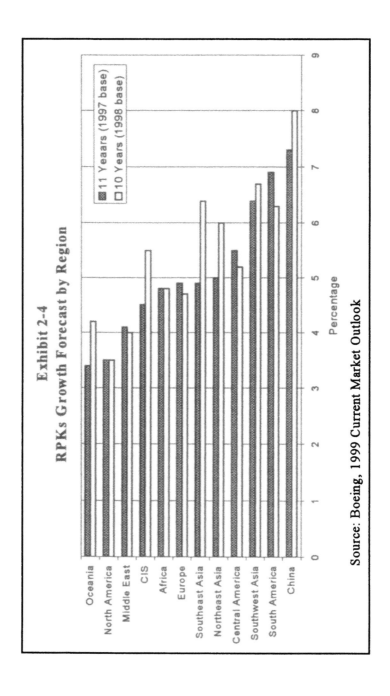

Exhibit 2-4
RPKs Growth Forecast by Region

Source: Boeing, 1999 Current Market Outlook

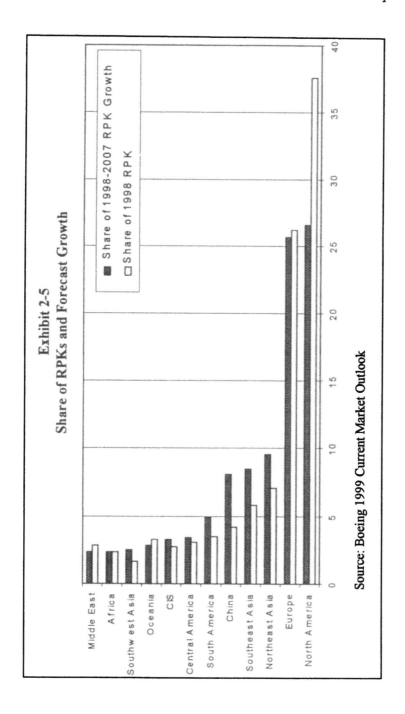

Exhibit 2-5
Share of RPKs and Forecast Growth

Source: Boeing 1999 Current Market Outlook

worst of all worlds: both yields and load factors declining simultaneously.

Despite the current economic crisis in Asia, the long-term economic growth in Asian countries, intensification of intra-regional trade, and continuing air transport liberalization will sustain Asia-Pacific's high traffic growth in the future, especially in countries with large travel potential but low traffic bases at present, such as China. Asia Pacific's importance in the world's aviation industry is expected to increase beyond the year 2010 because its nations are at varying stages of economic development. In 1997, for example, in terms of Purchasing Power Parity, GDP per-capita was $1,600 in India, $3,200 in the Philippines, $3,460 in China, and $4,600 in Indonesia, while it was $13,700 in South Korea, $24,500 in Japan, $24,600 in Singapore, and $26,800 in Hong Kong.[4] As growth of airline markets in economically advanced countries slow down, airline demands in currently developing and less developed countries are expected to increase faster, sustaining growth of air traffic to, from and within the Asia Pacific region.[5]

2.2 Nature of the Airline Industry in Asia Pacific and Future Prospects

Even with the fastest growing aviation market, Asia's major airlines have remained relatively small in terms of network size, traffic volume, and operating revenue, as compared to major U.S. and European carriers (see Exhibit 2-6). One reason is that growth of Asian carriers has been severely limited by restrictive bilateral agreements. In addition, most Asian airline networks are concentrated at one airport in the carrier's home country, resulting in inefficient operations and traffic collection/distribution. Until now, airlines have passed the cost of these inefficiencies onto their passengers, most being their own nationals. Prices for intra-Asia travels and those originating from Asia have typically been higher than those originating outside Asia. These countries are in fact penalizing their own nationals (passengers) and benefiting foreign carriers by keeping air fares higher than would prevail in a competitive market.

In most Asian countries, airline policy decisions are made through consultations between governments and air carriers. The consumer has no voice. However, as economies and middle income brackets grow, governments and the industry cannot continue to ignore consumer interests. After all, a major objective of airline policy is to enhance the interests of consumers, that is, a nation's generalpublic. As economies grow, and social and economic systems become more democratic, passengers will demand lower fares and a wider variety of improved services. Internal and external forces will increase competition in Asia's airline industry. This increased

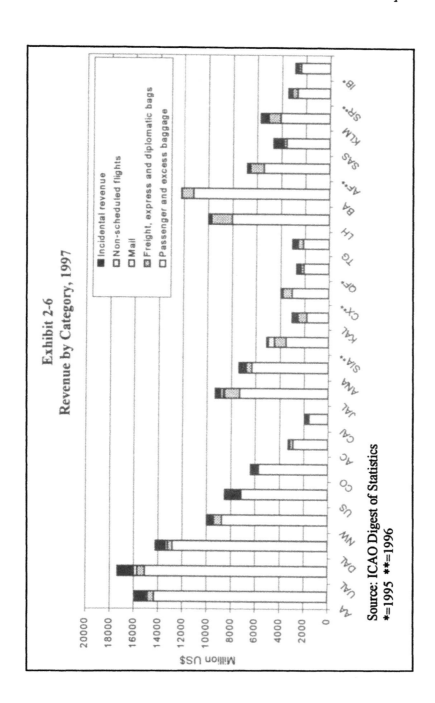

Exhibit 2-6
Revenue by Category, 1997

Source: ICAO Digest of Statistics
*=1995 **=1996

competition will put enormous downward pressure on fares charged by Asian carriers.   So far, most Asian carriers are getting away with substantial directional fare differentials (the practice of charging higher fares to intercontinental passengers originating travel in Asia).   There are also substantial fare differentials between North Pacific and North Atlantic routes, even after removing effects of the differences in average stage length and traffic density (Dresner and Tretheway, 1992).[6]   The ability to charge higher fares is clearly a major reason why North American and European carriers are eager to expand services into Asia.   However, Exhibit 2-7 shows that the average yield per passenger-miles measured in real terms (worldwide) has declined about 2.2 percent per year over the last two decades (Boeing, 1997).   Airfares to, from and within Asia are likely to decrease faster than in North America or Europe because their fares are traditionally higher.

Asian carriers (except Japanese carriers) currently enjoy cost competitiveness relative to their North American and European counterparts, mainly because of lower input (particularly labour) prices, see Exhibits 2-8a, 2-8b, and 2-8c. However, this unit cost advantage will diminish rapidly as input prices increase faster in most parts of Asia (especially NICs) relative to North America and Europe (Oum and Yu, 1998).   Oum and Yu (1998) show that on average, Asian carriers were about 4 percent less efficient than the U.S. carriers in 1993 (Exhibit 2-9). We do not have such comprehensive measures for more recent years at this point.   However, simple productivity measures, namely revenue passengers per employee and revenue passenger kilometres per employee, which are commonly used by industry analysts, indicate that there is still a gap between the Asian carriers and the U.S. carriers.   Exhibit 2-10 shows that in 1995, Asian carriers achieved an average productivity of 925 passengers per employee, as compared to 1,219 passengers for the North American carriers. This labour productivity improved to 996 and 1,269 passengers per employee in 1997, respectively.   Similarly, Exhibit 2-11 shows that in terms of revenue passenger kilometres per employee, Asian carriers achieved an average productivity of 1.89 million RPK/employee in 1995 and 1.90 in 1997, compared to 1.93 million and 2.01 million for the North American carriers.   While the gap in terms of passengers per employee appears to have reduced slightly, the gap in terms of revenue passengers kilometres per employee has more than doubled.   In addition, it is noted that there is a larger dispersion among the Asian carriers than that among the North American carriers. Passengers per employee ranges from 165 for Air India to 3,319 for Japan Air Systems (JAS) in 1997, while RPK per employee ranges from 340,000 for Indian Airlines to 2.65 million for JAS. These measures indicate that there is still a considerable distance for the Asian

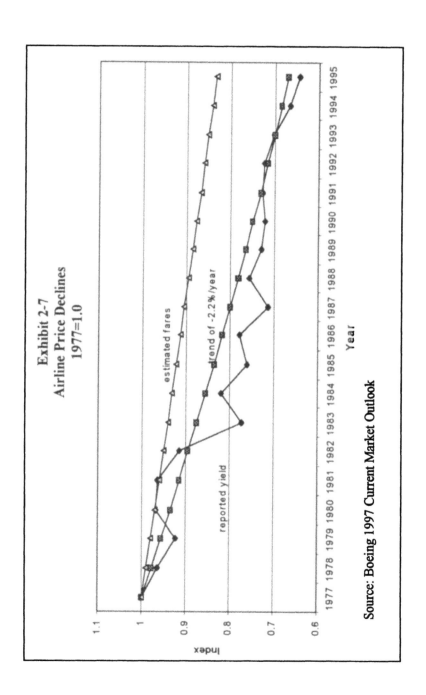

Exhibit 2-7
Airline Price Declines
1977=1.0

Source: Boeing 1997 Current Market Outlook

Exhibit 2-8a
Labour Price Index

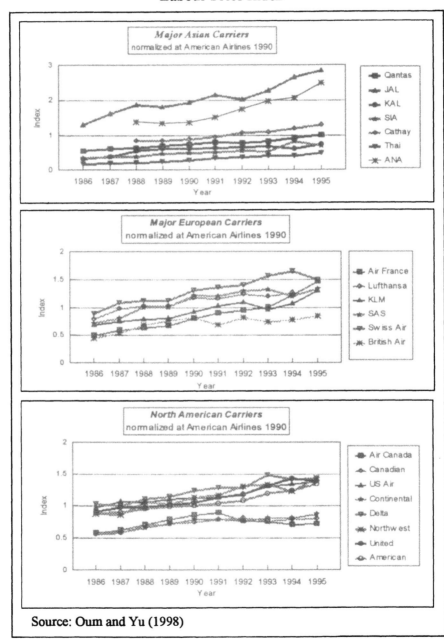

Source: Oum and Yu (1998)

Exhibit 2-8b
Non-Labour Price Index

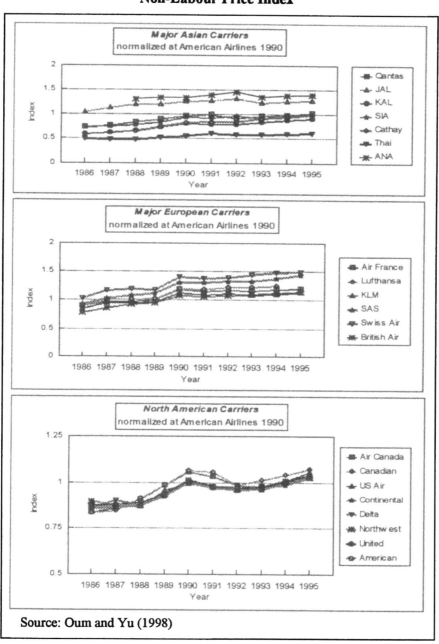

Source: Oum and Yu (1998)

Exhibit 2-8c
Total Input Price Index

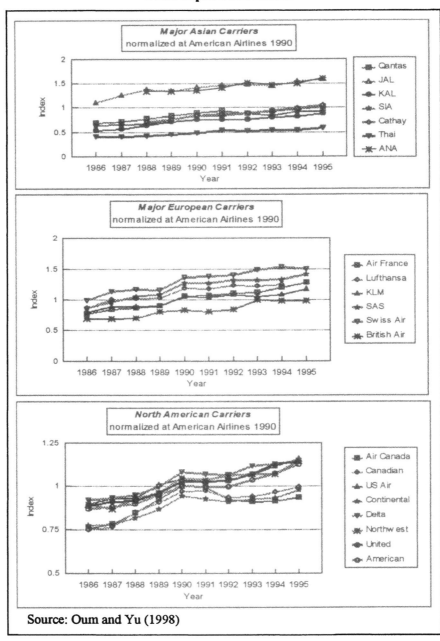

Source: Oum and Yu (1998)

Exhibit 2-9
Residual Total Factor Productivity Index

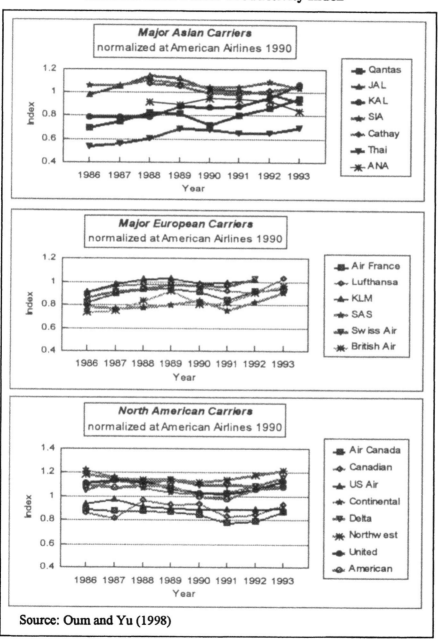

Source: Oum and Yu (1998)

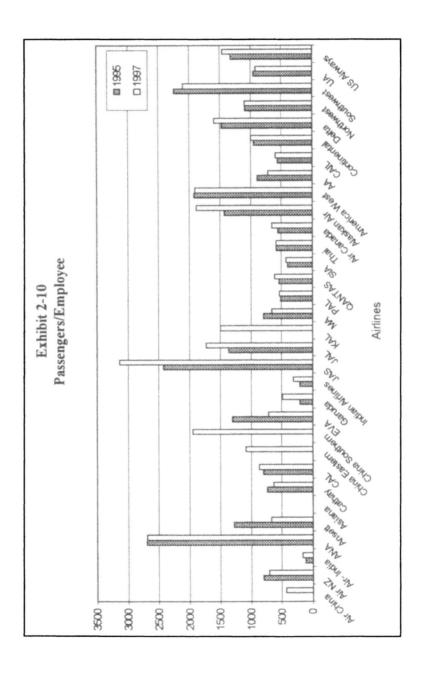

Exhibit 2-10
Passengers/Employee

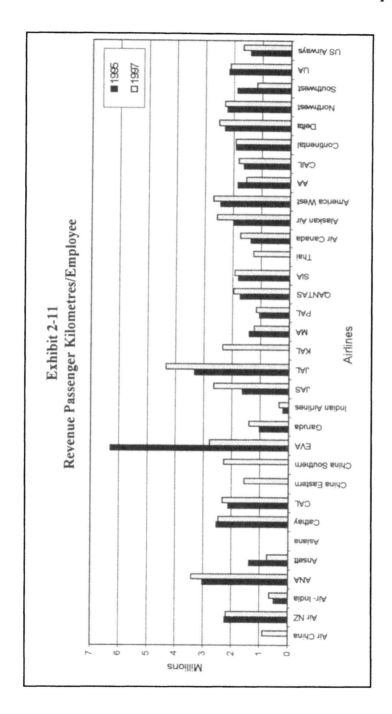

Exhibit 2-11
Revenue Passenger Kilometres/Employee

carriers to catch up with their North American counterparts, and to become truly competitive. It is important to point out that these are partial measures, which do not truly reflect the overall productivity of the airlines. High labour productivity may come at the expense of low productivity of other inputs.   Moreover, the output measure used here is not a comprehensive measure of the true total economic output; an obvious omission is the cargo output.   Also, Asian carriers' productivity is over-estimated as compared to the U.S. carriers if one considers that Asian carriers generally have long haul flights. As input prices are expected to increase faster for Asian carriers than for U.S. carriers, Asian carriers' unit costs may approach or even exceed those of U.S. carriers in the long run.

For a long time, Asian carriers have been able to enjoy low input prices and relatively high output prices. These two factors have helped keep many Asian carriers profitable despite their low productivity and efficiency.   However, input prices have been rising fast in Asia than in other parts of the world, and increasing competition has brought tremendous downward pressures on the yields. The recent economic crisis has further highlighted this pressure, thus forces the airlines to improve their productivity and to cut costs. Exhibit 2-12 shows that Asian carriers still enjoy a slightly higher revenue per employee ($214,000) than North American carriers ($194,000), primarily because of higher output prices. However, this advantage is disappearing rapidly, as Asian carriers try to retain their market shares under strong competitive pressures from both within and outside the region. For example, in 1998 many airlines reported double digit decline in yield.[7] In fact, the yield picture could very likely be reversed if 1998 statistics were used.

The recent economic crisis has forced the carriers to realize that there are serious problems with their operations, and changes are inevitable in order to survive and remain competitive in this increasingly competitive industry.   Many carriers have since undertaken, sometimes painful, restructuring to improve efficiency.   For example, Japan Airlines is undertaking a restructuring plan to quicken its decision-making. Part of the plan is to reduce the number of its full-time directors to 13 from the current 28 and appoint 10 new executive directors.[8] The airline will gradually transfer operations on its Southeast Asia, Oceania and Pacific resort routes to its international flight unit, Japan Air Charter, which will receive full airline status in October 1999. JAL will transfer short-hop domestic flights to JAL Express, another unit. The moves are aimed at enhancing cost competitiveness. Japan Airlines also plans to raise its marketing capability by developing an integrated group sales system. The company is aiming for pre-tax profit of 30 billion yen every year through fiscal 2001 to pay stable dividends. At the same time, ANA will set up a holding company and cut

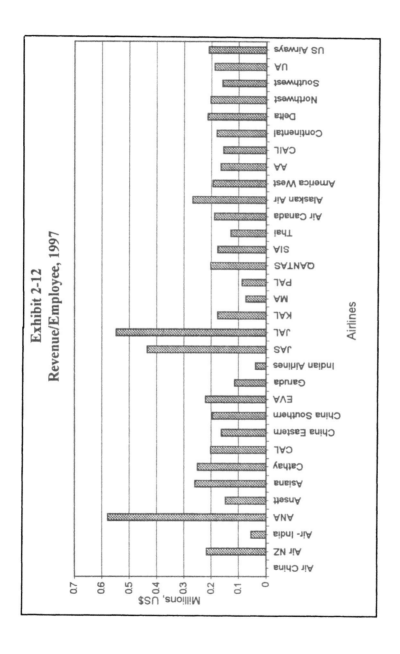

Exhibit 2-12
Revenue/Employee, 1997

its group work force by 10 percent as part of its medium-term business plan. The holding company will likely to be set up in 2000, and will plan airline group overall operations and handle accounting and finance. It will also oversee All Nippon Airways, Air Nippon Co (ANK), and sales companies as wholly owned subsidiaries. ANA aims to reduce parent-company debt by 17 percent over four years to about 610 billion yen, to reduce lease liabilities by 30 percent and to procure 10 aircraft instead of the 19 planned. The airline will also restructure its hotel operations and sales arms, strengthening cooperation with ANK.

One good thing about the economic crisis is that it has served as a survivability test for the carriers in Asia Pacific. It sorted out the weaker, inefficient players while the strong became stronger. The carriers that were overburdened with debt or (inefficient) management suffered the most, while those who did the right thing at the right time have had an easier time to minimize its negative impacts. Some, such as Singapore Airlines, even attempted to take advantage of the softer market conditions and the Asian crisis to expand and grow. Instead of retrenching, Singapore Airlines continues to explore strategic opportunities in a number of markets, such as Thailand, India, and South Africa, to create a truly global network, and to help consolidate its position as a world leader in the air travel market.

Although many Asia Pacific carriers are facing a difficult time, the future looks bright. According to the latest IATA forecasts, air traffic will grow at an average annual growth rate of 4.5 percent during 1998-2002 in Northeast Asia, and 4.4 percent in Southeast Asia. Indeed, Northeast Asia actually had a -1.6 percent growth rate in 1998 and Southeast Asia grew by just 0.6 percent. China's average annual growth is expected to tumble from earlier predictions of 14 percent to 8.8 percent. These forecasts are considerably lower than that made before the economic crisis. However, there are signs of recovery. Air passenger traffic has made an upturn later in 1998, and continues into 1999. For example, there has been an 11.4 percent increase in passenger traffic and 8.5 percent increase in cargo traffic at Singapore's Changi Airport in the first quarter of 1999, bouncing back to the 1997 levels. There is optimism that many regional economies are bottoming out; thus some countries start to resume new construction and major expansion projects which have been put on hold because of the economic crisis. For example, Thailand recently announced plans to resume the construction of its planned second international airport in Bangkok.

The above discussions indicate that there is a tough road ahead for most of the Asian carriers to establish themselves as viable players in the global air transport market. However, there are many untapped markets in the region with great growing potentials, and the countries have learnt a valuable lesson from the present economic turmoil and are expected to regain some of the high economic growth experienced before 1997. It is important for the carriers to strategically position themselves in their traditional markets and beyond.

2.3 Fifth Freedom Traffic in Asia

Despite the fact that Asian countries do not have a liberalized air transport regime, these countries have granted substantial 5th freedom rights to foreign carriers, particularly to U.S. carriers. They also negotiated for some 5th freedom traffic opportunities between themselves. As a result, fifth freedom traffic accounts for a substantial portion of total traffic handled at major Asian airports.

Singapore and Bangkok are the busiest fifth freedom hubs in the region. Singapore hosts the most intra-Asian fifth freedom sectors, while Bangkok has the most overall[9] (see Knibb, 1994). Both are strategically located as gateways to and from the Indian subcontinent, Middle East, and Europe, and straddle the Kangaroo Route between Australia and Europe. Together they account for a third of all fifth freedom flights within Asia. Kuala Lumpur, by contrast, hosts fewer fifth freedoms than most Asian capitals largely because of its proximity to Singapore.

Hong Kong and Tokyo are the next busiest fifth freedom hubs. They can be compared in the same way as Singapore and Bangkok, in that Hong Kong[10] has a few more intra-Asian fifth freedom sectors than Tokyo, but Tokyo has more total fifth freedoms. Together they account for over a quarter of all fifth freedom flights within Asia. Geographically, Hong Kong is the crossroads between east and Southeast Asia, while Tokyo is the stopover between Asia and North America. Both continue to carry out these respective roles with some reluctance. Consequently, Taipei, which sits between, benefits from the congestion in both Hong Kong and Tokyo. Singapore Airlines and Malaysia Airlines stop en route to North America; U.S. carriers stop en route to Thailand. Taiwan actively promotes Chiang Kai Shek airport as a regional hub. As a result, Asian carriers have more fifth freedom sectors through Taipei than any other Asian airport: half the airport's fifth freedom flights are to Hong Kong or Seoul. Seoul is the other Tokyo bypass for flights to and from North America. Three U.S. carriers (United, Northwest and Delta) hub in Seoul; a fourth (American) is studying the prospect. Thai Airways and SIA use Seoul as a stopover on their flights to North America. Now that Korea and Taiwan are both open skies partners with the U.S., more U.S. carriers have fifth freedom access to the rest of Asia. The new U.S.-Japan aviation accord somewhat reduces fifth freedom tensions, but such freedoms beyond Japan are still available only to U.S. incumbent carriers and are limited by Japan's slot restricted airports.

Most fifth freedom sectors within Asia are actually operated by Asian carriers. Asian airlines operate 31 per cent of all fifth freedom sectors within Asia, and 58 per cent of all such sectors beyond Asia. They trade fifth freedom rights with their neighbours. U.S. carriers operate 30 per cent of all fifth freedom sectors within Asia - nearly as many as Asian airlines. U.S. airlines dominate Tokyo and have major hubs at Seoul and Taipei. European carriers operate 19 per cent of the fifth freedom sectors within Asia, but they do not rely heavily on fifth freedom traffic. Carriers from the Indian subcontinent, the Middle East, Australia, and New Zealand aggregate another 19 per cent of Asia's fifth freedom sectors. Throughout Asia, fifth freedom flights account for a quarter to half of all frequencies on those routes where they are permitted. The average for fifth freedom sectors out of Tokyo, for example, is 29 per cent.

Exhibit 2-13 shows 1993 intra-regional 5th freedom traffic volumes at twelve major airports in the Asia-Pacific region. Fifth freedom traffic varies greatly among the airports. It ranges from 60,000 passengers at Kuala Lumpur to 2.3 million passengers at Tokyo. Tokyo, Singapore and Bangkok had the strongest intra-regional 5th freedom traffic volume. However, in terms of 5th freedom traffic as a percentage of total sector traffic, Seoul and Bangkok were the leaders. In 1993, 5th freedom traffic accounted for 27 percent of sector traffic at Seoul and Bangkok, but only 2 percent at Kuala Lumpur.

2.4   Summary

Asia Pacific's air transport market has experienced tremendous growth during the past two decades. Demand for air travel in the Asia-Pacific region is growing faster than in any other world region. During the 1991-1997 period, Asia-Pacific airlines achieved international traffic growth of 12.1 percent per year. Over the same period, European scheduled airlines experienced annual system-wide growth of 11.6 percent, while system traffic of U.S. airlines grew at 5.7 percent per year. In early 1997, IATA forecasted that air passenger traffic in Asia Pacific will grow at 7.4 percent per annum between 1995 and 2010, more than twice as high as the growth rate for rest of the world (3.4 percent). Asia-Pacific's share of worldwide

Exhibit 2-13
Intra-Regional Fifth Freedom Traffic, 1993

Airports	Total Sectors	Sectors with 5th Freedom Capacity	5th Freedom Passenger Traffic (000)	5th Freedom Share of Sector Traffic
Auckland	9	4	464	23%
Bangkok	13	10	1,865	27%
Hong Kong	13	7	1,232	10%
Jakarta	12	5	255	9%
Kuala Lumpur	12	2	60	2%
Manila	12	4	275	10%
Osaka	7	2	160	6%
Seoul	11	4	1,425	27%
Singapore	13	8	1,527	14%
Sydney/Melbourne	12	5	840	20%
Taipei	12	4	1,300	14%
Tokyo	12	6	2,315	24%
Total			**11,718**	

Source: IATA, 1995

international scheduled traffic increased from 26.2 percent in 1985 to 36.2 percent in 1995 and is forecasted to reach 49.8 percent by 2010. By 2010, there will be 1.1 billion passengers travelling to, from and within Asia-Pacific. This is almost equivalent to the worldwide passenger traffic total in 1995. In light of the recent economic crisis, this forecast needs to be adjusted.

The reasons behind this rapid growth leading to 1997 include strong economic growth in the region, thus increased personal disposable income; relaxation of travel restrictions (mainly Korea and Taiwan); and air transport reform/liberalization (even though still in early stages). Despite the economic crisis, the long-term economic growth in Asian countries, intensification of intra-regional trade, and continuing air transport liberalization will sustain Asia Pacific's high traffic growth in the future, especially with countries with large travel potential but low traffic bases at present, such as China, Indonesia and Vietnam.

Total scheduled international traffic to, from and within the Asia-Pacific region amounted to 134 million passengers in 1995, and is forecasted to triple to 393 million passengers by 2010. In 1995, 65 percent of the traffic was recorded within the region. This percentage will increase to 68 percent by 2010. Most of this traffic concentrates within Northeast Asia and between Northeast Asia and Southeast Asia. Moreover, the strongest sub-regional growth for the next two decades is forecasted to be within Northeast Asia followed by Southeast Asia. Air traffic in Northeast is predicted to grow from 92 million passengers in 1993 to 325 million in 2010. And international traffic between Northeast Asia and the rest of the region will amount to 109 million passengers by 2010, representing 41 percent of total traffic within the whole of Asia-Pacific.

Substantial fifth freedom rights have been granted to foreign carriers by Asian countries. These rights have mainly been granted to U.S. carriers, but some intra-Asian rights have been negotiated. Singapore and Bangkok together comprise the largest share of fifth freedom flights within Asia, accounting for 36 percent of all fifth freedom traffic. About 31 percent of fifth freedom sectors within Asia are operated by Asian airlines. U.S. carriers closely follow Asian airlines by operating 30 percent of these sectors. Moreover, large variations exist for 5th freedom traffic among the airports. In 1993, Kuala Lumpur handled 60,000 passengers while Tokyo dealt with 2.3 million passengers for intra-regional traffic. Other cities that experienced strong intra-regional fifth freedom traffic volume include Bangkok, Singapore, Seoul, Taipei, and Hong Kong.

Despite the dramatic growth of the aviation market during the last two decades, major airlines in the Asia Pacific region are still relatively small in terms of network size, traffic volume, and operating revenue, as compared to major U.S. and European carriers. They also lag behind the U.S. carriers in terms of productivity and efficiency. With their traditional advantage of low input cost starting to diminish, carriers in the region need to explore strategic opportunities in all potential markets in efforts to establish their positions in the increasingly globalizing air transport market. However, many parts of the region are still in the early stage of development with large potential travel base, such as China, Indonesia, and Vietnam. The air traffic in the region is expected to recover from the current economic crisis, and to grow at a higher rate than other regions of the world.

Notes

[1]   *Air Transport World*, July, 1998.
[2]   IATA's 20 year forecast has not been updated.
[3]   Note that traffic growth rates with a 1998 base can seem misleading because of the deep drops in traffic in the base-year Asia flows.

[4] *CIA World Factbook* 1998.

[5] Both Boeing and Airbus are targeting Asia as the most important region to sell their aircraft in the future.

[6] Oum, Park and Zhang (1996) show that air fares on Asia-Oceania routes are estimated to be about $406 higher than Asia-North America routes, while it is about $211 higher than America-Oceania routes, even after removing effects of distance and travel volumes on fares.

[7] Li (1999) shows an average of 10 percent decline in yield.

[8] 'JAL to Implement Management Reform from April', *Asia Pulse*, March 17, 1999.

[9] Forty per cent of Bangkok's fifth freedom flights start or end in Singapore or Hong Kong.

[10] Code-sharing is only permitted under the Hong Kong - Switzerland and Hong Kong - Vietnam bilaterals, for airlines from other countries, the only way to use Hong Kong as a regional hub is through fifth freedom (Feldman, 1999).

3 Aviation Development in Northeast Asia

Northeast Asia has played an important role in the economic and social development of the Asia Pacific region, and in the global context. Air transport is essential in facilitating the movement of people and goods between countries in the region. Air transport market in Northeast Asia has grown faster than any other world region during the past two decades, both in terms of passengers and cargo. It now accounts for 11.5 percent of the global market. Five Northeast Asian airports are ranked in the top 20 in the world in terms of passenger volume in 1998. Among the Northeast Asian countries, Japan, China, South Korea, Taiwan and Hong Kong hold the key to the shaping of the air transport system in the region in terms of geography and population. Their air transport markets will play an important role in determining the network patterns that Northeast Asian carriers will need to set up in the future. This chapter discusses the development of air transport industry in these countries as well as their major carriers.

Exhibit 3-1a shows the IATA forecasts of scheduled international passenger volumes for countries in Northeast Asia, while Exhibit 3-1b illustrates forecasts of traffic growth rates for the same countries. In light of the Asian economic crisis, these forecast will likely be overestimated. The long term country specific traffic forecast updated after the Asian crisis is not available to us at this point, however, the most recent Boeing forecast indicates that the revised forecast of the Asia's GDP for the year 2018 is about 16 percent lower than the forecast conducted before the economic crisis (Boeing, 1999). Most of the reduction in GDP growth forecast occurs due to negative and/or lower growth in the 1997-2001 period. Boeing's most recent forecast indicates that air traffic in Northeast Asia will grow at an average annual rate of 6 percent over the next 10 years.

Japan accounted for 32 percent and 31 percent of total Asia-Pacific scheduled international passengers in 1985 and 1993, respectively. Japan's share is expected to decrease further to 23 percent in 2010, as Japan's aviation markets become mature. However, air transport markets in other Asian countries are still in their growth stages. The number of scheduled international passengers in Japan is expected to increase from 35 million in 1993 to 91 million in 2010, and Japan will be the second largest aviation

31

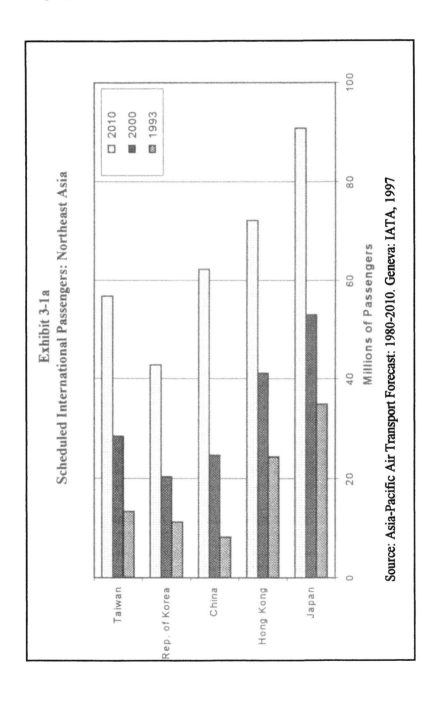

Exhibit 3-1a

Scheduled International Passengers: Northeast Asia

Source: Asia-Pacific Air Transport Forecast: 1980-2010. Geneva: IATA, 1997

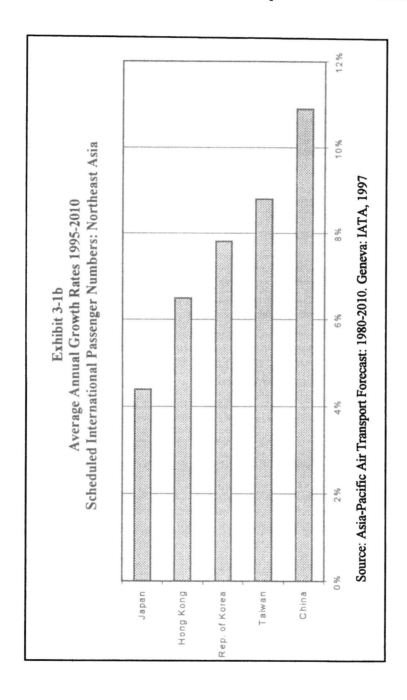

Exhibit 3-1b
Average Annual Growth Rates 1995-2010
Scheduled International Passenger Numbers: Northeast Asia

Source: **Asia-Pacific Air Transport Forecast: 1980-2010.** Geneva: IATA, 1997

market in the region, falling behind the combined volume of China and Hong Kong.

China's aviation industry has expanded at an average annual growth rate of 20.6 percent during the last 15 years, and its scheduled domestic and international flights have increased nearly five-fold in the same period. China's market is forecasted to grow much faster than most other Asian countries: 8.3 million scheduled international passengers in 1993 to 62.3 million in 2010, an average growth of 12.6 percent per annum. Hong Kong's traffic is forecasted to grow from 24.4 million scheduled international passengers in 1993 to 72.3 million in 2010, average growth of 6.6 percent per annum.[1] Although it is difficult to believe that Hong Kong's traffic will grow so dramatically, it is clear that China and Hong Kong together will become the largest aviation market in Asia: their combined traffic is forecast to grow from 37.7 million passengers in 1995 to 133 million by 2010.

Taiwan's air traffic is predicted to grow from 13.5 million in 1993 to 56.8 million in 2010, while air traffic in Korea is to grow from 11.3 million in 1993 to 42.8 million in 2010. Together, the Northeast Asian market will become increasingly important as a source of and destination for air travel, accounting for one half of all intercontinental trips to or from the Asia Pacific. It is predicted to grow from 92 million passengers in 1993 to 325 million in 2010 (6.8 percent annual growth). Naturally, Northeast Asia is a very important and high growth market.

3.1   Japan

The Air Transport Market

Due to Japan's strong economic growth, the strength of its currency, and commercial expansion overseas, international business and leisure travel increased very rapidly until the early 1990s. As a result, total international scheduled passenger traffic in and out of Japan increased at an average annual rate of 9.8 percent between 1985 and 1993, reaching nearly 35 million passengers in 1993. This further increased to nearly 38 million passengers in 1996. Traffic to/from Japan accounts for close to 20 percent of revenue for most Asia Pacific carriers (Jones, 1998). International traffic in Japan is highly concentrated at four major airports, Narita, Haneda, Kansai and Itami. In 1996, the four airports handled 82 percent of all international traffic to/from Japan.[2] However, a growing share of the international traffic is handled at regional airports to alleviate congestion at major airports. Since the number of air visitor arrivals increased much slower than traffic originating from Japan between 1985 and 1993, it was essentially the outgoing Japanese travel market that contributed to the past strong growth in airline passenger traffic (IATA, 1995). See Exhibit 3-2 for a time-series illustration of incoming and outgoing Japanese traffic. It can be seen that the number of foreigners visiting Japan was less than one-third the number of Japanese going abroad. In 1996, the number of foreign visitors was 3.8 million, compared to 16.7 million Japanese going abroad. Japan's outbound passenger travel has been shifting in character since the Japanese economic slowdown in the early 1990s. Corporate travel has weakened significantly, while the leisure market has undergone a structural shift towards individual travel instead of tour groups. This provides cheaper tickets and a broader choice of destinations, and has led to the falling demand for flights to expensive destinations such as Hong Kong. Nevertheless, the United States remains as the top destination for Japanese overseas travellers. There were close to 5 million passengers travelling from Japan to the U.S. in 1998.

According to early IATA forecast, total international scheduled passenger traffic to and from Japan is expected to reach 91 million by 2010 (IATA, 1997). The council for civil aviation, 'Koku Shingikai', of the Japanese government published its own forecast for air traffic as follows:

	1989	*1997*	*2000 (E)*
Domestic			
Passenger (million)	60.12	82.1	103.0 (+17%)
Cargo (000' MT)	661	833	1,250 (+32%)
International			
Passenger (million)	29.94	46.5	57 (+27%)
Cargo (000' MT)	1,518	2,231	3,100 (+29%)

By 1998, there were more than 2,291 weekly scheduled direct flights between Japan and major cities around the world, including 722 to/from North and South America, 247 to/from Europe, 285 to/from Korea, 213 to/from Hong Kong, and 145 to/from mainland China. According to the most recent IATA forecast, international scheduled passenger traffic to/from Japan will grow at an average annual rate of 4.1 percent over the 1998-2002 period, and reach 55.5 million by 2002 (IATA, 1998).

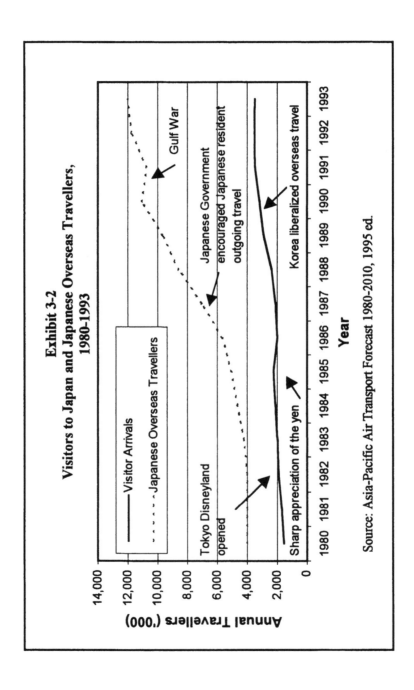

Exhibit 3-2
Visitors to Japan and Japanese Overseas Travellers,
1980-1993

Source: Asia-Pacific Air Transport Forecast 1980-2010, 1995 ed.

Development of Major Carriers

Japan's first airline enterprise, the Nippon Koku Yuso Kenkyujo (NKYK), or the Japan Air Transport Research Institute (JATRI), came into existence on June 4, 1922 with ten Yokosho floatplanes. NKYK began its first regular air service on November 12, 1922 over the route Sakai (a suburb of Osaka) to Tokushima, across Osaka Bay on the island of Shikoku. By the end of first year, NKYK had carried only 27 passengers and 1107 kg of cargo, while under the support of government subsidy. Throughout the 1920s, several other pioneering air transport enterprises started air transport operations as well.[3] Since then, the Japanese airline industry experienced dramatic changes during the pre-war and the Second War periods, and a five-year total ban on aviation after the War. The present airline industry was born during the 1950s.

Japan Air Lines Japan Air Lines Company (JAL) was formed as a private company on August 1, 1951, and started its flight on October 25, from Tokyo to Osaka, with leased aircraft. On August 1, 1953, JAL was designated as the sole international airline of Japan. Consequently, JAL was reorganized on October 1, 1953, and the Japanese government held half of the new Japan Air Lines Company LTD's shareholdings. Four months later, JAL's first trans-Pacific flight began from Tokyo to San Francisco, via Wake Island and Honolulu. Since then, Japan Air Lines has undergone steady expansions: routes to Southeast Asia during the second half of 1950s, to Europe in the early 1960s, and subsequently to Australia and South America. It is noteworthy that no Japanese airman was allowed to pilot the JAL aircraft when JAL first started its operation, by September 1955, all domestic flights were flown by Japanese crew, while foreign pilots and aircrew operated most of the international services. By 1982, JAL was still employing as many as 200 foreign pilots.

In November 1987, Japan Air Lines was privatized, and the government sold its 34.5 percent shareholding on December 15 of the same year. Japan Air Lines became Japan Airlines. JAL now employs 19,682 people, and a total of 137 aircraft. It serves 25 domestic cities and 74 foreign airports in 31 countries and territories. In the 1998 fiscal year, JAL carried 31.6 million passengers and 839,646 tons of cargo. It posted a net profit of 26 billion yen (US$220 million) in the year, compared with a net loss of 94.2 billion yen for the preceding year. This includes a 15 billion non-operating profit from sales of aircraft and other factors. However, overall revenue fell 5 percent to 1.15 trillion yen. Total passenger traffic on international flights increased by 1 percent, but first and business class passenger fell. It experienced lower demand on its European, Pacific and Southeast Asian routes. This depressed passenger revenue by 7.5 percent. Domestic passenger revenue fell by 5 percent due to lower fares. Operating profit dipped 23 percent to 24 billion yen. Lower fuel costs and cuts in the salaries of pilots and cabin crew failed to offset the fall in revenues.

JAL is a high cost carrier; it had a 38 percent cost disadvantage relative to American Airlines in 1993 (Oum and Yu, 1998). With a total of US$ 9.5 billion debt, JAL announced its cost restructuring plan in April 98 to reduce costs by 10 percent by 2001. The plan includes cutting 2,300 ground jobs to reduce the staff to 17,000. The economic crisis has forced JAL to trim some Asian frequencies, but it has boosted services to North America. JAL has entered extensive alliance agreements with members of the OneWorld alliance group, and has code-sharing alliances with Swissair on Osaka and Tokyo to Zurich.

All Nippon Airways All Nippon Airways (ANA) came into existence on March 1, 1958 as a result of the merger of Japan Helicopter and Aeroplane Transport Company, usually known as Nippeli, and Far Eastern Airlines. Both Nippleli and Far Eastern were regional feeder carriers.   After the merger, ANA started to upgrade itself, and began trunk route operations a year later. However, ANA still focused on the feeder routes, and undertook measures to fully explore the opportunities in its designated market.[4] During the first half of the 1960s, All Nippon Airways was able to maintain an incredible rate of traffic growth: an average annual growth rate of 54 percent for passenger traffic and 46 percent for cargo traffic over the 1960-1964 period. This high growth rate reflected the astonishing rate of growth the Japanese economy enjoyed as a whole.

With the economic boom, a number of small companies started to enter the airline industry. All Nippon Airways quickly recognized that these small airlines could usefully co-operate with the larger airlines such as itself, in a manner that was strikingly similar to today's alliances. On August 22, 1962, ANA entered its first cooperative agreement with TOA Airways, an airline based at Hiroshima and specialized in routes in Kyushu and to the Ryukyu Islands to the southwest. Less than a month later, ANA signed similar agreements with Central Japan Airlines (Naka Nihon Koku) and Nagasaki airlines, as well. ANA later transferred some of its lesser routes on the fringes of its 'beam' network to TOA. As the expansion proceeded, All Nippon Airways also purchased some small airlines to strengthen its position, Fujita Airlines in August 1963, Naka Nihon Koku in January 1965, Nasagaki Airways in December 1967, and Yokohama Airlines in October 1970. While these co-operative agreements and takeovers were undoubtedly beneficial to ANA, the process was encouraged by the Japanese civil aviation authorities as well. The authorities were concerned about the safety standards of the small airlines. In addition, the merger and acquisition would make it easier for the authorities to monitor and enforce regulations.

ANA continued steady growth in the 1970s, its network covering essentially the entire Japan. However, the domestic market was close to saturation, there was no more room for further growth. All Nippon Airways' real potential growth could only come from the international market. In June 1970, ANA was given permission to operate shore-range international routes. Its first international flight started on July 25 with a charter flight from Fukuoka to Pusan, Korea. ANA's international charter services flourished in Southeast Asia during the 1970s, and by the mid-1970s, flights were leaving almost every day. Between 1971 and 1978, All Nippon Airways carried more than half a million Japanese tourists to more than half a dozen destinations. Then in April 1981, ANA was given permission to operate charter services to Guam and Saipan.

In September 1978, ANA founded Nippon Air Cargo Lines in partnership with four shipping companies. In November of the same year, Nippon Air Cargo Lines applied for a licence to operate scheduled air cargo services. Early in 1984, Nippon Air Cargo Lines was renamed as Nippon Cargo Airlines (NCA), and applied for a license to fly to the United States. NCA was given permission to fly to San Francisco and New York, and started its first trans-Pacific services in May 1985.[5]

On March 3, 1986, ANA opened its first scheduled international route, to Guam. This was followed four months later by routes from Tokyo to Los Angeles and Washington, D.C. During the next four years, ANA opened twenty new international routes (including the first three). On January 1, 1989, All Nippon Airways joined the International Air Transport Association.

Today, ANA employs 15,200 people, and has a fleet of 168 aircraft. ANA accounts for about half of Japan's domestic air travel markets, and flies to 30 foreign destinations. It carried 46.2 million passengers in the 1997-1998 fiscal year, and ranked 7th among IATA member airlines in 1997 in terms of passenger volume. ANA has signed a marketing agreement with SAS and is to become a full member in the Star Alliance in October 1999.

Like JAL, ANA is also a high cost carrier. It had a 40 percent unit cost disadvantage relative to American Airlines in 1993 (Oum and Yu, 1998). ANA lost US$20 million in the fiscal year 1997-98, compared with

US$ 30 million net profit a year earlier. It has implemented a three-year cost-cutting plan, but the results have been below expectations because of a dispute with pilots' union remaining unresolved since 1996. Its cost cutting plan include hiring freeze and senior staff salary reductions, and job cuts of 700 or 4.6 percent of workforce in administration through attrition. Because of the economic crisis, ANA has increased services to North America, while cutting some Asian frequencies. In addition, it has lowered domestic fares by half to maintain its market share.

3.2   Korea

The Air Transport Market

Korean civil aviation industry was negligible over the period of 1948 to 1969 because of the Korean War, political turmoil, and poor economic growth. During this period, international air transport was provided mostly by a number of foreign carriers, including Northwest Airlines, Japan Airlines, and Cathay Pacific (Lee, 1997). The following 25 years, 1970-1995, however, saw the rapid growth of the Korean airline industry, thanks to the strong Korean economy and the aggressive expansion of the airlines. Domestic air traffic grew at an average annual rate of 14.2 percent over the 1975 to 1995 period, and international air traffic achieved an average annual growth rate of 21.5 percent during the same period.   Total international passenger traffic in and out of Korea grew from 457 million RPKs in 1970 (Lee, 1997), to 63,161 million RPKs in 1997 (IATA, 1998). The growth of international air arrivals in Korea was particularly dramatic in the late 1980s, spurred by the 1988 Olympic Games (Ahn and Ahmed, 1994). The number of foreign visitors increased from 84,216 in 1967 to 4.3 million in 1998.[6] The result was an increased number of carriers operating flights to Seoul.   By 1997, major international airlines were conducting over 766 scheduled direct or non-stop flights per week between Seoul and major cities in North America, South America, Europe, North Africa, the Middle East and Asia.   Today, Korea has air service agreements with 72 countries: 23 in the Asia-Pacific region, 9 in the Middle East, 9 in Africa, 24 in Europe and 7 in North and South America.

   Korea's aviation industry has maintained rapid growth in recent years, due mainly to the country's rising economic power and relaxed regulations on overseas travel by Koreans.[7]   Since most international travellers arrive in and depart from Korea by air, Korea's travel industry relies almost entirely on the ability of airlines to negotiate routes, upgrade equipment, and meet demands for travel[8].   As a result, the Korean government broke up flag carrier *Korean Air*'s monopoly by designating a new carrier, *Asiana* in 1988.[9] By August 1997, Asiana operated 44 international routes (Korean Air 74). Increased competition between Korean Air and Asiana, and their competitive entry in new international routes, has further facilitated the increased demand for outbound travel. Korean Air and Asiana together now serve 85 cities in various parts of the world, and in 1996, carried more than 16.1 million passengers on their international flights.

In order to handle Korea's rapidly growing international air traffic better, the Government has made large investments in improving airport facilities. A dedicated international air terminal was developed at Kimpo Airport in Seoul in 1980. The terminal was built to accommodate 4.8 million passengers and 320,000 tons of cargo annually. As part of Olympics preparations, a new 4,000m runway was built to handle the upsurge in flights. Despite these expansions, Kimpo Airport, with a capacity of 16.5 million passengers and 1,500,000 tons of cargo annually, reportedly reached its peak capacity in 1995.[10] To relieve congestion at Kimpo Airport,[11] a new airport, named Inchon International, is being constructed on Yeongjong Island, about 50 kilometers west of Seoul.

Early IATA forecast (IATA, 1997) predicts that total international scheduled passenger traffic to and from Korea will amount to 42.8 million passengers by 2010. The number of air visitor arrivals is expected to grow less rapidly than airline passenger traffic during the forecast period. This indicates that the Korean resident outgoing travel market is expected to contribute to a larger share of sustained growth in international passenger traffic. This forecast did not foresee the subsequent economic crisis and the severity of its impact on the air travel industry. Korea is one of the hardest hit countries by this crisis. As a result, Korean out-bound traffic declined by 40.5 percent in 1998, while international visitor arrivals to Korea during 1998 were up 8.7 percent over 1997. The most recent IATA 5-year passenger forecast indicates that Korea's international scheduled traffic will grow 4.0 percent in 1999, 6.1 percent in 2000, 6.5 percent in 2001 and 8.0 percent in 2002, and reach 17.5 million passengers in 2002 (IATA, 1998).

The Development of Major Carriers

The First Airline In 1949, Korean National Airlines (KNA) began operation with a fleet of three Stinson Voyagers, providing services to four coastal points. KNA's operation was soon interrupted by the Korean War. Early in 1952, KNA resumed its commercial services, and replaced the

Stinsons with DC-3s. Later in the year, under an agreement with Civil Air Transport (CAT) in Taiwan, KNA started its first international route, Seoul-Iwakuni-Tokyo, with aircraft chartered from Taiwan. By July 1959, KNA had obtained an U.S. foreign air carrier permit to fly to Seattle. Unfortunately, around this time, KNA began running into political and operational troubles. Consequently, it ran into a financial crisis, and was on the verge of bankruptcy. As a result, the Korean government decided to start a new airline.

Korean Air Lines (KAL) was founded on March 3, 1962 to take over Korean National Airlines and its routes. The government had 60 percent of KAL's ownership, the remainder was owned by private investors. Soon after, KAL started to expand its network in East Asia, and became a member of the Orient Airlines Association in September 1966. However, KAL soon run into troubles again, partly because of managerial inexperience in a highly demanding business. Also, there were some recriminations against the idea of government control over an essentially commercial enterprise.

On March 1, 1969, Korean Air Lines was turned over to the Hanjin Group. By this time, the Hanjin Group had already established the Korea Airport Service Company and the Korean Air Terminal Service, providing airline fueling services and ground handling services at all Korean airports. Korean Air Lines was revitalized, and started to move from failure to success. Its regional network was considerably expanded, and its fleet was modernized and augmented. Then, on April 26, 1971, KAL began an all cargo service to Los Angeles. A year later, on April 19, 1972, Korean Air Lines opened full trans-Pacific passenger services from Seoul to Los Angeles via Tokyo and Honolulu with Boeing 707-320c. In October 1973, KAL expanded its network into the European market with an all cargo service to Paris, jointly with Air France. Full passenger services to Paris began on March 14, 1975 via the Polar route. KAL's network was further expanded to the Middle East in May 1976 with a twice-weekly passenger service to Bahrain. KAL's capital was doubled in the mid-1970s due to its explosive growth, reaching to almost 12 billion won by the end of 1976, and then almost doubled again, to 23 billion won by the end of 1978.

KAL continued its growth during the 1980s, adding more routes and purchasing more aircraft. The 1988 Olympic Games and the designation of KAL as the official airline of the games as well as the lifting of restrictions on Korean nationals' overseas air travel on January 1, 1989 further boosted KAL's rapid growth. Korean Air Lines became a respected player in the airline world. At the end of 1989, KAL joined the International Air Transport Association (IATA).

In 1998, Korean Air carried 19.7 million passengers (25.5 million in 1997) and more than one million tons of cargo. The airline now operates 359 flights per week to 74 cities in 27 countries. This translates to an amazing growth of 73 times the number of passengers and 606 times the volume of cargo carried in 1969 (the first year of operation under Hanjin group). Today, Korean Air's fleet includes 112 aircraft, primarily Boeing and Airbus aircraft. It is one of the youngest fleets in the industry with an average age of 7.6 years. Korean Air is implementing plans to reduce the fleet's average age to approximately five years over the next five years. Measured in either passengers or passenger kilometers, Korean Air Lines ranks among the top twenty airlines of the world. Korean Air is also the world's second largest commercial airline cargo carrier in terms of international Freight Ton Kilometers (FTK) (right behind Lufthansa Cargo), carrying more air cargo than UPS.

Despite its remarkable achievement, there have been some shadows cast over KAL's success. Korean Air Lines seems to have a less than desirable reputation for safety, because of a number of infamous disastrous incidents. The most noticeable incidents include the loss of Flight 007 which was shot down by Soviet fighters over the sea of Okhotsk in 1983, killing 269 people; the exploration of a Boeing 707, allegedly caused by a bomb, off the Malaysian coast in 1987, killing 115 people; and the crash of Flight 801 at Guam in 1997, killing 227 people. Undoubtedly, this adverse publicity has had some negative impacts on Korean Air Lines operation. For example, both Air Canada and Delta cancelled their code-sharing alliance with KAL following KAL's most recent crash of a cargo plane in Shanghai in April 1999.[12]

The Second Carrier The dramatically increased demand for air travel as a result of growing affluence and the lifting of travel restrictions toward the end of the 1980s, coupled with the trend towards multi-carrier designations in other countries, led to the formation of Asiana Airlines in February 1988 by the Kum Ho Business Group. Thirty-five percent of the new carrier was owned by the Korean Development Bank. Asiana started its domestic services on December 23, 1988 with six modern Boeing 737-300s leased from the GPA group in Ireland. By April 1990, Asiana had carried three million passengers, adopting a policy of high quality rather than cheap fares and high density. It had begun service to four cities in Japan. Asiana's network was soon expanded into the other markets in Asia. In November 1991, Asiana inaugurated its first trans-Pacific route, Seoul-Los Angeles.

Today, Asiana employs 8000 employees, operates a fleet of 50 aircraft, and serves 14 domestic cities and 36 foreign cities in 15 countries. It carried 8.9 million passengers and 1,805 million tonne kilometres of cargo in 1998.

3.3 China

The Air Transport Market

On the back of vigorous economic growth, China's airline industry has experienced dramatic development since the early 1980s. Between 1980 and 1998, air passenger traffic carried by Chinese airlines increased 16-fold (Exhibit 3-3). According to the Civil Aviation Administration of China (CAAC), Chinese carriers recorded 57.55 million passengers in 1998[13]. CAAC now ranks fifth in the world in terms of passenger volume. Domestic air traffic in China was growing at an estimated 20 percent per year during the 1980-1996 period, despite being hampered by a relatively old air transport fleet.[14]   And according to IATA, total international scheduled passenger traffic to and from China increased from 1.9 million in 1985 to 8.3 million in 1993, an average annual growth rate of 20.5 percent (IATA, 1995). Since 1980, annual growth of China's air transport industry has been 2.2 times that of China's national economy and 4.3 times that of the world air transport industry.[15]   Such spectacular growth, both in domestic and international air traffic, has earned China the world's fastest growing aviation market. The dramatic growth of the Chinese airline industry is, in a large part, attributed to China's general economic growth. Its real GDP increased almost three times from 1980 to 1994, with an average growth rate of 8.7 percent per year, compared with that of 5.8 percent in the 1970s and 4.0 percent in the 1960s. The growth is also attributed to the airline industry reform. As the Chinese people's living standards continue to improve, and the government slowly opens the air travel market and gradually relaxes travel restriction,[16] air passenger traffic, especially out-bound traffic,[17] would continue to grow each year. IATA forecasts that China's international passenger traffic (excluding that of Hong Kong) will grow from 8.3 million in 1993, to 62.3 million in 2010. China's own forecast is even more upbeat than IATA's. According to the CAAC, the aviation sector is targeted to grow at 2.5 times the GNP growth rate over the next few years, or around 20 percent per year. By the end of the century, air transport capacity is to reach 10 billion tonne-kms (Lee, 1993). A report by the Economist Intelligence Unit (EIU) put China in 11th

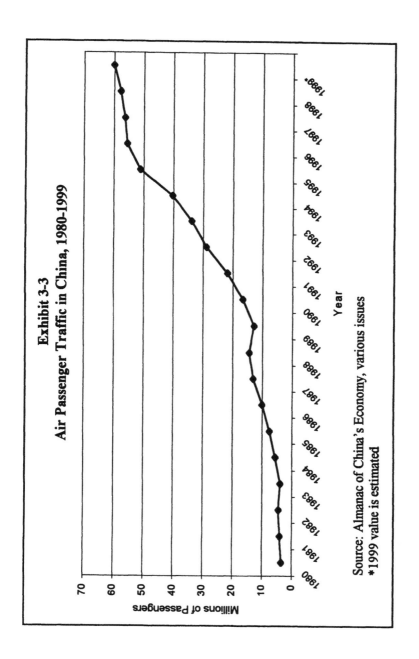

Exhibit 3-3
Air Passenger Traffic in China, 1980-1999

Source: Almanac of China's Economy, various issues
*1999 value is estimated

place as an origin country for regional traffic in 1993. By 2000, the number of air arrivals could rise to 6 million, growing further to a possible 10 million in 2005 (Edwards, 1995). These forecasts were made before the Asian crisis; thus, they may be too optimistic in light of the recent development in the region. Although a more realistic forecast would likely be lower than the above estimates, China is still expected to be a leader in traffic growth in the world. The most recent Boeing forecast expect China to maintain an annual growth rate of 8.1 percent over the next 20 year, compared to the world's average of 4.9 percent (Boeing, 1999). Similarly, IATA forecast indicates that China's international scheduled passengers will grow by 10 percent in 1999, 10.9 percent in 2000, 11 percent in 2001,and 11.3 percent in 2002, reaching 19.2 million passengers in 2002 (IATA, 1998).

In 1993, Chinese carriers operated 492 domestic routes to 109 cities and 58 international routes to 53 cities (Lee, 1993). By November 1995, China had 680 domestic aviation routes linking 134 cities across the country, and 87 international routes linking the country with 56 cities around the world.[18] By the end of 1998, China had 1,122 air routes linking 135 Chinese cities and 65 cities in 31 foreign countries and regions.[19] Despite pressures for rapid capacity growth, China has been trying to curb international capacity growth for fear of Chinese carriers losing out to their foreign counterparts.

Both *Airbus Industrie* and *Boeing* see China as a key market in the next few years. *Boeing* predicts that China will become the world's largest commercial aviation market outside the United States in the next 20 years, and is expected to purchase 1,800 jetliners[20] valued at US$125 billion (RM475 billion).[21] *Airbus Industrie* sees a total of 500 airliners going into China over the next 20 years. This is almost 20 percent of total deliveries forecast for the entire Asia/Pacific region, which itself is the world's fastest growing aviation market.[22] Exhibit 3-4 shows the actual and predicted air traffic in China and Hong Kong, as well as their share in world air travel markets. By 2018, combined air traffic in China and Hong Kong will reach 724.6 billion RPK, or 9.5 percent of the world market.

Since the CAAC split into 6 autonomous carriers in the late 1980s, a score of provincial and independent airlines have emerged as new players (Lee, 1993). This caused a reduction in the relative importance of Air China/CAAC during that period, particularly in Shanghai (IATA, 1995). In 1995, carriers in the CAAC system transported 41.87 million passengers, or 81.8 percent of the air passenger traffic in China. Local and other independent carriers accounted for the other 18.2 percent. According to CAAC, by early 1997, official count of airlines in China reached 37. However, it is estimated there are more than 40 international and domestic

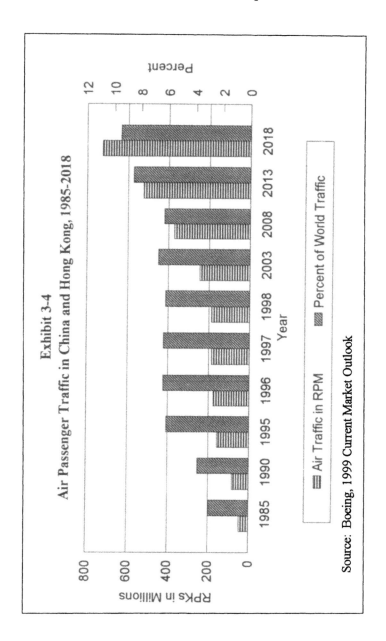

Exhibit 3-4
Air Passenger Traffic in China and Hong Kong, 1985-2018

Source: Boeing, 1999 Current Market Outlook

airlines operating in China.[23] The large number of airlines operating in China has caused some problems, particularly safety concerns.[24] Also, many small local carriers were losing money. These, among other things, led CAAC to limit the pace of airline growth. Accordingly, CAAC has endeavoured to encourage take-overs and mergers and to discourage newcomers. As a result, we have seen that China Northwestern taking control of Nanjing Airlines, China Southwestern merging with Guizhou Airline, and China Eastern acquiring General Aviation Airlines, another CAAC carrier.[25] In 1998, the airlines under CAAC carried 47.5 million passengers, accounting for 82.6 percent of the total passenger volume industry-wide. This slightly increased market share may in part be attributable to the consolidations. The consolidation continues in various forms. Recently, six local carriers, namely, Sichuan, Hainan, Shenzhen, Zhongyuan, Shandong and Wuhan, formed a 'New Star Alliance Group'. Despite this consolidation trend, however, CAAC still faces demands from dozens of regions and cities across the country, all wanting their own carrier.

The large majority of international air travel activity in China is concentrated around the east and Southeast regions (IATA 1995), with Guangdong Province leading China's air transport market. The 6 civilian airports in Guangdong handled 19.7 million passengers and 395,000 tonnes of freight in 1995, with a total of 178,000 aircraft movements. Guangzhou's Baiyun International Airport handled 12.6 million passengers (12.5 million in 1997), the bulk of traffic in the province, and the second largest throughput in China after Beijing.[26] (See Exhibits 3-5a and 3-5b for locations, traffic shares, and volumes handled at Pearl River Delta area airports).

Over the past decade, China's economic growth has stretched the nation's air transport system beyond capacity, even though the system was growing around 20 percent annually during the 1980s and the first half of 1990s.[27] A restrictive factor in China's air transportation growth is its inadequate infrastructure, particularly its airports and air traffic control systems. China built 13 new airports, rebuilt 7 and expanded more than 30 airports during the 1986-1995 period. At present, China has 121 civil airports,[28] not including Hong Kong, of which 31 are registered for international flights. The density of China's airports averages one in every 79,000 square kilometres,[29] far less than other countries.[30] China plans to build 20 feeder airports by the year 2010.[31] This is part of efforts to meet the needs of the rapid development of the national economy, international trade and foreign exchanges as well as tourism.

As discussed above, China's tremendous growth puts severe strain on facilities, personnel, and resources. Almost every aspect of the industry,

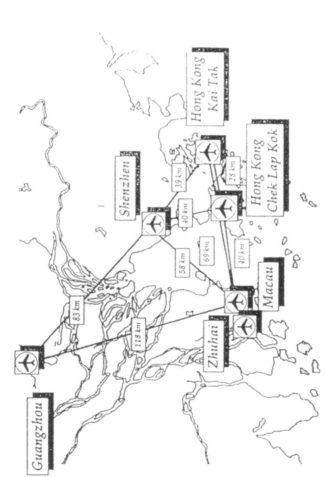

Exhibit 3-5a
Airports in the Pearl River Delta Area

Note: The Hong Kong Kai Tak Airport has been replaced by the new Chek Lap Kok Airport

Source: Asia-Pacific Air Transport Forecast 1980-2010, 1995 ed.

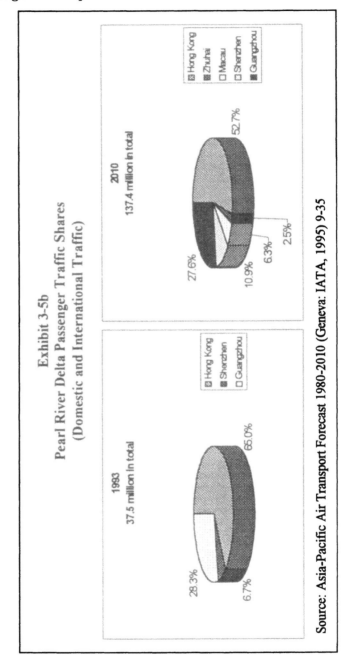

Exhibit 3-5b
Pearl River Delta Passenger Traffic Shares
(Domestic and International Traffic)

Source: Asia-Pacific Air Transport Forecast 1980-2010 (Geneva: IATA, 1995) 9-35

from the upgrading of obsolete air traffic control and ground support systems to the replacement of antiquated reservation methods and the training of inexperienced flight personnel, has to be improved.[32] For this reason, the CAAC has opened China's aviation sector to foreign investment to seek new technology, investment, and management methods.[33] This is at least partially motivated by China's desire to achieve international air transport standards so that Chinese airlines can compete in global markets as well as fulfill domestic demand (Lee, 1993). However, the industry has many challenges, Chinese airlines have poor safety records and reputations for lacklustre service, unreliable schedules, frequent delays, and cancellations due to bad weather (Lee, 1993).

Since 1993, there have been a significant increase in the number of aircraft, from 315 to 485 in 1997 (Chen and Zhang, 1999), consequently, the number of flights have been dramatically increased. By the end of 1998, there were 801 aircraft nation-wide used for transportation and general aviation. This includes 523 transport aircraft, of which 402 are under CAAC. At the same time, there is a slowdown in the growth of air travel in China. The average annual growth rate of air passenger traffic in the mid-1990s was about half of that prior to 1993. As a result, over-capacity is a serious problem in terms of aircraft and available seats. This has led to productivity stagnation during the 1990s in the airline industry (Chen and Zhang, 1999). To retain traffic shares, the airlines engaged in large-scale price wars. However, the price war was not able to reverse the slowdown in traffic growth.[34] In 1998, the Chinese airline industry saw its first collective loss of over RMB 7 billion[35] (about US$843 million), a first loss in 20 years. There is urgency for China's airlines to adapt to the needs of market, and improve efficiency. In addition, even the 'top three' carriers in China are very small by global standards. In 1997, Air China, China Eastern and China Southern, the top three carriers in China, carried 6.46 million, 6.83 million and 15.24 million passengers, respectively. In comparison, American Airlines, United Airlines, and Delta carried 81.0 million, 84.2 million and 101.15 million passengers, respectively, in the same year. Further consolidation of carriers may be needed to achieve economies of scale.

The Development of Major Carriers

China's first airline, China National Aviation Corporation (CNAC), was established on April 12, 1929 with 60 percent U.S. ownership and 40 percent Chinese ownership. CNAC's first objectives were to link Shanghai with Peking (Beijing), Hankow (Hankou), and Canton (Guangdong) by air. Flights were to be operated by Aviation Exploration Inc. of the United States through contract arrangements. Four months later, China Airways Federal Inc was incorporated as a wholly owned subsidiary of Intercontinent Aviation (parent company of Aviation Exploration Inc.) to provide the operations. The strong foreign involvement in both ownership and operations caused a furious protest from many sectors of the Chinese governments. CNAC was denied the use of the existing airfields, and had to use amphibious aircraft to circumvent the restrictions on airfield use. At the same time, the Ministry of Communication imported four Stinson Detroiters, along with two pilots and a mechanic, and created a truly Chinese airline on July 29, 1929, Shanghai-Chengtu Air Mail Line. The newly created airline flew between Shanghai and Nanking (Nanjing), the then Chinese capital, carrying 354 passengers during its first year of service.

On July 8, 1930, CNAC, together with its U.S. partner - China Airways Federal, and Shanghai-Chengtu Air Mail Line, merged to become the new China National Aviation Company. The Chinese government held 55 percent ownership of the new CNAC and China Airways Federal 44 percent. In March 1933, Pan American Airways purchased China Airways Federal, and effectively took over the operations of CNAC.

Almost parallel to the development of CNAC, another airline, Eurasia Aviation Corporation, was created in February 1930 through a joint venture. Chinese interests held two third of the ownership, while Deutsche Lufthansa owned the other third. Eurasia's first route linked Shanghai, Peking, and the border station of the Trans-Siberian Railway at Manchouli in northern Manchuria. Eurasia was able to establish a presence in China during the late 1930s, with a network that challenged CNAC in its influence.

In January 1935, a regional airline was created in the southwest of China, the South-Western Aviation Corporation, with capital from military agencies, civil administration, and merchants. A little over a year later, South-Western became the first airline in China which operated an international route, to Hanoi in French Indo-China (Vietnam).

Civil Aviation Administration of China The Civil Aviation Administration of China (CAAC) was established in March 1954 as China's national flag carrier by the merger of two airlines, China Civil Aviation Administration and SKOAGA.[36] The new airline was under the general jurisdiction of the China Civil Aviation Bureau. There were six major regional bureaux, at Beijing, Shanghai, Guangzhou, Shenyang, Xi'an, and Wuhan.

By the late 1950s, CAAC had a fleet of over 400 aircraft, almost entirely Soviet designs (most of them built in China), with a network covering the whole country. While a route map and a timetable existed, most flights were made according to local demand, and this was restricted almost entirely to government officials and dignitaries. Traveling in an airplane was out of reach for ordinary citizens.

In the international front, CAAC's first transborder route (other than to the USSR) was opened on April 11, 1956, from Kunming to Rangoon via Mandalay. This was followed by services to Hanoi (May 1956), Pyongyang (April 1959), then to Phnom Penh (1964). CAAC's initial international route network was limited to China's close political allies and friendly neighbours.

Early 1970s was a busy time for CAAC: expanding network, and upgrading and modernizing its fleet with a flurry of orders for new jet aircraft. In April 1973, CAAC inaugurated its first route to Europe, a weekly flight from Beijing to Tirana, Albania, via Teheran and Bucharest. Then, in September 1974, it began services to Tokyo, which was soon followed by the opening of services from Beijing to Paris in October of the same year. Also in October 1974, China joined ICAO as a full member. The second half of the 1970s saw CAAC actively expanding its international route network. In April 1978, a new route to a new continent was opened with services to Addis Ababa (Eithiopia) via Karachi. In May of the same year, it began services to Zurich with a technical stop at Urumchi and a traffic stop at Belgrade. A year later, in May 1979, it began services to Frankfurt, via Teheran and Bucharest. In July of the same year, a direct connection to the Middle East was made with services to Sharjah and Baghdad. CAAC made its first trans-Pacific flights to the United States in October 1980 with a special charter for General Motors. Scheduled flights to San Francisco and New York began in January 1981.

CAAC was considered as a national instrument in carrying out government policies, not as an economic entity. It did not seem to have a mandate for financial responsibility. From 1958 to 1978, China's airline industry incurred fourteen years of financial losses even with the central government's subsidy (Zhang, 1998). There was little commercial air transport. Most air travel was for administrative affairs for various levels of governments and large state-owned enterprises. Air travel for personal purposes was non-existent.

In September 1984, CAAC was decentralized, forming 4 regional airlines, and an autonomous international unit (Air China). Although given more autonomy, the new airlines were still part of the CAAC, which would continue to be responsible for regulatory functions, particularly those affecting airline infrastructure (airways, airports, navigational aids), international bilateral agreements and other aspects that were of a national rather than a regional importance. By the end of 1984, the original four regionals, China Eastern, China Southern, China Southwestern, China Northwestern, had been joined by two others: China Northern and a new China Northwestern based in Xi'an while the original China Northwestern (based in Urumchi) had become China Xinjiang Airlines. During the following few years, the new airlines gradually re-organized themselves, and started to improve operation standards and service quality. Then on July 1, 1988, the airlines officially became independent entities. Around the same time, many new airlines, not hived off from the CAAC, started to enter the air transport market in China. By the end of 1997, there were 43 airlines with a total fleet of 760 operating in China.

The 'Big Three'   The 'Big Three' refers to Air China, China Eastern, and China Southern. They are the only Chinese carriers that provide international services.[37] Air China was formed out of the international division of the CAAC, and operates out of its hub in Beijing. It operates scheduled passenger and cargo services, special and chartered flights and also general aviation. It has a fleet of 64 aircraft, and operates 42 international and regional routes and 61 domestic routes, serving 39 cities in 28 countries and regions and most of the provincial capitals, major cities and tourist attractions in China. It has two subsidiaries in Tianjin and Inner Mongolia. In 1998, Air China carried 6.4 million passengers. China Eastern is the third largest airline in China, and operates out of its hub in Shanghai. It has a fleet of 68 aircraft and flies on more than 120 routes to the U.S., Belgium, Spain, Germany, Japan, South Korea, Thailand, Singapore, Australia, Hong Kong area and some 50 domestic points. In early 1997, China Eastern became the first Chinese carrier to be listed on the stock markets in Hong Kong and New York. It carried 8.4 million passengers in 1998. China Southern Airlines is the largest carrier in China in terms of passenger volume, accounting for over 27 percent of air passenger traffic in China. Like China Eastern, China Southern is listed on the stock markets in Hong Kong and New York. It operates out of its hub in Guangzhou, and serves a total of 328 routes, of which 273 are domestic. China Southern has a fleet of 91 aircraft, most of which are on lease, and operates an average of 2,522 flights per week. In 1998, China Southern carried 15 million passengers.

3.4   Hong Kong

The Air Transport Market

The history of HK airline operations is one of increasingly long haul service. The advent of the Boeing 747-400 and Airbus 340 put Hong Kong within full-load, non-stop range of both Western Europe and the U.S., putting the city at the centre of traffic development in the booming Asia/Pacific region. Meanwhile, there has been tremendous growth in Chinese traffic, increasing the flow of regional passengers via Hong Kong who are candidates for long-haul connections in Hong Kong

Between 1985 and 1993, scheduled passengers to/from Hong Kong increased from 9.3 million to 24.4 million, an average growth rate of 12.7 percent per year. In 1995, 28 million passengers and 1.5 million tonnes of cargo were handled at Kai Tak airport. Kai Tak was the world's third busiest airport in terms of international passengers, after London Heathrow and Frankfurt, and was second in terms of international cargo volume after Tokyo Narita. In 1998, a total of 27.8 million passengers and 1.7 million tonnes of cargo went through Hong Kong's international airports. Hong Kong was ranked 23 among the world's airports in terms of total passenger volume, the only airport among the top 25 airports that handles only international traffic.

Hong Kong is home to three privately owned international airlines: Cathay Pacific, Hong Kong Dragon Airlines, and Air Hong Kong. Together, they provide passenger and cargo services to 67 cities in 31 countries.[38] In 1996, 60 scheduled airlines linked Hong Kong to 99 cities in 41 countries.[39] In addition, between April 1995 and March 1996, 19 non-scheduled carriers operated 1,720 passenger flights and 172 cargo flights to and from Hong Kong, the majority of which were to and from mainland China.

According to IATA, total international passenger traffic to and from Hong Kong is forecast to increase from 24.4 million in 1993 to over 73 million in 2010 (IATA, 1997).[40] The new Hong Kong (Chek Lap Kok) airport has an annual capacity of 87 million passengers and 9 million tonnes of cargo when the two runways are fully operational. Thus, airport capacity will not put any constraint on expected traffic growth. Exhibit 3-6 shows the regional distribution of Hong Kong's air passenger traffic. This exhibit indicates that the strongest traffic growth area will be within the 'Southwest Pacific' region. The most recent IATA forecast expects that Hong Kong's international scheduled passengers will grow 7.5 percent in

Exhibit 3-6
Asia Pacific Traffic to and from Hong Kong (thousands)

	South Asia	Northeast Asia	Southeast Asia	Southwest Pacific	Total Asia-Pacific
1985	161.0	4,305.3	2,924.4	627.7	8,018.4
1986	200.0	4,809.9	3,258.1	678.7	8,946.7
1987	189.1	5,908.8	3,849.0	697.7	10,644.7
1988	185.3	7,801.7	4,305.5	752.0	13,044.6
1989	215.7	8,213.1	4,650.8	791.7	13,871.2
1990	232.4	10,063.5	4,986.6	726.0	16,008.5
1991	240.9	10,373.1	4,961.6	748.6	16,324.1
1992	292.2	12,132.5	5,528.3	821.1	18,774.1
1993	256.1	13,525.8	6,145.4	900.4	20,827.7
1996	401.0	15,086.0	7,732.0	1,340.0	24,559.0
1997	385.0	13,889.0	7,269.0	1,298.0	19,622.0
2002	491.0	18,219.0	8,645.0	1,926.0	29,281.0
2010	774.7	37,387.4	18,963.3	3,480.3	60,605.7

Source: IATA, 1995, 1998.

1999, 7.2 percent in 2000, 7.4 percent in 2001, and 7.8 percent in 2002, reaching 35.2 million in 2002 (IATA, 1998).

Tourism is the second biggest industry in Hong Kong, attracting 9.57 million tourists in 1998. The industry supports 74,100 jobs in Hong Kong or 3.1 per cent of total employment, accounting for 2.8 percent of GDP. It is expected to rise to 352,600 jobs or 3.2 percent of total employment by 2010. The past evaluation of Hong Kong resident outgoing travel shows a smooth trend contrasting with an erratic evolution of incoming visitor arrivals (Exhibit 3-7). IATA believes that the number of air visitor arrivals to Hong Kong will increase at a slightly lower rate than total airport passenger traffic. This means that outgoing resident travel and transfer passenger traffic will grow more rapidly than incoming visitor traffic.

Hong Kong's future hopes for developing an air traffic hub will be significantly influenced by future relations with and between Taiwan and China. The relaxation of travel restrictions imposed on Taiwanese residents in the mid-1980s resulted in a dramatic increase in Taiwanese visitors to Hong Kong (see Exhibit 3-8). In addition, because Taiwan's government prohibits any direct air services between Taiwan and mainland China, most passengers have to go to China via Hong Kong or Macao. Furthermore, as referred to earlier in Exhibit 3-5a, there are four Chinese airports in close proximity to Hong Kong (Macau, Shenzhen, Zhuhai and Guangzhou). Any of these airports could be used by mainland China to influence the status of and activities at Hong Kong airports and to indirectly control Hong Kong's air transportation policy.

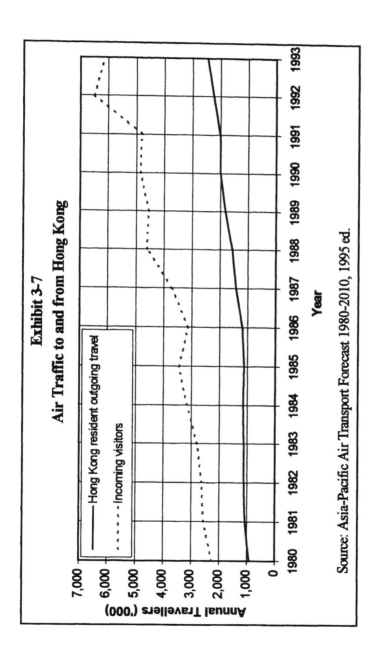

Exhibit 3-7

Air Traffic to and from Hong Kong

Legend:
— Hong Kong resident outgoing travel
· · · · Incoming visitors

Annual Travellers ('000)

Year

Source: Asia-Pacific Air Transport Forecast 1980–2010, 1995 ed.

Exhibit 3-8
Air Traffic Arrivals to Hong Kong from Key Selected Markets

	Japan		Taiwan		Australia		United Kingdom	
	Air Visitor (000)	Annual Growth (%)	Air Visitor (000)	Annual Growth (%)	Air Visitor (000)	Annual Growth (%)	Air Visitor (000)	Annual Growth (%)
1980	472		1,237		166		121	
1981	508	7.6%	136	9.7%	202	21.4%	167	38.1%
1982	516	1.5%	153	12.9%	217	7.3%	156	-6.4%
1983	502	-2.6%	157	2.3%	228	5.4%	165	5.2%
1984	584	16.3%	168	6.5%	278	21.9%	171	4.1%
1985	636	8.9%	177	5.9%	275	-0.9%	188	9.6%
1986	596	-6.3%	217	22.9%	238	-13.4%	186	-1.1%
1987	871	46.1%	345	58.8%	219	-8.3%	216	16.4%
1988	1,092	25.5%	844	144.8%	223	1.9%	245	13.1%
1989	1,078	-1.3%	902	6.9%	228	2.4%	238	-2.9%
1990	1,219	13.1%	976	8.1%	224	-2.0%	243	2.3%
1991	1,129	-7.4%	899	-7.9%	203	-9.3%	237	-2.6%
1992	1,161	2.8%	1,113	23.8%	222	9.3%	270	14.2%
1993	1,103	-5.0%	1,205	8.2%	223	0.5%	293	8.3%
2000	1,730	6.6%	1,717	5.2%	303	4.5%	406	4.8%
2010	2,464	3.6%	2,578	4.1%	449	4.0%	601	4.0%

Source: IATA (1995)

The Development of Major Carriers

Cathay Pacific Airways   Before the Second World War, Hong Kong was served by two airlines, Imperial Airways of Great Britain, and Pan American Airways of the United States. With the end of the War, an indigenous airline industry came into existence. Cathay Pacific Airways was Hong Kong's first airline. It was created by a group of demobilized pilots, four Americans and an Australian, in 1945 with the purchasing an old DC-3. Initially, the group provided non-scheduled charter operations mostly on the Hong Kong-Australia route. The company was named Cathay Pacific Airways, and was formally registered in September 1946. In December of the same year, Cathay started its first scheduled services, a weekly service to Singapore via Bangkok, but its main business was still in charters.

Cathay Pacific was reorganized under pressures from both political and business interests in Hong Kong in 1948. The shareholders of the reorganized company, Cathay Pacific Limited, included China Navigation Company (a Swire-owned shipping company) 35 percent, Australian National Airways 35 percent, John Swire & Sons 10 percent, de Kantzow (one of the original founder) 10 percent, and Cathay Pacific Holdings, representing the original founders, 10 percent.

Parallel to this development, the British Overseas Airways Corporation (BOAC), a state owned airline, established a subsidiary, Hong Kong Airways, in March 1947. Hong Kong Airways started its first scheduled service in December 1947, to Shanghai. It soon expanded into other cities in the Chinese mainland, and to Manila. Its mission was to extend and to help protect British commercial interests in China.

With two airlines operating out of Hong Kong, the government ordained a division of the designated routes in May 1949. All routes to the north of Hong Kong became the exclusive catchment area for Hong Kong Airways (including China, Japan, and Korea), while all routes to the south were allocated to Cathay Pacific. The route to Manila was shared between both airlines.

Hong Kong Airways' services to Mainland China were cut off after the People's Republic of China was born in 1949. Consequently, in November, 1949, BOCA sold its entire holdings in Hong Kong Airways to the legendary trading company, Jardine, Matheson, which subsequently sold Hong Kong Airways' fleet of DC-3s. Thereafter, the airline confined its operations to Taiwan, with aircraft chartered from Northwest Airlines.

In June 1959, the two airlines merged to form the new Cathay Pacific Airways. Butterfield and Swire held the majority and controlling interests, either directly or through the China Navigation Company, BOCA[41] held 15 percent, and the Australian Ansett Airways, which had taken over Australian National Airways, retained 12 percent of the newly capitalized airline.[42] The new Cathay Pacific undertook an accelerated route expansion right after the merger. By 1970, Cathay Pacific firmly established as one of the most successful carriers in the Far East. By March 1973, Cathay had carried 5 million passengers. The airline started to look beyond Asia, and its first scheduled passenger services outside the Asia-Pacific region were to the Middle East, with flights to Bahrain starting in 1976, and to Dubai a year later. Many Asians worked in the Middle East, then at the height of the oil boom, and the new routes were extremely successful.

During the 1980s, Cathay Pacific further expanded its Asian base, and at the same time, started to spread its wings across different continents.

It started with Europe and Oceania, then the Pacific. Cathay's first entry into the North American market was to Vancouver, Canada, on May 1, 1983. The trans-Pacific route was expended to San Francisco by July 1986; this included the fifth freedom right to carry traffic between Vancouver and the U.S. points. It gradually established itself as one of the leading airlines in the world. On July 1, 1990, Cathay Pacific joined the International Air Transport Association.

The 1990s has not been an easy time for Cathay Pacific. High inflation has forced Cathay Pacific to face the challenge of how to remain truly competitive against other premier carriers. It has undertaken measures to adapt to changing customer needs, as well as the cost structure. For example, Cathay Pacific moved some functions, such as accounting, outside its expensive home base. At the same time, it started to offer highly personalized customer service to cater to the differing needs of individual groups of passengers. The recent Asian economic downturn has further taken a heavy toll on the airline. The widespread economic weakness saw reductions in both passenger loads and yields, particularly on routes to Japan and Southeast Asia. Its cargo traffic fell, and its airline-related businesses of catering, ramp-handling and aircraft maintenance were also adversely affected. As a result, Cathay Pacific suffered a loss of US$69.9 million during 1998, the first time the airline has incurred an annual loss since 1963. However, despite the difficulties, Cathay Pacific has pressed ahead with its extensive investment program to improve its products and services. To cut down the cost, Cathay laid off over 1,000 staff in the 1997-1998. It also positioned itself to meet the challenges in the increasingly competitive global market by becoming a founding member of the new OneWorld alliance in 1998. In addition, Cathay Pacific has struck a code-share agreement with Swissair on Hong Kong-Zurich, and announced a long-term partnership with JAL covering codesharing and frequent flyer program.

In 1998, Cathay Pacific carried 10.3 million passengers. Today, Cathay Pacific employs 13,795 people, has 60 aircraft in operation[43] with an average age of 5.15 years.[44] It serves 47 cities in 28 countries.

Dragonair   Cathay had enjoyed essentially a monopolistic position in Hong Kong until April 1985 when Hong Kong Dragon Airlines Ltd (Dragonair) came into existence, as a wholly owned subsidiary of Hong Kong Macau International Investment Co. Dragonair started its first commercial (non-scheduled) flight, Hong Kong to Kota Kinabalu, on July 26, 1985, only two days after it took delivery of its first aircraft. In November of the same year, it was granted Air Transport Licensing Authority to operate 'regular charter services' to eight points in China (Beijing and Shanghai were excluded). A year later, scheduled services began to two points in Thailand. By March 1987, Dragonair had three Boeing 737s, and on May 15, 1987, it joined the International Air Transport Association (IATA).

However, rapid expansion led to some financial problems at Dragonair. On February 1, 1990, Cathay Pacific and Swire Group acquired 43 percent of shareholdings in Dragonair, and CITIC Pacific took 38 percent.[45] Dragonair continued its autonomous existence,[46] and was able to lease large aircraft from Cathay Pacific. In April 1990, Cathay Pacific relinquished its key Chinese routes to Beijing and Shanghai to Dragonair.

Dragonair has remained as a regional airline, serving 27 destinations across Asia, including 17 on the Chinese mainland.[47] However, its catchment area spans half of the world's population, and includes the most dynamic and fast-growing economies in the world. Dragonair has benefited considerably from limited competition on its main routes, and from the perception in China that as a Western airline, it is safer than its mainland competitors. In 1996, it enjoyed a 25 percent net profit margin. The profit margin was 25 percent for 1995, and 23 percent for 1994. Dragonair is currently looking at the possibility of adding long-haul routes outside the region to compete with Cathay Pacific.

Today, Dragonair has 1,148 employees, and its fleet now comprises seven single-aisle A320 aircraft and five wide-body A330. It carried 2.1 million passengers in 1998, a 2.9 percent decline from a year earlier.

3.5 Taiwan

The Air Transport Market

Despite its limited geographical area and population, Taiwan generates over 35 million air passengers and 1.2 million tons of air cargo annually. Total international scheduled passenger traffic to and from Taiwan increased from 4.8 million passengers in 1985 to 15.8 million passengers in 1995, an average growth rate of 12.7 percent per annum (IATA, 1997). This traffic further increased to 16.7 million passengers in 1996 (Exhibit 3-9a). Domestic air traffic achieved an even greater growth rate, an average annual rate of 18.4 percent since 1987 (Exhibit 3-9b). Total air passengers in Taiwan average annual growth rate was 15.4 percent between 1985 and 1995, ranking the 3rd among the major Asia-Pacific countries. Northeast Asia was by far the most important region for Taiwan's international air

Exhibit 3-9a
Total International Scheduled Passenger Traffic to/from Taiwan
(thousands of passengers)

	Europe	Americas	Asia-Pacific	Rest of World	Total
1985	29.2	267.2	4,497.9	2.9	4,797.0
1986	36.1	349.2	4,938.3	2.7	5,326.3
1987	53.6	358.4	5,774.1	18.2	6,204.4
1988	50.9	329.6	7,069.1	24.7	7,474.3
1989	59.9	382.1	8,229.2	36.5	8,707.7
1990	68.5	552.2	9,766.7	40.8	10,428.2
1991	71.4	737.4	10,178.6	30.9	11,018.3
1992	104.5	897.4	11,532.0	33.2	12,567.0
1993	135.1	1,203.4	12,126.3	27.1	13,491.9
1996	564.0	1,982.0	14,110.0	100.0	16,756.0
1997	369.0	1,169.0	13,265.0	7.0	14,809.0
2002	584.0	1,559.0	16,133.0	7.0	18,282.0
2010	524.0	7,653.6	48,485.0	171.6	56,834.3

Source: IATA, 1995, 1998

Exhibit 3-9b
Airline Traffic in Taiwan

	1988	1997	1998
	International Traffic		
Passengers (000)	7,129	17,069	16,440
Freight (000'MT)	516	1,204	1,205
	Domestic Traffic		
Passengers (000)	7,614	37,400	33,294
Freight (000' MT)	27	104	94

Source: Directorate-General of Budget, Accounting and Statistics of
the Executive Yuan, Taiwan

traffic, with 60.6 percent of the total traffic in 1997. The number of visitor arrivals to Taiwan increased by 18.7 percent between 1988 and 1998 (Exhibit 3-10), while the Taiwan residents outbound departures increased by 3.4 times during the same period (Exhibit 3-11). This indicates that it is the Taiwanese resident outgoing travel element that contributed mostly to the strong growth in airline passenger traffic during that period. The most important country of origin-destination for Taiwan was Hong Kong, with over 5 million passengers in 1997 (Shon, Chang, and Lin, 1999).[48] Taiwan is the second largest source market for Hong Kong after Mainland China. According to early IATA forecast, Taiwan's domestic passengers will

Exhibit 3-10
Visitor Arrivals to Taiwan (thousands)

	1988	1997	1998
Asia			
Japan	917	908	831
South Korea	87	98	63
Southeast Asia	233	439	454
Others	26	31	32
America			
United States	228	326	332
Canada	24	43	46
Others	13	14	13
Europe			
United Kingdom	32	56	58
Germany	27	38	39
France	16	27	29
Others	52	79	79
Africa			
	16	9	8
Oceania			
	24	40	41

Source: Directorate-General of Budget, Accounting and Statistics of the Executive
Yuan, Taiwan

reach 104 million by 2010, and its international passengers will reach 52.8 million. Total air passenger average annual growth rate is estimated to be 8.8 percent over the period 1995-2010. The number of air visitor arrivals to Taiwan is expected increase at a lower rate; IATA's forecast before the Asian crisis puts it at 5.7 percent per year between 1993 and 2000 and 5.9 percent per year thereafter. This implies that most growth anticipated for the future will be the contribution of the Taiwanese resident outgoing travel market and transfer passengers at Taipei Airport. The most recent IATA forecast indicates that Taiwan's international scheduled passengers will grow by 5.5 percent in 1999, 5.1 percent in 2000, 5.5 percent in 2001, and 5.6 percent in 2002, reaching 18.3 million in 2002 (IATA, 1998).

Since 1949, Taiwan has banned direct transportation links with mainland China. China-bound passengers from Taiwan must transit in a third country, such as Hong Kong or Macau. However, due to rapid increases in travellers between Taiwan and the mainland, Taipei authorities may have to abandon this policy.[49] A study by the National Taiwan University estimates that Taiwanese authorities could save US$96 million a year in fuel and other costs if direct flights were available from Taiwan to Beijing, Shanghai, and Xiamen.[50]

Exhibit 3-11
Outbound Departures by Residents in Taiwan (thousands)

	1988	1997	1998
		Asia	
Hong Kong	622	1,948	1,746
Japan	340	652	674
Singapore	46	284	261
Thailand	155	343	362
Others	212	1,401	1,424
		America	
United States	183	589	577
Canada	5	117	127
Others	5	0	0
		Europe	
Netherlands	9	48	67
France	2	24	29
Others	11	115	100
		Africa	
	7	1	0
		Oceania	
Australia	4	35	35
Others	1	49	39

Source: Directorate-General of Budget, Accounting and Statistics of the Executive
　　　Yuan, Taiwan

Apart from *China Airlines* (CAL) and *EVA Airways*, Taiwan has two other international carriers: *Mandarin Airlines*[51] and *TransAsia Airlines*. EVA, which is backed by the powerful Evergreen Group, was instrumental in Taiwan's adoption of an open skies policy in the late 1980s. Since taking off in July 1991, EVA has aggressively developed its international routes, effectively forcing Taiwan's Civil Aeronautics Administration (CAA) to adopt a new liberalized policy. Until EVA arrived, CAL enjoyed monopoly status as Taiwan's only airline that flew overseas. The presence of another carrier has thus forced the government to divide up international routes.[52] The CAA may, in the future, have to accommodate other privately owned Taiwan-based international carriers (Baum, 1995).

In 1995, Taiwan's China Airlines and Hong Kong's Cathay Pacific Airways underwent a series of talks to negotiate renewal of their 5-year agreement regarding the lucrative Taiwan-Hong Kong route. Taiwan's priority was to expand the route, making it available to other carriers such as EVA Airways. The new agreement was finally signed on June 13, 1996 after receiving approval by Beijing. This new agreement ended the monopoly on Hong Kong - Taiwan routes formerly held by Cathay Pacific and China Airlines. EVA won the rights to 16 passenger flights per week between Hong Kong and Taiwan. And Hong Kong-based Dragonair, controlled by state-owned China National Aviation Corp. (CNAC), was allowed to operate three-times daily services to Kaohsiung, a southern port city which is Taiwan's second largest city. China Airlines and Cathay Pacific carry over 84 percent of the total traffic between Taiwan and Hong Kong.[53] In 1996, it was estimated that the Taiwan-Hong Kong route could generate a total of about $270 million of annual passenger revenue for all carriers flying it.[54] This appears to be underestimated. Shon, Chang and Lin (1999) estimate the revenue at US$600 for China Airlines and Cathay Pacific.

On another front, in 1995, *China Airlines* replaced Taiwan's national flag with a plum blossom on all of its planes as part of a corporate image make-over, one that should make it easier for it to realize its goal of someday flying to the mainland (Baum, 1995). The change will also ease the airline's access to countries politically sensitive to possible negative reactions from the PRC.[55]

The Development of Major Carriers

China Airlines Founded in 1959 by a group of retired Chinese Air force officers in Taipei. CAL is the dominant national carrier in Taiwan today. The airline grew successfully in its early days, establishing new regional services in Asia and across the Pacific. However, the political strains between Taiwan and mainland China in the 1970's, devastated the airline when United Nations (UN) officially recognized the PRC to be the official Chinese government and UN member, and expelled the ROC from the organization. Consequently, Taiwan was also expelled from ICAO, and several neighbouring Asian governments suspended CAL's traffic rights to their major hubs, e.g. Malaysia, Vietnam, Korea and Japan. Political ostracism hurt CAL badly as many nations were unwilling to sign bilateral agreements with it, in fear of offending the giant PRC. At the height of the travel boom in 1987, only 17 nations recognized ROC, but these were not huge air traffic generators. CAL was able to bounce back, following the high export trade growth of Taiwan, and revived many of its Asian services and its position in the world industry in the 1980's. New air markets were also expanded in Europe.

In 1980, CAL suffered its first financial loss when surface transportation in Taiwan was substantially advanced. Most of the island's population and industrial areas are concentrated on the Western coastal strip. Through this quasi- megalopolis, the railway was electrified and a new express highway was constructed to relieve the busy urban traffic congestion. Given these developments and the actual geography of the island, the domestic air transport market did not appear promising. However, the growing population and congestion due to increased business and trade activity still called for more air transport in the later years. The comfort and speed of air shuttle services was favoured by many over the crowded trains and freeways. Although this increased air travel demand in Taiwan, profits were marginal, as the domestic routes were often too short to generate high earnings. For example, the main domestic route between northern capital Taipei and the southern port Kaohsiung, is only 200 miles and could only produce break-even results. Thus, the intercity services in Taiwan have great traffic potential but the profit potential remains slim.

In 1991, CAL entered a joint venture with the Koo's Group to incorporate a subsidiary, Mandarin Airlines, to help operate both domestic and international routes. CAL also owns 42 percent of Formosa Airlines Corp. CAL itself is 85 percent owned by the China Aviation Development Foundation.

CAL's poor flight- safety records have been a major concern for the carrier as it has turned away both foreign and local travellers. Government has cancelled some of its routes because of concern over safety record. To improve safety, CAL has brought in experts from Delta Airlines and Flight Safety Foundation.

CAL is implementing a 10-year fleet expansion plan to replace, modernize and increase its fleet size and routes. CAL's biggest traffic market remains to be people travelling to Mainland China via Hong Kong, Macao and Tokyo. As of April 1999, China Airlines employs 9,162 people with a fleet of 55 aircraft. It flies to 34 cities in 18 countries. In 1998, China Airlines carried 7.3 million passengers.

EVA Air   This new Taiwanese airline was formed by the Evergreen marine and investment company, one of the world's largest freight container shipping lines. EVA began operations in 1991 to service major neighbouring East Asian cities. Today, it flies to 27 cities in 18 countries across five continents. After 7 years of tremendous growth with the last 2 years being profitable, EVA is currently setting sights on consolidation and increasing efficiency in its operations. In 1991, EVA carried 140,000 passengers and achieved a 60 percent load factor. By 1996, the number of passengers shot up to 4.2 million with a load factor rate of 73.6 percent. Overall company revenues jumped from $37.8 million in1991 to $1.32 billion in 1998. In July 1998, EVA transferred its domestic flights to UNI Air,[56] its domestic subsidiary. As a result, its passenger volume fell from 4.2 million in 1997 to 3.7 million in 1998.

Despite good returns on its domestic flights, EVA's primary Asian regional markets have slumped in the past 2 years. Top management is now looking at aggressive cost cutting. The cuts in 1998 included the abandonment of plans to make the southern port city of Kaohsiung its 'sub-hub' for international flights. It dropped its seven-month-old Kaohsiung - Los Angeles service at the beginning of 1999, months after cutting Kaohsiung-Singapore services. EVA's fleet expansion plans have been scaled back and it will continue to terminate losing routes such as to Bangkok and Kuala Lumpur. New markets to be considered at include regional services to Osaka and Phnom Penh and European services to Vienna and Paris, via codesharing agreements with new partners. Currently, EVA codeshares with Air New Zealand, ANA, Ansett, Garuda and Continental Airlines. It is projecting substantial growth in the Australian and U.S. markets soon.

On the Asian side, the biggest market potential is the Taiwan-China market that is being served via Hong Kong or Macau right now. Cargo services are receiving more attention. EVA estimates that in the not-too-distant future cargo will account for half of EVA's businesses compared with just over one-third now. Major cargo routes will be trans-Pacific and to London, England. EVA's cargo expansion plans are in line with the Taiwan government's efforts to promote Taipei as a regional cargo hub. The carrier is forecasting more than 20 percent cargo growth in 1999 in terms of tonnes carried, and cargo tonne-kilometre is expected to grow by about 32 percent.

Turning to politics, many believe that EVA was created to plug the many international gaps in the world air map, created by the ongoing PRC vs. ROC tension. These strained relations insisted that national airlines from the two sides of Taiwan Strait would not serve the same destinations and that other countries must decide which side to co-operate with for air services. The European market was especially a concern for Taiwan since it was poorly represented there and most of the European nations chose to favour PRC instead of Taiwan. Since EVA did not carry as strong a Taiwanese nationalism as CAL, it could establish new air routes to these previously un-welcoming European hubs such as London in 1992. Soon afterwards, EVA was servicing Vienna, Seattle, New York and Los Angeles, helping to transform and improve Taiwan's stature in the international aviation community. So far, China has been quiet about EVA's emergence and many predict that EVA will eventually take over CAL's dominant position within Taiwan, too.

EVA is currently considering going public. Taiwan's Over the Counter Authority is assessing its application for a listing. EVA expects the company's stock to start trading early 2000. At the same time, EVA has been assessing membership in a global alliance, and has held preliminary discussions with OneWorld Alliance, Star Alliance and the KLM/Northwest group. But for now, it focuses on intensifying its bilateral alliances. EVA's alliances include passenger code-sharing with Air Canada, Air New Zealand, ANA, Ansett, American West Airlines, and Continental, and cargo agreements with Lufthansa and British Airways.

3.6   Summary

Air transport market in Northeast Asia has experienced tremendous growth during the past two decades. It now accounts for 11.5 percent of the global market. Japan has been the region's dominant travel market (domestic and international travel combined) in the past. Its share of total Asia-Pacific traffic was 30.8 percent in 1995. However, China will become the Asia Pacific's leader for total domestic and international scheduled passenger traffic by 2010. China's share of total Asia-Pacific traffic was 5.3 percent (11.6 percent including Hong Kong) in 1985. This increased to 16 percent (23 percent including Hong Kong) in 1995 and will reach 26 percent (32 percent including Hong Kong) by 2010, while Japan's share will fall to 20.1 percent by 2010. The combined total traffic (domestic and international) of China and Hong Kong is expected to grow from 88.9 million passengers in 1995 to 362.3 million passengers in 2010. Their combined international traffic is expected to grow from 37.7 million passengers in 1995 to 133 million in 2010.

Total international scheduled passenger traffic to and from Korea is predicted to increase from 11.3 million passengers in 1993 to 42.8 million passengers in 2010. A large part of this growth is expected to be sustained by Korean residents' outgoing travels and transfer passengers at Seoul airport. Taiwan is also expected to have strong growth in international traffic: 13.5 million passengers in 1993 to 56.8 million in 2010 (7.1 percent annual growth). Similar to Korea, most of Taiwan's future traffic growth will be the contribution of Taiwanese residents' outgoing travels and transfer traffic at Taipei airport.

International air traffic in Northeast is predicted to grow from 88.8 million passengers in 1997 to 110.6 million in 2002. And international traffic between Northeast Asia and the rest of the Asia Pacific region will amount to 109 million passengers by 2010, representing 41 percent of total traffic within the whole of Asia-Pacific.

Notes

1   It is hard to imagine that Hong Kong's traffic, with its population of six million, will increase from 24 million in 1993 to 72 million in 2010. In any case, Hong Kong is now officially a Chinese territory, the methods for measuring Hong Kong's international traffic will change.

2   They also handled 76 percent of domestic passenger traffic in the same year.

3   These operators shared a common characteristic: transporting holiday-makers to seaside places, almost entirely in seaplanes.

4   In fact, ANA was already using the hub-spoke system, with routes radiating from Osaka, later from Tokyo, which it called its Abeam routes.

5   The Japan – U.S. Air Agreement was signed on 30 April 1985.

6   Korea was the world's 18th largest nation in terms of tourism revenues in 1998 with \$5.8 billion.

7   On January 1, 1989, Korea's new administration lifted travel restrictions on overseas travel. As in Japan, the government hoped to encourage overseas travel as a way to redress the growing trade surplus Korea had at the time (Flint, 1989).

8   *Korean Tourism Annual Report* (Seoul: Ministry of Transportation, 1990) 50.

9   *Aviation Week and Space Technology* 130.19 (8 May 1989): 37.

10   Kim, J. 'The Regulation and Growth of Civil Aviation in South Korea', in Hufbauer, G.C. and C. Findlay ed. *Flying High*, Institute for International Economics, Washington D.C, November, 1996.

11   According to Kim (1996), Kimpo's congestion, to some extent, stems from congestion at Tokyo's Narita Airport and the consequent emergence of Kimpo as an alternate destination for trans-Pacific flights.

12   Taking responsibility for recent aircraft accidents, 29 senior executives (managing vice-president and higher) submitted their resignation to the company following the Shanghai accident. A new president and CEO was appointed in April, 1999.

13   'China to Build 20 Feeder Airports', *Asia Pulse*, June 7, 1999.

14   'Pacific Rim Airlines Pushing Boeing to Launch New Large Air Transport Program,' *Aviation Week and Space Technology* 136.1 (6 January 1992): 21.

15   'China's Air Transport Industry Developing Fast,' *Xinhua News Agency*, 29 September 1995.

16   Australia has recently been nominated as the first approved Western destination for Chinese travellers *(Asia Pulse*, May 16, 1999).

17   Out-bound travellers increased five percent in 1998 (*Asia Pulse*, May 16, 1999).

18   *Xinhua News Agency* (29 September 1995).

19   'China to Build 20 Feeder Airports', *Asia Pulse*, June 7, 1999.

20   Chinese airlines presently have 477 jetliners, 327 of which are Boeing products.

21   'China to be Boeing's Top Market Outside U.S. in Next 20 Years', *Asia Pulse*, March 15, 1999.

22   '1993 Forecasts-Part 7 of 7--Asia Pacific,' *Flight International* 23 December 1992.

23   *Orient Aviation*, February/March, 1997.

24   There were 9 crashes and 10 hijackings in China between 1992 and 1993.

25   CAAC has achieved limited success in its drive for domestic consolidation. In most cases, the takeovers result in a consolidation favouring the carriers in CAAC system.

26   'Reports,' *Airport Analyst-Asia Pacific* 7 February 1996.

27   J. Lee, 'The Sky's the Limit; China's Aviation Sector,' *The China Business Review* 20.3 (May 1993): 12.

28   There are also 48 airports which are for both military and civilian use.

29   About one in every 59,000 square kilometers if including the 'mixed-use' airports.

30   The United States' airports average one in every 1,672 square kilometers.

31   'China to build 20 feeder airports', *Asia Pulse*, June 7, 1999.

32   Ibid.

33   China Eastern Airlines has recently completed the initial public offering of 32 percent of its shares on the New York and Hong Kong stock exchanges, raising about US$250 million from the sale.

34   At the same time, railway and highway services have been considerably improved, thus some traffic has been diverted from airlines.

35   'China's Aviation is Waiting for Spring', *Civil Aviation Economics and Technology*, No. 206, February 1999 (in Chinese languange).

36   SKOAGA was a joint Sino-Soviet company, each with 50 percent of shareholding.

37   Yunnan Airlines, based in Kunming, flies to Hanoi.

38   'Key Transportation Issues in Hong Kong,' speech delivered at APEC Transportation Ministerial, Washington D.C., 12-13 June 1995.

39   *Report on Civil Aviation Hong Kong 1995-1996.*

40   Although IATA's Asia-Pacific Forecast (1995) 9-33 shows that Hong Kong international traffic will grow from 24.4 million in 1993 to 72.3 million passengers in 2010, this figure obviously includes air passenger traffic between Hong Kong and mainland China, which will no longer be counted as 'international' traffic.

41   BOCA bought out the shareholdings of Jardine, Matheson.

42   The original founders pulled out from the airline in 1951.

43   It also has 2 on firm order, and 25 on option.

44   Passenger aircraft's average age is 4.53 years.

45   In 1990, China National Aviation Corporation (Group) Limited (CNAC Group) purchased approximately 35.86 percent of the shares in Dragonair and became the largest shareholder of the airline. CITIC Pacific retained 28.50 percent, Swire/Cathay Pacific 25.50 percent. In December, 1997, China National Aviation Company Ltd, a subsidary of CNAC Group Ltd., having taken up the 35.86 percent shareholding in Dragonair from CNAC Group Ltd., was listed on the Hong Kong Stock Exchange. As a result of the listing, CNAC's stake in Dragonair increased from 35.86 percent to 43.29 percent. The shareholding structure of CITIC Pacific, Swire Pacific and Cathay Pacific remain unchanged. CNAC also owns the entire issued share capital of Air Zheijiang, a Mainland China domestic carrier, and has a 51 percent stake in Air Macau.

46   Since 1990, Cathay Pacific's network of overseas offices have acted as general sales agents for Dragonair around the world. In January 1991, this relationship was expanded to include cargo traffic as well.

47   Flights flown between Hong Kong and Mainland China account for 67 percent of Dragonair's total ASK in 1996. Passenger services for Mainland China routes accounted for 68.3 percent of total traffic revenue and approximately 83 percent of operating profit in 1996 (Machey, 1998).

48   In 1985, Japan was the most important country for international traffic to and from Taiwan, followed by Hong Kong.

[49] Direct shipping routes between Taiwan and Mainland China were opened at the end of April 1997. There were strong believes that direct flights would be possible by mid 1998, however that has yet to be materialized.

[50] *AsiaMoney* (July/August 1995): 61.

[51] Mandarin Airlines is a subsidiary of China Airlines. It was formed in 1991 to operate international routes. It does not operate any domestic routes.

[52] TransAsia Airways, Great China Airlines, and Makung Airlines were entitled to operate international charter flights.

[53] Singapore Airline, Thai Airways, Japan Asia Airlines, British Airways and Garuda Indonesia also provide service between Hong Kong and Taiwan through fifth freedom rights. Together, they account for about 11 percent of traffic (Shon, Chang and Lin, 1999).

[54] *Asian Aviation News*, June 14, 1996.

[55] 'Asia/Pacific Report,' *Air Transport World* 32.11 (November 1995): 17.

[56] UNI Air was created by the merger of EVA's subsidiary carriers: UNI Airways, Great China Airlines, and Taiwan Airlines.

4 Aviation Development in Southeast Asia and South Pacific

Economic development in Southeast Asia and South Pacific has boosted air traffic growth in the region during the 1980s and 1990s, on both domestic and international routes. Several airlines based in the region, such as Singapore Airlines, Thai Airways and Qantas, are among the world's largest. The region's hub airports are ranked among the busiest in the world. Exhibits 4-1a and 4-1b show that some markets in the region, such as Vietnam, are expected to experience the strongest growth in the world. IATA forecasts indicate that the international aviation market in Southeast Asia (Singapore, Thailand, Indonesia, Malaysia, Philippines, and Vietnam) will grow from 53 million passengers in 1993 to 205 million passengers in 2010, an average growth of 8.2 percent per year. This chapter provides an overview on the development of air transport markets in selected countries in Southeast Asia and South Pacific as well as their major carriers.

4.1 Thailand

The Air Transport Market

Over the past two decades, Thailand's national income has increased by approximately eight percent per year. The Thai economy took off into double digit growth in 1988, with GDP increasing by more than 13 percent. This performance was repeated in 1989 and 1990, with growth of 12.3 percent and 11.5 percent respectively. The economy has slowed down somewhat, registering an average annual growth of 8.9 percent between 1990-1995.[1] Real per-capita income had risen consistently despite steady increases in population. At current prices, it increased from 4,000 baht (US$191) per head in 1970 to 53,215 baht (US$2,102) per head in 1993. Thailand's economy collapsed, however, when the government floated the Baht on 2 July 1997, starting the remarkable meltdown of the Asian economy.

Tourism has been Thailand's highest income generator since 1982,

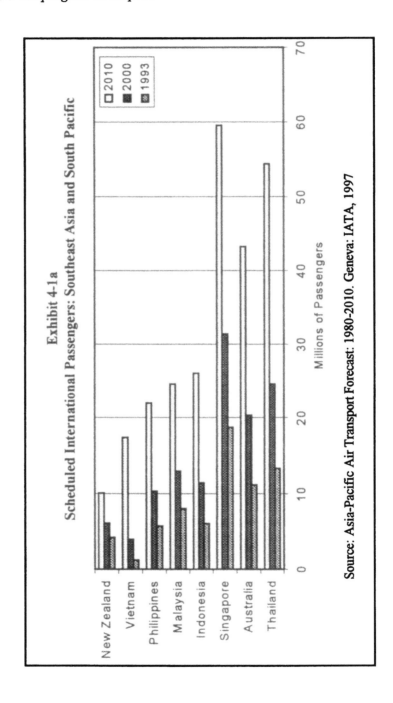

Exhibit 4-1a

Scheduled International Passengers: Southeast Asia and South Pacific

Source: Asia-Pacific Air Transport Forecast: 1980-2010. Geneva: IATA, 1997

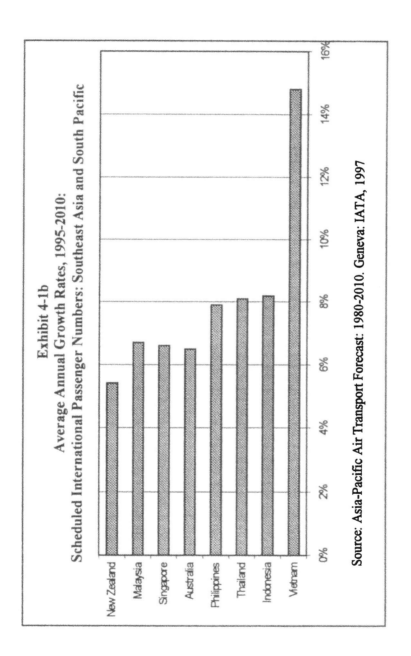

Exhibit 4-1b
Average Annual Growth Rates, 1995-2010:
Scheduled International Passenger Numbers: Southeast Asia and South Pacific

Source: Asia-Pacific Air Transport Forecast: 1980-2010. Geneva: IATA, 1997

having grown at a healthy 16 percent per annum since 1980. Visitor arrivals in Thailand soared from 1.9 million in 1980 to 4.2 million in 1988, and then to 6.6 million in 1994. In 1998, Thailand attracted 7.72 million tourists, ranking at 21st in the world. Most visitors came from Asia, with the largest contingent from Japan, followed by Europe. During the late 1980s and early 1990s, the number of visitors from Taiwan had the highest growth rate (see Exhibit 4-2).

Exhibit 4-2
Air Traffic Arrivals to Thailand from Key Selected Markets

	Japan		Hong Kong		Taiwan		Malaysia	
	Air Visitor (000)	Annual Growth (%)	Air Visitor (000)	Annual Growth (%)	Air Visitor (000)	Annual Growth (%)	Air Visitor (000)	Annual Growth (%)
1980	245		130		51		339	
1981	246	0.3%	156	19.5%	50	-3.4%	339	0.0%
1982	251	2.0%	150	-3.4%	69	38.4%	515	51.5%
1983	235	-6.4%	129	-14.3%	65	-5.1%	545	6.1%
1984	228	-2.6%	127	-1.4%	61	-6.7%	572	5.0%
1985	227	-0.8%	132	3.8%	69	13.4%	554	-3.3%
1986	262	15.5%	165	24.9%	127	84.5%	653	17.9%
1987	350	33.6%	251	52.6%	203	60.1%	742	13.7%
1988	452	29.4%	380	51.1%	233	14.3%	843	13.6%
1989	556	22.9%	377	-0.8%	411	76.6%	736	-12.7%
1990	652	17.4%	383	1.6%	503	22.5%	752	2.1%
1991	560	-14.2%	362	-5.4%	476	-5.4%	711	-5.4%
1992	569	1.7%	276	-23.8%	405	-14.9%	729	2.5%
1993	582	2.2%	265	-3.8%	525	29.5%	811	11.4%
2000	1,058	8.9%	459	8.1%	1,005	9.7%	1,094	4.4%
2010	2,129	7.2%	737	4.8%	2,419	7.9%	1,658	4.2%

Source: IATA (1995)

The total number of air visitor arrivals to Thailand increased by 11.3 percent per annum between 1985 and 1993 (Exhibit 4-3). Total international scheduled passenger traffic grew at an average annual rate of

Exhibit 4-3
Total Air Visitor Arrivals to Thailand by Region
(thousands of passengers)

	Europe	Americas	Asia-Pacific	Rest of World	Total
1985	448	181	1,371	438	2,438
1986	540	204	1,665	409	2,818
1987	705	250	2,098	430	3,483
1988	888	288	2,542	513	4,231
1989	1,089	328	2,948	443	4,810
1990	1,200	354	3,306	438	5,299
1991	1,135	335	3,128	415	5,013
1992	1,306	340	2,960	530	5,136
1993	1,411	338	3,568	444	5,761
2010	6,321	1,560	12,666	1,702	22,248

Source: IATA, 1995

12 percent over the same time period (Exhibit 4-4), slightly higher than the total air visitor arrivals. This indicates that Thailand resident outgoing travel and Bangkok Airport transfer traffic increased more rapidly than incoming air visitor arrivals to Thailand. However, the currency devaluation has substantially reduced the affordability of overseas travel by Thailand residents. On the other hand, the currency devaluation has made Thailand a well-priced destination for oversea visitors. As a result, international departures by Thai nationals declined by 14.9 percent in 1998, while international tourist arrivals to Thailand rose by 7.5 percent during the same period. A majority of this increase came from Europe (19.1 percent increase), Australia (29.5 percent increase), and China (29.9 percent increase). In 1998, Europe provided 24.1 percent of total arrivals to Thailand, up from 21.7 percent in 1997. IATA forecast predicts that total international scheduled passenger traffic to/from Thailand will reach 54.4 million passengers by 2010.

In light of the economic downturn, this appears to be over-estimated. A more recent IATA forecast indicates that Thailand's international

Exhibit 4-4
Total International Scheduled Passenger Traffic to/from Thailand
(thousands of passengers)

	Europe	Americas	Asia-Pacific	Rest of World	Total
1985	759.2	36.7	4,013.3	564.5	5,373.7
1986	850.6	47.4	4,410.5	553.8	5,862.4
1987	1,050.7	49.0	5,490.3	565.0	7,154.9
1988	1,350.8	75.1	7,208.5	571.7	9,206.1
1989	1,635.4	95.3	7,916.8	555.8	10,203.3
1990	1,840.5	96.0	8,789.1	408.4	11,134.0
1991	1,834.7	128.1	8,644.3	245.9	10,853.1
1992	2,021.7	176.1	9,268.6	279.8	11,746.3
1993	2,324.5	136.7	10,521.0	317.4	13,299.5
1996	2,762.0	206.0	13,853.0	530.0	17,351.0
1997	2,874.0	190.0	13,400.0	497.0	16,961.0
2002	4,021.0	323.0	17,360.0	678.0	22,381.0
2010	8,805.2	667.2	44,059.1	867.4	54,399.0

Source: IATA, 1995, 1998

scheduled passengers will grow at 6.4 percent in 1999, 6.6 percent in 2000, 6.4 percent in 2001, and 6.2 percent in 2002, reaching 22.4 million in 2002 (IATA, 1998).

Thailand's international airline industry was monopolized by its national flag carrier, Thai Airways International, for 17 years[2] until November 1995, when the government commenced a process to establish a second international carrier.   Recently, Angel Airlines was designed as Thailand's second international carrier.   It was granted eight routes initially, including Bangkok-Singapore, Phuket-Singapore, and Chiang Mai-Singapore, all lucrative, and it also wishes to expand service to Vietnam, China, Laos, Myanmar and Cambodia.[3]   In addition, Orient Thai Airlines operates a fleet of three 737-200s from Thailand to Myanmar, Laos and Cambodia, but is restricted to routes not operated by Thai

Airways. In the domestic market, competition is severely constrained because Thai law prevents other carriers from serving routes already operated by Thai Airways. Bangkok Airways, which started as a charter carrier 29 years ago and has offered scheduled services for 12 years, currently operates nine domestic routes, which Thai Airways regards as unprofitable.

Bangkok's Don Muang Airport, developed from a military facility, is one of the busiest in the region, and had hopes of supplanting Singapore as the region's traffic hub after expansion and modernization in 1987. International scheduled passenger traffic at the airport increased from 7.1 million in 1988 to 12.5 million in 1994, an average growth of 9.8 percent per year.[4] In 1998, the airport handled a total of 25.6 million passengers and 719,000 tons of freight.

The international terminal at Don Muang currently can handle 25 million passengers a year, and will be expanded to serve as many as 45 million annually by 2007. In addition, a second international airport, six times larger than Don Muang, is in the initial stages of construction, and the first phase is planned to open in 2004 with an annual capacity of 30 million passengers and an ultimate capacity of 100 million.

Development of Major Carrier

Thai Airways International Medium-sized Thai Airways International (THAI) began operations in 1960, as a joint venture between SAS and the state-owned carrier, Thai Airways Co (TAC), which served mostly domestic markets with a few intra-Asia routes . TAC held 70 percent of the shares and SAS 30 percent. THAI took over from TAC all the international routes, and immediately began to expand services, starting with new routes to Manila and to Jakarta via Singapore. It soon established itself in east Asia, and started to venture outside Asia. It started services to Sydney, Australia in April 1971. A little over a year later in June 1972, it entered the European market with services to Copenhagen. THAI began North American services in 1980.

In February 1977, Thai Airways International was designed as the sole international operator for Thailand, and a month later, the Thai government bought out SAS's shareholding in THAI. Today, THAI's main international hub is Bangkok, and its international flights account for over 85 percent of total kilometres flown, with major routes within the Asian region and to long- haul European destinations. It currently serves 73 destinations in 37 countries, and is a member of the Star Alliance, which has extended route networks to over 600 destinations.

Thailand is one of the hardest hit countries by the present economics crisis, As a result, THAI lost US$ 100 million in the third quarter of the 1997-1998 fiscal year. It has since sold 3 DC-10s, and failed to take delivery of nine aircraft in 1998. It has also asked Boeing for a delay of 17 out of 21 aircraft due through 2002, and had to cutback on some Asian routes.

As a condition of the IMF rescue package, THAI has to be privatized. It is planning a partial float in December 1999, or a private placement to a strategic partner in early 2000 in the first stage of its privatization program. Lufthansa and Singapore Airlines are considering taking a stake. Thai government says it wants to reduce its holding from 93 percent to 71.5 percent in near term to raise US$300m and is considering a further reduction to 51 percent later.

4.2   Indonesia

The Air Transport Market

Indonesia is archipelago of 17,000 islands (6,000 inhabited) with a population of 213 million. Since the oil boom in early 1970s, Indonesia's economy had been growing at an average annual rate of between 5 percent and 7 percent before it was hit by the economic crisis in 1997. The economic growth in 1997 was reduced to 4.7 percent, which was followed by a negative 13.7 percent growth with 77.6 percent inflation in 1998.

In the years leading up to the Asian economic crisis in 1997, Indonesia had begun steps to liberalize its aviation regime by permitting the entry of three private carriers, Bouraq, Mandala and Sempati Airlines, to compete against the established state-owned carrier, Garuda Indonesia, and its domestic subsidiary, Merpati Nusantra. While Bouraq and Mandala still remain on domestic routes, Sempati gained the authorization to offer international services in late 1990s. Before, it was forced out of business by the economic crisis, Sempati was focusing on international markets in ASEAN states. The emergence of private Sempati and gradual deregulation, has benefited the local travelers with reduced fares and increased air travel opportunities.

Indonesia signed a limited open skies agreement with Malaysia and Thailand, in efforts to liberalize trade and services within their Growth Triangle. This was also part of its plan to boost visitor arrival numbers and develop its national aviation industry. Tourist arrivals to Indonesia rose by

354 percent between 1983 and 1993, three quarters of all visits to Indonesia in 1993 were for holiday purposes (Edwards,1995). Scheduled international passenger numbers increased at an average 12.2 percent per year between 1983 and 1993 (IATA, 1995). Foreign tourists arrivals further increased from 3.4 million in 1993 to 5.2 million in 1997, this reflects an increased number of visitors from the Asia Pacific region, from 1.18 million in 1993 to 2.14 million in 1997 (Exhibit 4-5). Over the same period, international air passengers to/from Indonesia increased from 6.9 million to 10 million (Exhibit 4-6). Domestic air traffic increased from 21.6 million in 1993 to 27.2 million in 1996, but declined to 25.7 million in 1997.

The economic crisis, natural disasters and security disturbances in many regions since 1997 have had a substantial negative impact on the tourism industry and the airline industry. From August 1997 to March 1998, the number of foreign tourists visiting Indonesia declined to 3 millions from 3.4 million visitors for the same period in 1996/97, an 11.9 percent decrease. Domestic air passengers fell from 25.7 million in 1997 to 16 million in 1998, a 38 percent decline. International air passengers fell from 10.3 million in 1997 to 7.9 million in 1998, a 23 percent decline. The crisis has forced Sempati out of business, and Merpati needs government help to continue operations. Garuda has also suffered huge losses from reduced travel demand and inflated debt and operating costs.

Despite the current difficulties, Indonesia is expected to recover from this economic downturn with modest growth over the next few years. The most recent IATA passenger forecast indicates that international scheduled passenger traffic to/from Indonesia will grow at 1.0 percent in 1999, 1.3 percent in 2000, 2.4 percent in 2001, and 3.3 percent in 2002, reaching 8 million passengers.

Development of Major Carrier

Garuda Indonesia Indonesia's flag carrier, Garuda Indonesian Airways, was founded in 1950, and jointly owned by the newly formed Indonesian government and KLM. Then in 1954, Garuda acquired the KLM shareholding, and became a truly Indonesian airline.

Indonesia is a nation of islands, thus an efficient air transport system is vital for the country to stay economically, socially, and politically unified. Garuda began with a comprehensive domestic routes system, and then opened international services to nearby foreign points, Singapore, Manila and Bangkok, which later extended to Hong Kong and Tokyo. Its inter-continental debut was a flight to Amsterdam in March 1965 via

Exhibit 4-5
Foreign Visitor Arrivals to Indonesia by Country 1993-1997

Country	1993	1994	1995	1996	1997
USA	154,762	169,061	155,111	197,923	171,707
Canada	26,379	30,770	30,700	32,244	27,075
Others America	9,169	11,698	15,338	14,330	9,944
Total America	**190,310**	**211,529**	**201,149**	**244,497**	**208,726**
Austria	16,671	21,982	18,275	16,870	12,350
Belgium	14,168	18,274	17,436	20,331	22,338
Denmark	14,713	19,690	17,888	17,303	12,582
France	69,874	72,314	80,422	88,322	107,843
Germany	133,245	160,325	167,653	167,607	185,976
Italy	60,132	74,571	55,725	62,912	67,802
Netherlands	114,916	134,717	136,858	122,410	144,622
Spain & Portugal	16,771	18,962	14,780	16,139	32,989
Sweden, Norway,	30,962	35,570	39,480	37,749	41,443
Finland & Switzerland	34,522	40,869	44,016	34,163	30,188
United Kingdom	133,209	162,304	165,788	145,268	142,161
USSR	3,559	9,213	7,232	11,145	7,121
Other Europe	16,984	28,079	28,289	14,193	12,925
Total Europe	**659,726**	**798,870**	**793,842**	**754,412**	**820,340**
Africa	6,558	9,957	38,128	29,051	24,253
Middle East	29,596	31,259	27,212	23,860	30,479
Brunei	6,952	10,055	11,641	10,801	8,590
Malaysia	361,089	371,457	511,903	392,562	481,713
Philippines	76,936	78,438	96,242	51,487	50,925
Singapore	858,034	1,017,155	1,046,533	1,300,482	1,376,37
Thailand	37,444	41,446	38,908	43,408	45,676
Total Asean	**1,340,455**	**1,518,551**	**1,705,227**	**1,798,740**	**1,963,281**
Australia	287,850	305,209	320,494	380,475	539,156
Hong Kong	69,962	84,936	93,163	123,312	103,450
India	14,769	20,992	31,968	26,947	26,418
Japan	377,551	476,456	486,278	665,711	706,942
Korea Rep.	85,739	103,932	115,091	250,035	246,307
New Zealand	33,577	36,406	28,339	33,077	38,762
Pakistan, B'desh	11,919	14,109	18,933	19,423	13,162
Taiwan	244,121	317,505	352,797	607,015	404,929
Other Asia Pacific	**51,005**	**76,601**	**111,608**	**77,917**	**59,038**
Total Asia Pacific	**1,176,493**	**1,434,146**	**1,558,671**	**2,183,912**	**2,138,164**
Grand Total	**3,403,138**	**4,006,312**	**4,324,229**	**5,034,472**	**5,185,243**

Source: Statistics Indonesia of The Republic of Indonesia

Exhibit 4-6
International Air Traffic, Indonesia 1993-1998

		1993	1994	1995	1996	1997	1998*
				Aircraft			
Departures	000	35	39	42	46	45	
Arrivals	000	33	38	42	46	45	36
							36
				Passenger			
Departures	000	3 449	3 941	4 082	4 545	4 936	3 889
Arrivals	000	3 159	3 824	4 146	4 517	5 052	3 836
Transit	000	341	383	295	170	412	191
				Cargo			
Loaded	Mil.'Kg	122	140	152	169	171	171
Unloaded	Mil.'Kg	47	62	79	55	121	62
				Baggage			
Loaded	Mil.'Kg	57	66	60	59	60	58
Unloaded	Mil.'Kg	45	57	62	48	73	70
				Mail			
Loaded	Kg	1.2	1.2	1.2	1.1	1.2	1.0
Unloaded	Kg	1.5	2.3	1.8	0.9	1.9	2.0

* preliminary figures
Source: Statistics Indonesia of The Republic of Indonesia

Bangkok, Bombay, Cairo, Rome, Prague, and Frankfurt. But there was cause for concern with the administration of the airline, which had a reputation for lateness and unreliability in maintenance and flights. Its poor safety records had also shed a bad light on the carrier's image and even strained its regional capacity. As a state-owned corporation, it was considered as a branch of the government and used by government officials at will for any reason and free of charge. As well, all such bureaucratic inefficiencies were fully compensated with large subsidies from the state. This situation was later corrected by the change of government, and subsequent change of administration at Garuda. Garuda undertook a modernization program in the late 1960s and early 1970s, and at same time slowly and continuously expanded its international network. By 1975, it was serving 15 international routes. During the next few years, Garuda further expanded its network in Europe and the Middle East. Its first trans-Pacific flight was made in August 1985, between Bali and Los Angeles via Guam.

Although, except for a few intra-Asian routes, Garuda has remained the sole international carrier for Indonesia, it has faced some competition in its domestic markets since the late 1960s when the Indonesian government relaxed its regulations to allow private airlines to enter domestic routes. One of its main competitors was Merpati Nusantara. At its peak, Merpati was flying to more than 128 points, some of which in parallel to Garuda's routes. However, large financial losses forced Merpati to re-organize as a domestic branch of Garuda in 1978.[5]

Garuda started to lose money heavily in the mid-1980s, and has not been able to become truly profitable since then. The economic crisis further aggravated the problem, and Garuda is deemed technically bankrupt at present. It has difficulty servicing its US$400 million foreign debt. Garuda has laid off 4,000 of its 13,000 staff, and is trying to increase outsourcing. Some redundant pilots are being 'loaned' to other airlines (notably EVA). It plans to cut fleet to as little as 39 aircraft by terminating leases and has returned some newly-delivered Boeing 737s and 6 MD-11s, while 5 DC-10s are up for sale. It has also cut most routes to Europe replacing them by codesharing with foreign partners (KLM, Swissair, Lauda Air). It plans partial stock offering in next two years.

4.3   Malaysia

The Air Transport Market

In the last two decades Malaysia has achieved a sustained rate of growth averaging 6.7 percent each year. In particular, Malaysia's GDP grew at average 8.5 per cent between 1991-1997 with per capita income increasing two-fold in terms of US dollar by 1997. However, the Asian economic crisis put a sudden halt to the trend. Consequently, Malaysia experienced a negative growth of 6.7 percent in 1998.

Air transport has been an important contributor to the growth, facilitating and promoting trade and tourism. At the same time, the rapid economic growth has boosted air traffic growth significantly. International scheduled passenger traffic increased at an average rate of 11.3 percent between 1985 and 1993, reaching 8 million in 1993. This number further increased to 10.3 million in 1997 (Exhibit 4-7). Note that the 2010 forecast in Exhibit 4-7 was made before the economic crisis, thus it may be overestimated. The number of air visitor arrivals increased more rapidly than airline passengers traffic, increasing nearly 2.5 times between 1985 and 1993. This means that incoming visitors contributed to traffic growth to

Exhibit 4-7
Total International Scheduled Passenger Traffic to/from Malaysia
(thousands of passengers)

	Europe	Americas	Asia-Pacific	Rest of World	Total
1985	185.9	0.0	3,167.9	39.7	3,393.5
1986	177.7	8.6	3,119.3	48.4	3,354.0
1987	207.2	20.7	3,441.7	56.0	3,725.7
1988	233.2	24.9	3,747.6	71.8	4,077.5
1989	256.8	36.3	4,407.8	84.4	4,785.3
1990	319.9	51.7	5,214.7	158.1	5,744.5
1991	396.6	51.9	5,954.8	188.6	6,591.8
1992	461.0	61.3	6,516.8	189.4	7,228.5
1993	566.8	88.3	7,125.5	218.7	7,999.2
1996	853.0	161.0	9,376.0	320.0	10,711.0
1997	927.0	152.0	8,920.0	341.0	10,339.0
2002	1,221.0	272.0	10,397.0	452.0	12,341.0
2010	2,009.9	555.2	21,517.0	539.2	24,621.3

Source: IATA, 1995, 1998

a larger extent than Malaysian residents' outgoing traffic, This reflects the significant growth in foreign visitors to Malaysia. International visitor arrivals grew by 5 percent a year from 1985 to 1988, leaped by a third in 1989 and by a further 54 percent in 1990 (Visit Malaysia Year). There was a small decline in 1991, but visitor arrivals grew at average 5.5 percent a year between 1991 and 1994. In 1998, 10.8 millions foreign visitors[6] arrived in Malaysia, representing a 13.5 percent decline from 1997. About half of them (5.5 million) were tourists who stayed at least one night (Exhibit 4-8). Thailand and Singapore are the most important travel generating countries for Malaysia. There were 25.6 million outbound trips from Malaysia in 1998, of which 1.1 million were by air (Exhibit 4-9).

Exhibit 4-8
Tourist Arrivals in Malaysia (thousands)

	1996	1997	1998
	Top Five Generating Markets		
Singapore		3,489.0	3,007.6
Thailand		483.4	454.8
Japan		308.9	252.2
Brunei DS		179.2	183.1
United Kingdom		162.1	160.7
	Total Tourist Arrivals		
	7,200.0	**6,210.9**	**5,550.7**

Source: Department of Statistics, Malaysia

Exhibit 4-9
Malaysia Outbound Travel (thousands)

	1997	1998	97/98Change (%)
Air	1,546.0	1,082.3	-30.0
Sea	393.9	351.7	-10.7
Road	23,541.9	23,687.5	0.6
Rail	682.9	509.4	-25.4
Total	**26,164.7**	**25,631.0**	**-2.0**

Source: Department of Statistics, Malaysia

Malaysia has taken various measures to revive the economy, and there are signs of recovery. In 1999, the real economy is projected to register a positive real GDP growth of one percent. The air travel industry is also expected to recover as the economy improves. The most recent IATA forecast expects international scheduled passenger traffic to/from Malaysia will grow at 3.7 percent in 1999, 4.1 percent in 2000, 4.7 percent in 2001 and 5.1 percent in 2002, reaching 12.3 million passengers in 2002.

Development of Major Carrier

Malaysia Airlines   The Malaysian national carrier began as Malayan Airways in 1937 and after several name changes and break-up with Singapore, it became Malaysia Airlines in 1987. By then, intercontinental and regional services had been gradually introduced directly from Kuala Lumpur. MAS had become an important player on the Europe-Australia trunk route, including routes to major hubs in London and Frankfurt, and started trans-Pacific services to Los Angeles via Tokyo in the previous year. This did not come without cost, however. Indeed, MAS' balance sheet suffered, and economies were made in the domestic services, as the airline did not wish to pull back from the penetration into oversea markets that it had successfully made.

Today, MAS uses more than 100 aircraft to serve more than 110 destinations across six continents. In 1997, MAS' revenues dropped slightly but its loss position improved from 1996. It also carried more passengers but the overall load factor still decreased. Currently, MAS' ownership is evenly split between the public and the Malaysian government but full- scale privatization is being considered. MAS lost US$70million in the fiscal year ended March 1998, compared with US$100 million profit in 96-97 financial year, and it has reported losing US$115 million in first six months of the fiscal year 1998-99. As a result of the loss, it is considering laying off up to 6,000 of 21,000 staff. Also, MAS has cut fleet and arranged US$ 100 million credit with a Saudi bank for aircraft sale and lease-back. It sold two 747s to Qantas in August 1998, and three more on offer, and leased out 15 aircraft. It has delayed eight 777 and six 747 deliveries from 1999-2001 by up to three years. MAS has also made cuts in domestic and international operations, closing on-line stations at Madrid, Cebu, Macau, Vientiane and Pusan. It has recently entered code sharing with KLM.

By the end of the decade, MAS expects to expand its network to over 100 destinations, of which 70 will be international. At the same time, it plans to undertake an intensive US$5 billion replacement and renewal programme to transform its fleet into the youngest in the region.

4.4   Philippines

Philippines is an archipelago of 7,100 islands with a population of 77.7 million. The Philippine economy experienced considerable difficulty in the

1980s. Real gross national product grew at an annual average of only 1.8 percent, less than the 2.5 percent growth rate of population. However, the economy made a turn-around in the 1990s, and was able to sustain continued positive economic growth for a number of years before the Asian crisis.

International air traffic increased consistently in the 1980s, despite economic difficulties, and this increase continued into the 1990s. Total international scheduled passenger traffic rose at an average annual rate of 7.8 percent between 1985 and 1993, amounting to 5.7 million passengers in 1993. This traffic further increased to 7.5 million passengers in 1997 (Exhibit 4-10). Before the Asia crisis, IATA forecast predicts that total international scheduled passenger traffic to/from Philippines will reach 22 million by 2010. This forecast appears to be over-estimated in light of recent developments. The most recent IATA 5-year forecast predicts that total international scheduled passenger traffic will reach 9.5 million in 2002. North America, Europe, Southeast Asia, and South Pacific all expect to have strong growth. Northeast Asia is the most important air traffic generating region for Philippines, accounting for over 52 percent of total international traffic to and from the Philippines in 1997. This percentage is expected to be maintained over the next 5 years.

Exhibit 4-10
Total International Scheduled Passenger Traffic to/from Philippines
(thousands of passengers)

	Europe	Americas	Asia-Pacific	Rest of World	Total
1985	147.0	83.4	2,429.7	447.7	3,107.8
1986	146.6	91.3	2,499.6	429.4	3,166.8
1987	165.9	137.4	2,4749.5	469.7	3,522.5
1988	210.8	163.4	3,103.9	565.5	4,043.6
1989	204.6	180.1	3,449.1	490.5	4,324.3
1990	220.4	190.9	3,219.9	485.7	4,117.0
1991	249.3	179.7	3,519.3	487.8	4,436.0
1992	291.8	220.4	4,154.3	600.4	5,266.9
1993	307.9	213.0	4,517.5	644.9	5,683.3
1996	348.0	977.0	5,664.0	635.0	7,624.0
1997	426.0	1,025.0	5,478.0	611.0	7,540.0
2002	581.0	1,328.0	6,993.0	627.0	9,530.0

Source: IATA, 1995, 1998

There are a total of 301 airports in Philippines, 237 are usable. There are four international airports, namely, the Ninoy Aquino International Airport in Metro Manila, the Mactan International Airport in Cebu, the

Clark International Airport in Angeles City and the Subic Bay International Airport in Olongapo City. However, most of the international traffic was handled in Manila (Ninoy Aquino). Manila has been experiencing serious congestions. The government had planned to increase its airport capacity and facilities to meet forecasted strong traffic growth. However, the current economic downturn has prompted some concerns regarding the capacity expansion.

Political instability, coupled with economic difficulties, largely hampered the tourism industry in Philippines during the 1980s. In particular, air arrivals experienced negative growth during the first half of the 1980s. Tourist arrivals rose rapidly in 1988 and 1989, then declined in 1990 and 1991, but have since increased considerably. Exhibit 4-11 shows the visitor arrivals by region for the 1993-1998 period. This represents a significant increase from the 1.0 million in 1988. It also shows that East Asia remains the largest generator for visitors to Philippines, followed by North America. However, the latter experienced a much larger growth rate. Visitor volumes from ASEAN countries and from Europe have also had strong growth during the period. Over 95 percent of all visitors arrive by air. There were 1.4 million air visitors in 1993, this number is expected to increase to 5.6 million by 2010 (IATA, 1995). Furthermore, the number of air visitor arrivals is expected to increase more rapidly than airline passenger traffic, which means that incoming visitors will contribute to traffic growth to a larger extent than outgoing residents.

Development of Major Carrier

Philippine Airlines Ltd PAL is the national carrier for the Philippines and is probably Asia's oldest airline, although having been restructured and renamed several times. PAL started as a private company, the government of Philippines became a minority shareholder shortly after its incorporation, and later became a majority shareholder. PAL enjoyed a monopoly status during the early years of its development, but started to face competition in the late 1950s. PAL became a state-owned company in November 1977. While going through many vicissitudes of political and industrial strife, PAL maintained its steady growth by expanding its international network while maintaining its domestic network. In 1988, the Aquino administration decided that the government shareholding in PAL would be substantially reduced as part of the administration's measures to introduce wider competition in the airline industry. By 1998, the Lucio Tan Group held 70 percent of the shares while the government held 15 percent.

Exhibit 4-11
Visitor Arrivals in Philippines by Region of Residence

	1995	1996	1997	1998
Asean	92,965	139,324	155,226	137,030
East Asia	750,938	896,096	971,870	816,449
South Asia	20,856	24,646	26,189	29,883
Middle East	20,242	21,543	18,334	19,810
North America	387,914	430,805	491,523	535,564
Central America	800	955	1,238	1,430
South America	2,595	3,068	3,452	3,602
Western Europe	108,529	127,628	133,198	140,420
Northern Europe	94,360	112,925	126,094	134,771
Southern Europe	22,613	25,210	27,959	27,089
Eastern Europe	3,842	4,213	4,368	4,778
Oceania	85,244	98,473	105,391	97,438
Africa	2,634	2,891	2,913	3,142
Others and Unspecified Residences	16,728	18,837	20,227	23,674
Overseas Filipinos	149,903	142,753	134,541	174,277
Grand Total	**1,760,163**	**2,049,367**	**2,222,523**	**2,149,357**

Source: Department of Tourism (DOT), Philippines

One of PAL's constant challenges has been to make its numerous, nation-serving domestic routes more efficiently run and profitable as well as creating a stronger presence in Asia. Many of PAL's domestic services to the many remote islands are low-volume routes that do not contribute to network earnings. In 1996, PAL Chairman, Lucio Tan proposed a series of reforms to turn around PAL and make it the best airline in Asia, including a US$4 billion re-fleeting and modernization program. However, his plan has substantially increased the company costs and leverage, weakening its cashflow position. The Asian economic crisis devalued the Peso, reduced air travel and also added to PAL's troubles. By mid- 1998, the PAL pilots went on strike over pay and work conditions. Operations were grounded and PAL could not meet its interest and debt obligations of $2.1billion. It went into receivership and fired 5000 employees. In September 1998, PAL shut down its operations to protect its remaining assets. Operation was partially resumed in October 1998 after the union agreed to a 20 percent ownership in the company. At present, PAL has 8,770 employees with a fleet of 24 aircraft.

Under the current rehabilitation plan, PAL has reduced its fleet size by nearly a half, as well as route capacity and employees. The rehabilitation program has shifted into a new phrase following an infusion of $200 million in new capital in June 1999. The program hopes to improve route profits, fleet efficiency and cashflow demands in the long-term. At least for now, PAL is assured of 10 years of labour stability.

4.5 Singapore

The Air Transport Market

The Singapore economy is small by international standards: Gross Domestic Product of US$84 billion in 1998. But, it is a relatively rich economy with per-capita GNP in 1998 of US$22,800. It is highly open to international trade and investment: trade to GDP ratio of 250 percent. Singapore has been able to maintain high economic growth with low inflation for the past four decades.

Given its small market base, Singapore relies heavily on air traffic from other countries such as Indonesia, Malaysia, China and Japan, to sustain its aviation industry. Total international scheduled passenger traffic to and from Singapore increased at an average annual rate of 10.2 percent between 1985 and 1993, amounting to 18.7 million passengers in 1993. This number further increased to 23.3 million in 1997 (Exhibit 4-12). The regions that achieved the strongest growth during that period were the Americas, with an average annual rate of 29.6 percent, and Northeast Asia at 13.3 percent per year. Southeast Asia remains the most important region for air traffic to/from Singapore, accounting for 46.4 percent of total international scheduled passenger traffic in 1993, and 43.3 percent in 1997. Note that the forecast for 2010 was made before the Asian crisis, thus it is likely to be over-estimated in light of current developments.

Tourist traffic is an important component of Singapore's air traffic.

Exhibit 4-12
Total International Scheduled Passenger Traffic to/from Singapore
(thousands of passengers)

	Europe	Americas	Asia-Pacific	Rest of World	Total
1985	903.4	40.6	7,537.7	162.3	8,644.0
1986	980.3	86.2	7,573.9	176.2	8,816.6
1987	1,061.8	93.7	8,620.5	170.0	9,945.9
1988	1,210.0	144.5	10,271.9	193.9	11,820.3
1989	1,421.5	160.1	11,433.7	236.8	13,252.1
1990	1,532.0	271.2	12,239.0	210.0	14,252.2
1991	1,543.6	229.5	13,299.6	226.3	15,298.9
1992	1,639.0	239.1	14,590.1	264.7	16,732.9
1993	1,869.1	323.0	16,203.5	346.0	18,741.6
1996	2,302.0	572.0	19,726.0	487.0	23,087.0
1997	2,466.0	609.0	19,701.0	489.0	23,266.0
2002	3,189.0	808.0	23,521.0	612.0	28,130.0
2010	5,889.2	1,086.1	51,456.0	1,046.8	59,478.2

Source: IATA, 1995, 1998

Exhibit 4-13 shows recent visitor arrival (excluding visitors entering from Malaysia by land) volumes to Singapore. The most important tourist generating market is ASEAN countries, accounting for about 30 percent of tourist arrivals in 1998. Exhibit 4-13 also lists Singapore's top five tourist generating markets in 1998. Visitor arrivals increased 12 percent between 1993 and 1997, while international scheduled passenger traffic increased 24 percent during the same period. Outbound departures of Singapore residents by air rose from 2.16 million in 1993 to 3.67 million in 1997, an increase of 70 percent (Exhibit 4-14). This clearly shows that Singapore residents outgoing traffic contribute the most to the growth of Singapore international air traffic.

The Asian crisis has undoubtedly had considerable impact on the air traffic to/from Singapore. Inbound traffic into Singapore decreased by 13.3 percent to 6.2 million arrivals in 1998. Singapore also lost much air market share to competitors in the region. Passenger traffic at Changi Airport fell by 5.4 percent, while cargo traffic fell 3.9 percent. The Asian crisis slowed

Exhibit 4-13
Visitor Arrivals in Singapore
(thousands)

1993	1996	1997	1998
	Total Visitor Arrivals		
6,425.8	7,292.5	7,198	6,241.0

Top Five Tourist Generating Markets for Singapore

ASEAN		1,870.6
Japan		843.7
Australia		427.2
Taiwan		362.4
UK		357.9

Source: Singapore Department of Statistics

Exhibit 4-14
Outbound Departures of Singapore Residents by Mode of Transport
(thousands)

	1993	1997	1998
Air	1,587.4	2,391.8	2,197.8
Sea	568.8	1,279.3	1,547.2
Total	**2,156.2**	**3,671.1**	**3,744.9**

Source: Singapore Department of Statistics

the Singaporean economy down a great deal in the second half of 1998. This especially impacted the long-haul outbound air traffic as many travelers were unwilling to fly to popular vacation spots in other continents. As a result, Singapore's air passenger traffic growth was the highest to travel destinations in Malaysia, Thailand and Indonesia. The number of travelers to China and Hong Kong declined slightly.

Despite the slow performance, Singapore has not been hurt as severely as other Asian countries. It uses its strategic location to gain traffic and reciprocal air rights from other countries that need access to the regional markets. The U.S., in particular, has had to set a very liberal bilateral agreement with Singapore in order for its mega carriers to use the Singapore hubs. The most recent IATA forecast predicts that international scheduled passenger traffic will grow at 4.0 percent in 1999, 4.4 percent in 2000, 4.5 percent in 2001, and 4.5 percent in 2002, amounting to 28.1 million passengers. The strongest growth is expected to be from South Asia, followed by North America and South Pacific. Southeast Asia will remain as the most important market, accounting for 40 percent of total international scheduled passenger traffic to/from Singapore in 2002.

Development of Major Carrier

Singapore Airlines   Singapore's flag carrier, was born in February 1972[7] with Singapore's share of the failed Malaysia-Singapore Airlines (MSA). Singapore Airlines (SIA) received about 83 percent of MSA's asset. It inherited almost all the overseas points on the previous MSA network; all the long range aircraft and most of the medium range ones; and the MSA head office and engineering base in Singapore. The new national flag carrier of Singapore had a modest fleet comprising 10 aircraft, a staff of 6,000 and a route network spanning 22 cities in 18 countries.

During the 1970s, Singapore Airlines undertook fast and furious expansion of the international and intercontinental route system it had inherited from MSA, particularly to the European market. Only six years after its independent existence, SIA was voted 'Airline of the Year' in January 1978 by the *Travel News* magazine of Great Britain. By April 1980, Singapore Airlines was operating 17 weekly services to Europe, all with Boeing 747s.

On September 23, 1977, Singapore Airlines was granted landing rights to fly to San Francisco, via Hong Kong, Guam and Honolulu. In exchange Singapore had to grant generous rights to U.S. airlines for access to its Southeast Asian hub. Its first trans-Pacific service, on April 1, 1978, was a cargo flight. Its plans for passenger services met some obstacles with British authorities over the traffic rights through Hong Kong. In resolving these, SIA decided to omit Guam as a stop, and thus became the first airline to operate non-stop from Hong Kong to Honolulu. By July 1980, Singapore Airlines was operating nine weekly flights across the Pacific between four major Asian gateways and three major destinations in the United States.

Today, Singapore Airlines is internationally recognized as one of the world's leading carriers with 13,690 employees. Singapore Airlines has the most modern fleet in the industry with 89 aircraft[8] in operation at an average age of 4 years and 9 months. SIA has formed major alliances with Lufthansa, Air New Zealand, Ansett, Scandinavian Airlines System, and United Airlines. SIA has also signed Memoranda of Understanding to form alliances with South African Airways, and Air Canada. As of March 31,

1999, SIA operated 572 weekly flights out of Singapore. Together with its alliance partners, SIA's route network spans over 115 cities in more than 42 countries. In the fiscal year 1998-99, SIA carried 12.8 millions passengers, and 768,500 tonnes of cargo.

4.6 Cambodia, Laos and Vietnam

Cambodia Cambodia borders the Gulf of Thailand, between Thailand, Vietnam, and Laos, with a population of 11.3 million. Its per capita GDP was US$289 in 1995. Measured by purchasing power parity, its per capita GDP was $715 in 1997. Political instability has severely hampered the country's economic development. Human resource levels in the population are low, particularly in the poverty-ridden countryside. The almost total lack of basic infrastructure in the countryside will continue to hinder development.

There are about 20 airports in the country which are served mainly by its national carrier, Royal Air Cambodge. Four foreign carriers also provide services to Cambodia, namely, Air France, China Southern, Thai Airways International and Bangkok Airways. Tourism industry is relatively small, but growing. In 1997, there were 218,843 visitors arrived in Cambodia (Exhibit 4-15). Most of them came from Asia. Information on air traffic to and from Cambodia is not available to us at this point.

Laos Laos is a land-linked country bordered on the north by China, on the south by Cambodia, on the east by Vietnam, on the north-west by Myanmar, and on the west by Thailand. Laos has a population of 5.3 million. The population is growing by 2.6 percent per year, among the highest growth rates in the region. Forty five percent of the population is below the age of fifteen. Over the period 1994 to 1996, GDP growth in

Exhibit 4-15
Tourist Arrivals in Cambodia

	1993	1994	1995	1996	1997
Asia				178,015	150,205
Europe				53,761	43,331
America				27,812	24,561
Africa & Middle East				901	746
Total	**118,183**	**176,617**	**219,680**	**260,489**	**218,843**

Source: Ministry of Tourism, The Royal Government of Cambodia

Laos averaged over 7 percent per year. Despite the Asian crisis, growth in 1997 was 7.2 percent. There are 52 airports in Laos, and the national carrier, Lao Aviation, provides services from Vientiane to most of the provincial capitals. Four foreign carriers fly to Laos: Silk Air, Yunnan Airlines, Vietnam Airlines, and Thai Airways. There are 9 direct international routes linking Laos with its Asian neighbors.

Vietnam   Vietnam borders the Gulf of Thailand, Gulf of Tonkin, and South China Sea, alongside China, Laos, and Cambodia. It is a densely populated country with a population of 76 million. It has achieved substantial progress in its economy over the past decade, moving forward from an extremely low starting point. During the 1991-1995 period, the economy grew at an average rate of 8.5 percent per year. Economic growth continued at a strong pace during 1997 with industrial output rising by 12 percent and real GDP expanding by 8.5 percent. The tourism industry has grown at an average rate of nearly 50 percent per year since 1991. Vietnam forecasts that the country will receive 3.8 million foreign tourists per year by the year 2000 and 8.7 million foreign and 15~18 million local tourists by 2010.

Vietnam has about 48 airports, but most of its international traffic is handled at Ho Chi Min Airport. Vietnam's national carrier, Vietnam Airlines, flies to 16 domestic destinations, and 23 international destinations in Europe, Asia, Australia and the Middle East. In 1998, Vietnam Airlines carried 1.57 million domestic passengers and 0.9 million international passengers, accounting for 93.7 percent and 38.6 percent of the market shares, respectively. Exhibit 4-16 shows air passenger traffic in Vietnam between 1991 and 1998. Total domestic and international air travel in Vietnam increased at an average of 40.9 percent per year between 1985 and 1995, reaching 3.6 million in 1995. Total international scheduled passenger traffic to and from Vietnam increased at an average annual rate of 33 percent between 1985 and 1993. Most of this growth took place after 1988. Total international scheduled traffic reached 1.2 million passengers in 1993, and further increased to 1.7 million in 1997. Northeast Asia is Vietnam's largest market, followed closely by Southeast Asia. Vietnam is expected to achieve the strongest growth in air travel over the next two decades, and become an important player in the air transport market in Southeast Asia. The most recent IATA forecast predicts that international scheduled passenger traffic will grow at 7.5 percent in 1999, 8.6 percent in 2000, 8.2 percent in 2001, and 7.6 percent in 2002, reaching 2.4 million passengers in 2002.

Exhibit 4-16
Total Airline Passengers in Vietnam
(thousands)

	Domestic	International
1991	235.7	565.7
1992	457.2	876.3
1993	678.7	1,146.6
1994	1,038.8	1,626.3
1995	1,424.4	2,060.6
1996	1,623.4	2,263.8
1997	1,652.5	2,324.6
1998	1,675.5	2,360.8

Source: Vietnam Airlines

4.7   South Pacific

The Air Transport Market

Air transport market in South Pacific is characterized by long distance between regional airports and low population density. Airlines in the region have often been criticized for high fares and/or low frequencies. Air traffic growth has been somewhat slower, as compared to other parts of Asia Pacific. Total international scheduled passenger traffic in the region increased from 16.4 million in 1993 to 19.4 million in 1997, an 18 percent increase, compared to the 29 percent increase over the same time period in Asia (IATA, 1995, 1998). Australia is the largest country in the region, this section will focus on Australia.

Australia The nature of air traffic in Australia has changed substantially over the last two decades. In 1984, nearly two-thirds of the traffic was Australians travelling to Asia, but a decade later, two-thirds of the traffic originated in Asia. In 1998, there were 3.16 million Australians travelling overseas, compared to 4.17 million visitors arriving in Australia. New Zealand is the most popular destination for Australians travelling overseas, accounting for 14.9 percent of total resident departures in 1998. Japan is the largest source market for visitors to Australia, providing 18 percent of total visitor arrivals in 1998. Exhibit 4-17 shows visitor arrivals increased at a greater rate than the resident departures during the 1991–1998 period.

Exhibit 4-17
Resident Departures and Visitor Arrivals in Australia
(thousands)

	Visitor Arrivals	Resident Departures
1991	2,370	2,099
1992	2,603	2,276
1993	2,996	2,267
1994	3,362	2,354
1995	3,726	2,519
1996	4,165	2,733
1997	4,318	2,933
1998	4,167	3,161

Source: Australian Bureau of Statistics

A total of 61 international scheduled airlines operated services to and from Australia in 1998, carrying 7.2 million inbound passengers and 7.1 million outbound passengers as well as a total of 631,900 tonnes of freight. Qantas Airways carried 36.4 percent of the passengers and 28.9 percent of the freight. Sydney International Airport accounted for 48.7 percent of total passenger traffic and for 53.1 percent of total freight traffic. Exhibit 4-18 lists international scheduled traffic to/from Australia since 1978. Passenger traffic increased four-fold during the period, while freight traffic increased over five-fold. Recent IATA forecast indicates that international scheduled passenger traffic to/from Australia will increase at 4.6 percent in 1999, 5.7 percent in 2000, 4.7 percent in 2001, and 4.2 percent in 2002, reaching 17.8 million passengers in 2002 (IATA, 1998).

Development of Major Carrier

Qantas Airways   Australia's international airline is the 10th largest airline in the world and 2nd largest in the Asia Pacific. Founded in 1920, it also claims to be the second oldest carrier in the world. Originating as an Australian/Britain mail carrier, it was nationalized in 1947 and grew rapidly due to the tourism boom in Australia. Qantas provided only international services before its merge with Australian Airlines, a domestic carrier, in 1993. A month before the merger decision was made, 25 percent ownership was sold to British Airways as part of Australia's air transport deregulation. It was fully privatized in 1995.

In 1997, Qantas joined forces with two of the world's largest and most profitable airlines, British Airways and American Airlines, in the

Exhibit 4-18
International Scheduled Traffic to/from Australia

Year	Flights			Passengers		
	Inbound	Outbound	Total	Inbound	Outbound	Total
1978/79	10,405	10,359	20,764	1,790,154	1,716,599	3,506,753
1979/80	10,253	10,225	20,478	2,059,450	1,959,866	4,019,316
1980/81	10,251	10,236	20,487	2,127,234	1,981,031	4,108,265
1981/82	11,212	11,134	22,346	2,192,327	1,993,844	4,186,171
1982/83	10,799	10,687	21,486	2,164,525	2,084,724	4,249,249
1983/84	10,622	10,460	21,082	2,239,728	2,211,980	4,451,708
1984/85	11,319	11,066	22,385	2,519,447	2,469,551	4,988,998
1985/86	12,729	12,579	25,308	2,767,413	2,656,964	5,424,377
1986/87	14,893	14,805	29,698	3,154,920	3,040,061	6,194,981
1987/88	17,005	16,843	33,848	3,692,976	3,518,767	7,211,743
1988/89	19,560	19,294	38,854	4,022,634	3,907,954	7,930,588
1989/90	21,340	21,013	42,353	4,175,315	4,077,454	8,252,769
1990/91	22,743	22,557	45,300	4,257,165	4,167,346	8,424,511
1991/92	24,264	24,155	48,419	4,539,042	4,503,847	9,042,889
1992/93	26,207	26,088	52,295	4,902,693	4,856,372	9,759,065
1993/94	27,504	27,277	54,781	5,340,017	5,281,959	10,621,976
1994/95	30,501	30,157	60,658	5,830,311	5,735,811	11,566,122
1995/96	34,403	33,984	68,387	6,391,884	6,288,528	12,680,412
1996/97	37,432	36,898	74,330	6,895,374	6,823,453	13,718,827
1997/98	39,054	38,546	77,600	7,066,748	6,997,080	14,063,828

	Freight (tonnes)			Mail (tonnes)		
	Inbound	Outbound	Total	Inbound	Outbound	Total
1978/79	65,613	46,226	111,839	5,838	3,869	9,707
1979/80	69,614	52,370	121,984	6,071	3,803	9,874
1980/81	72,243	55,597	127,840	6,133	3,972	10,106
1981/82	89,871	67,837	157,708	6,661	4,110	10,771
1982/83	89,569	77,134	166,703	6,834	4,283	11,117
1983/84	108,927	85,001	193,928	7,262	4,080	11,342
1984/85	122,253	100,615	222,868	7,826	4,791	12,617
1985/86	111,075	124,710	235,785	7,719	4,974	12,693
1986/87	111,324	157,071	268,395	7,408	5,555	12,963
1987/88	130,135	165,932	296,067	7,691	6,237	13,928
1988/89	165,318	159,328	324,646	8,492	6,747	15,238
1989/90	176,338	177,560	353,898	9,128	6,829	15,957
1990/91	174,208	183,298	357,507	9,910	6,864	16,774
1991/92	179,042	200,801	379,843	10,018	7,263	17,281
1992/93	191,500	241,310	432,810	9,893	7,280	17,173
1993/94	211,729	264,606	476,336	10,469	8,196	18,665
1994/95	251,240	293,208	544,448	10,566	7,627	18,193
1995/96	253,988	313,134	567,122	11,192	8,530	19,722
1996/97	285,850	331,752	617,602	12,920	8,530	21,450
1997/98	308,313	338,935	647,248	13,249	8,721	21,969

Source: Department of Transport and Regional Services, Australia

formation of Global Explorer, in efforts to dominate their consolidated positions in world air transport. Today, this alliance has expanded into OneWorld. Qantas has extensively used international alliances in past years to maintain its customer base and market share, given Australia's remote geographic location. It is looking for a continental hub in Europe, Paris or Zurich is most likely. Financially, Qantas reached its targeted cost-savings plan, while its revenues and profits have grown consistently in the last 5 years. Qantas revenues have increased from US$4 billion in 1993 to over US$6 billion in 1998. Net profits were about US$200 million in 1998, an increase of 21 percent from the previous year. International route earnings have declined but domestic revenues have increased. Today, Qantas employs around 29,000 staff across a network that spans 104 destinations in Australia, Africa, the Americas, Asia, Europe, the Middle East and the Pacific. It operates a jet fleet of 100 aircraft. In 1997/1998, Qantas carried 16.4 million passengers (18.9 million by the Qantas group).

During the Asian economic crisis, Qantas suspended some Asian services, but claims that this did little to affect company profits since Asian route revenues do not contribute much to overall income. Despite being the fastest growing markets, Asian routes often brought poor returns as compared to non- Asian routes. Today, top Qantas executives are faced with problem of expanding routes. Since Australia is disadvantaged in terms of location and has a small market, Qantas has relied on 3rd parties for rights to fly elsewhere and is often restricted in its capacity by major Asian countries to do so. On the contrary, other Asian carriers have exploited their 6th freedom rights to fly over their countries between Europe and Australia.

4.8 Summary

Air transport market experienced tremendous growth in the 1980s and 1990s in the Southeast Asia and South Pacific region, and is expected to continue to have strong growth in the future. Tourist traffic is a very important component of the air traffic in the region. In many parts of the region, growth in inbound visitors contributed to traffic growth to a larger extent than resident outgoing traffic. Malaysia and Philippines are such examples. On the other hand, in Thailand resident outgoing travel and Bangkok Airport transfer traffic had increased more rapidly than incoming air visitor arrivals before the recent economic crisis.

Singapore and Thailand are the dominant markets in the region at present. However, Vietnam is expected to have the strongest growth over the next two decades, followed by Philippines and Thailand. Vietnam's international scheduled passenger traffic is predicted to grow at an average rate of 7.9 percent between 1999 and 2002. The total international scheduled passenger traffic is expected to grow at an average rate of 5.3 percent over the same period in Southeast Asia, and 5.1 percent in South Pacific. Majority of this traffic is within the Asia Pacific region.

The region also hosts a number of the world's major carriers, including Singapore Airlines, Thai Airways, and Qantas. Singapore Airlines is one of the most efficient carriers in the world, and has been able to remain profitable in the midst of the recent economic crisis. However, other carriers in the region have experienced various degrees of financial difficulties, some long before the economic crisis. For example, Garuda started to lose money heavily in the mid-1980s, and has not been able to become truly profitable since then. Philippines Airlines was forced to seek bankruptcy protection in the fall of 1998. Privatization of national flag carriers appears to an ongoing trend in the region.

Notes

[1]   The Economist Intelligence Unit, *Country Profile - Thailand, 1995-96*.

[2]   Thai Airways International and Air Siam operated separate international route networks in the 1970s. Because of political reasons, however, Air Siam was forced out of business in 1977. Thai Airways then took over its routes and became Thai's sole designated international carrier.

[3]   'Thailand Designates Angel Airlines Its Second International Carrier', *Aviation Daily*, October 29, 1998.

[4]   IATA, *Asia-Pacific Air Transport Forecast: 1980-2010*, 1995.

[5]   This was also partly because of the continued attempts by Garuda to limit its services to feeder routes and remote services.

[6]   Including 5.3 million so-called excursionist arrivals that did not stay over night.

[7]   It was initially named as Mercury Singapore Airlines, and was later renamed as Singapore Airlines in June, 1972 (Davies, 1997).

[8]   SIA has 46 aircraft on firm order, and 33 on option.

5 Current Regulatory Approaches

The regulatory environment in which international airlines operate will continue to have major impacts on airline network structures, management strategies, and consequently, airline productivity and efficiencies. International air transport is traditionally regulated by a complex network of bilateral and multilateral agreements. This chapter reviews the current approaches to bilaterals by different countries in the Asia-Pacific region, and discusses problems and issues arising out of the current approaches.

5.1 History of the United States - Asia Aviation Relations

Some of the current approaches to air bilaterals in Asia can be traced to the historical development of the aviation relationship between the United States and Asian countries. It was at the Chicago Convention (1944) where the world aviation community decided that the international airline business would be governed by a bilateral rather than multilateral framework. During the following ten years, the U.S. signed air treaties with many Asian countries. The U.S. essentially obtained unlimited 3rd/4th freedom rights and extensive fifth freedom rights on intra-Asia/Oceania routes. The U.S. was also successful in limiting Asian carriers' access points to the United States. There were at least two reasons for the U.S.' success in obtaining such extensive traffic rights. First, Japan, a nation just defeated in WWII, was not in a strong position to argue for rights against the will of their conqueror.[1] Other Asian countries granted what the U.S. wanted because they were so grateful to the U.S., their saviour from Japanese invasion and colonial rule. Second, most countries did not pay much attention to international airline affairs as they did not have commercially viable airline industries. The U.S. (and to a lesser extent UK) had a commercial airline industry, aircraft, and trained personnel. They foresaw the value and enormous potential of the industry.

Asian countries eventually realized their disadvantage in asymmetric traffic rights from unfair bilateral air agreements with the U.S. From the mid-1980s, the Japanese government and its carriers began to register dissenting voices regarding these asymmetric rights. Japan Airlines began to lose market share to U.S. carriers, particularly to Northwest, United Airlines and Federal Express.[2] In recent years, Japanese bilateral negotiators have threatened the U.S. that Japan may repeal the 1952 U.S.-Japan Air Agreement and renegotiate a fair deal. Although other Asian countries, such as Korea, Taiwan, Philippines, etc., are not happy with asymmetric traffic rights, they are reluctantly getting along with the U.S. as the U.S. has been allowing these Asian carriers to access more U.S. cities. Thailand abrogated its bilateral ASA with the U.S. in 1990, and it took several years to sign a new agreement.

Many Asian carriers would like to box the U.S. into third and fourth freedoms, and completely discard fifth freedom rights. However, while the airlines may display a united front against the injustices of invading outsiders, individual carriers and countries have in fact made their own deals and reached accommodations to suit their own needs (Donoghue, 1996).

Naturally, there is a growing movement in Asia to develop some bloc unity to blunt the impact of U.S. carriers (Donoghue, 1996). For example, Japan's Ministry of Transport proposed a 'Competitive Skies' policy to counter the U.S.-initiated 'Open Skies' policy. The proposal was endorsed by civil aviation officials from 12 Asian and Oceanian countries at a two-day international forum held in Bangkok, March 1997.[3] This 'competitive skies' policy is intended to establish a framework enabling airlines of all countries to compete on equal footing.

5.2   Approaches to Bilateral Agreements in Northeast Asia

This section describes the airline policy stance and general attitude of Northeast Asian countries when negotiating bilateral air treaties and/or in multilateral policy fora. Major concerns of each country during the negotiations are also highlighted.

Traditionally, the Asia-Pacific international air service market was dominated by monopolistic flag carriers. However, since the late 1980s, second tier intra-Asia regional carriers have emerged (Knibb, 1993), and the competitive self interest of these carriers has had considerable impact on the development of air policy. Some countries have started to allow second tier airlines to enter the international market, although many of these smaller airlines are confined to relatively few international points and are frequently excluded from long-haul high density markets. However, once a government allows new carriers to emerge (often to encourage competition and to make domestic markets more efficient), inevitably they feel obligated to keep them alive and help them grow. For example, Korea allowed a new carrier, Asiana Airlines, to enter its domestic market in 1988. When Asiana complained that it incurred losses on domestic routes, it was allowed to expand to some profitable international routes. Since then, the Korean government has allowed Asiana to expand to many intercontinental routes as well as intra-Asia routes. Hooper (1996) describes general patterns in which multiple carriers emerged in various Asian countries, and how creation of multiple carriers has influenced international route allocation policies of Asian countries: Korea, the Philippines, China, India, and Japan. Eventually, existence of multiple carriers forces a country to ask for multiple designation of carriers when negotiating bilateral agreements.

The development and changes in the attitude and approaches to air bilaterals are discussed below for each country.

Japan

Japan has only modest liberalization in place. The government is encouraging competition, but fares are still under regulatory control. Japan's international aviation system is orchestrated by regulations and administrative procedures crafted by bureaucrats in the Ministry of Transport. Japan Airlines and other flag carriers are also influential on Japanese government attitudes toward international aviation matters, as in most other Asian nations. At a 1994 ICAO conference in Montreal, Japanese delegate Akiyoshi Kitada said that 'while liberalization may produce more efficient airline management, low fares, increased traffic, and greater networking between airlines, it also leads to predatory pricing, capacity dumping, a retreat from thin routes, and a tendency toward oligopolies' (Ballantyne and Muqbil, 1994). A passive attitude has generally been adopted towards international air service liberalization. This is, to a large degree, due to the severe shortage of airport slots and the lack of competitiveness of Japanese carriers.

Japan was tangled in a long bitter dispute with the U.S. over air services agreements between the two countries, and has remained firm in its stance against open skies. Its concerns centre on the weak competitive position of Japan Airlines and All Nippon Airways (Oum and Yu, 1998), and on the potential encroachment of market shares by U.S. carriers on trans-Pacific and intra-Asian markets to and from Tokyo (Kayal 1997a, 1997b). For example, the Japanese carriers' share of trans-Pacific markets was reduced from 40 percent in 1986 to about 30 percent in 1994 (Oum and Taylor, 1995; Yamauchi and Ito, 1996).

The U.S.-Japan air treaty was signed in 1952. As a defeated nation in WWII, Japan had little power to wrestle with the U.S. for a fair deal. Also, at the time, not many Japanese nationals travelled overseas, nor did Japan have a well-developed commercial airline system. The 1952 accord gave some U.S. airlines (Pan Am, Northwest, and Flying Tigers- later acquired by Federal Express) virtually unlimited 'fifth-freedom' rights, allowing them to use three important Japanese cities (Tokyo, Osaka and Naha[4]) as a jump-off point for operations to/from the rest of Asia. American carriers operated 23 routes linking Japan to the rest of Asia (Holloway, 1996). In contrast, Japanese carriers had virtually no fifth-freedom traffic rights from the U.S.. The only practical route Japan could use was the Los Angeles-Sao Paolo, Brazil route. In addition to the imbalance in beyond rights, Japan points out another imbalance in the U.S.-Japan ASA: the number of incumbent (full-right) carriers.[5] Although the number of designated carriers was not specified in the text of the 1952 treaty, it happened that the U.S. designated three carriers and Japan originally designated only one (Japan Airlines). Japan regards this as another imbalance of opportunity against Japanese carriers. Under the treaty, U.S. airlines can only fly to Tokyo, Osaka and Naha (after Okinawa returned to Japan), while Japanese airlines can fly to seven U.S. airports - Anchorage, Honolulu, Los Angeles, New York, San Francisco, Saipan, and Guam. Since flight-originating cities are not restricted to either party, Japan argues that U.S. carriers are able to serve from more U.S. cities than JAL, which can fly only to four U.S. mainland cities.

The U.S. often hears similar complaints from other Asian countries concerning asymmetric bilateral agreements favouring the U.S. carriers. To counter these arguments, the U.S. points out that it has the world's largest aviation market. Foreign carriers, in fact, enjoy greater benefits than they realize as they can access multiple U.S. airports. U.S. carriers, on the other hand, essentially serve only one or two cities in foreign countries. Thus, U.S. carriers are entitled to unlimited 5th freedom rights to/from Asian countries.

A series of 'provisional agreements' supplemented the original U.S.-Japan treaty: the Record of Communications (ROC) of 1982, and the Memorandum of Understanding (MOUs) of 1985 and 1989; ROC of 1995 and MOU of 1996 (see Murakami, 1997).[6] The agreements allowed for expansion of service destination points and more entry into U.S.-Japan markets. All Nippon Airways (ANA) and Nippon Cargo Air Lines (NCA) on the Japanese side and American Airlines, Delta, Continental and UPS on the U.S. side were allowed to enter the Japan-U.S. market as a result of these MOUs. They are thus referred to as 'MOU carriers' in the literature.

The U.S. carriers' rights to use the Tokyo-Narita Airport as an Asian hub has caused continuous frustrations for Japan. These two nations have directly opposing views regarding liberalization. For more than 20 years, Japan wanted to renegotiate an accord that would give its own airlines a larger slice of the trans-Pacific pie. Japanese airlines would like greater access to the U.S. market and restrict U.S. carriers' fifth freedoms beyond Japan, which they say have been unfairly exploited by American carriers. Japan argues that there is a need to rebalance existing bilateral agreements before going ahead with liberalization (Gallacher, 1995). In recent years, Japan has constantly expressed its desire to repeal the 1952 air treaty to establish a fair and equal agreement which would give carriers of both countries 'balanced opportunities.'

Although Japan argues that their carriers have been losing market shares because of unbalanced opportunities, it appears that more of its frustrations stem from the fact that its carriers have been losing their market shares because of their declining cost competitiveness.[7] Over time, Japan's attitude towards the U.S. has hardened as the U.S. carriers' share of Japan-U.S. traffic has increased from 58 percent in 1986 to over 70 percent in the 1990s, while the share of Japanese nationals among total international passengers to/from Japan has drastically increased (see Oum and Taylor, 1995). If Korea were to adopt Japan's argument, Korea would have far more reasons to cry as it has even greater 'unbalanced opportunities' than Japan. According to the Korea-U.S. ASA, any U.S. carrier may serve Korean cities via any intermediate point and beyond. Korean carriers' access to U.S. cities, on the other hand, have been restricted albeit having been expanded over time. Fifth freedom traffic rights of Korean carriers have also been severely restricted - 3 points beyond the U.S. (two points in Latin America and one point in Europe). However, the Korean government has not cried as loud as Japan, since U.S. carriers could not increase market shares in markets to/from Korea due to Korean carriers' aggressiveness and cost competitiveness.

It appears that Japan's concerns about fifth freedom rights are justified. According to IATA (1995), fifth-freedom traffic on intra-regional routes (including Asia and Oceania) to/from Tokyo was over 2.3 million passengers, which accounts for 24 percent of total intra-regional traffic handled at Tokyo (Narita). U.S. carriers control 20 percent of the lucrative Tokyo-Hong Kong market. Japan feels that U.S. airlines control too many slots in Tokyo's Narita airport. According to a JAL official, U.S. airlines control 800 slots, one third of all weekly slots. This is only slightly less than the total number of weekly slots used by all Japanese airlines combined for all flights world wide. Of these 800 slots, about 260 slots are used for beyond traffic (Nagata, 1997). And Northwest's 324 weekly slots at Narita are second only to Japan Airlines (Jennings, 1992). Japan regards U.S. 'incumbent' carriers' fifth-freedom rights as similar to cabotage rights in the U.S. market.

Why then, has Japan not abrogated the 1952 bilateral air treaty with the U.S like the French and Thai governments did a few years ago? There are two reasons. First, there are fears that the U.S. may decide to retaliate such a move in other Japan-U.S. trade areas where Japan enjoys enormous trade surpluses. Japanese airlines realize that their government will not be able to initiate an aviation war against the U.S. Second, Japan and its carriers know that they would not be able to successfully compete with the U.S. and other carriers in open markets even if the perceived 'imbalance of opportunities' is corrected. Japan Airlines currently suffers a 50 percent cost disadvantage relative to U.S. mega carriers (Oum and Yu, 1998). This leads one to conclude that, while the Japanese policy protects its carriers, it will be rational for Japan to use delay tactics for the time being.

Japan's views have spilled over to its bilateral air relations with other Asian neighbours. For example, from 1994, in various international and bilateral *fora*, Japan began to express growing concerns for increasing sixth freedom traffic (traffic diversion from Japan's direct international routes to connecting routes via Seoul and other Asian cities). According to some Japanese airline executives, on routes such as a UAL flight from LA to Seoul or Singapore, 90 percent of the passengers were sixth freedom passengers from Tokyo (Jennings, 1992).[8] Although there is no objective data to verify this figure, it does indicate Japan's growing concerns on this issue. It is clear that Korean carriers enjoy very good access to numerous profitable routes to/from Japan. In fact, an additional reason why Japan has raising concerns regarding sixth freedom traffic via Seoul is to warn Seoul that Japan has a means to retaliate if Korea signs an open skies agreement with the U.S.[9]   Therefore, Korea was in a delicate situation when negotiating open skies with the U.S. because of potential retaliatory actions by Japan.

Japan frequently blames a lack of airport capacity for its inability to expand opportunities for foreign carriers. Narita Airport unquestionably suffers a severe shortage of landing/takeoff slots. However, it is not known for sure how much of this blame is genuine and how much of it is to discourage foreign carriers from entering the market and expanding their market shares.

Of course, Japan protects its carriers at an enormous expense to passengers, most being Japan's own nationals.[10] It is clear that at present, Japan's overriding concern is to protect its flag carriers from competition.

Japanese regulators are under a spell by their inducers, the airline industry. Unless consumer voices are louder than the carriers', and policy priorities are changed, there will be no rationale for the Japanese government to voluntarily agree to an open skies agreement with the U.S., or any other country.

After lengthy intense, sometimes bitter, negotiations, Japan and the U.S. signed a new Memorandum of Understanding on aviation on March 14, 1998. The new agreement provides for unrestricted U.S.-Japan and beyond rights for the so-called incumbent carriers: United, Northwest, Federal Express, Japan Airlines, All Nippon Airways and Nippon Cargo Air Lines. These carriers are now able to operate between the U.S. and Japan without restrictions on frequency and city-pair.[11] The agreement allows the United States to designate two additional passenger carriers to serve Japan, one immediately and another in two years. The new agreement also allows for the first time extensive code-sharing between U.S. carriers, U.S. and Japanese carriers, and U.S. and third-country carriers on services between the United States and Japan, and beyond Japan. Under the agreement, further liberalization will take effect automatically after four years if a fully liberalized agreement is not in place by then. Slot allocation at Tokyo Narita, however, is not addressed by the new agreement, so carriers may still have some difficulties exercising the new rights.

Korea

In 1988, the Korean government diluted its flag carrier, *Korean Air*'s (KAL), monopoly power. A new entrant, *Asiana*, was allowed to compete, both domestically and internationally. The decision to establish a competitor to KAL was not necessarily an attempt to downsize KAL. Travel to and from Korea had increased dramatically, in tune with the country's economic transformation. Reportedly, KAL was unable to satisfy the rapidly rising demands for capacity. As a result, the share of international passenger traffic to and from Korea on Korean carriers fell. Creation of Asiana was a way to inject more Korean lift into the market, increase competition, and thus increase the total market share of Korean carriers.

Because the two Korean carriers compete with each other, international routes must be divided between Korean Air and Asiana based on the government's 'guidelines for the supervision and development of national flag carriers', established in 1990. The guidelines were subsequently revised in 1994, due to dissatisfaction by both carriers. Since the creation of Asiana, government policy towards bilateral air treaties has somewhat liberalized as it seeks dual designation of carriers.   However, with the exception of the liberal bilateral with the U.S, most of Korea's other bilateral air service agreements remain restrictive, even with its Asian neighbours. Another exception is with Japan, because Korean carriers together enjoy far higher market shares than Japanese carriers.

Korea has essentially granted unlimited 5th freedom rights to U.S. carriers. However, Korean carriers have succeeded in curbing U.S. carrier advances into Korea and beyond markets by strengthening their cost competitiveness vis-a-vis U.S. carriers.   The U.S. has gradually allowed Korean carriers to increase U.S. entry points, in exchange for the Korean side accommodation of various U.S. requests, such as U.S. carrier access to cargo terminals, easing ground service rules, relaxing CRS rules, etc.   The June 1991 revision to the U.S.-Korea bilateral air agreement is described as 'open designation, open route description and double disapproval pricing,' making the new Korea-U.S. bilateral one of the U.S.'s most pro-competitive (Jennings, 1992).

Korea is the United States' second-largest market in Asia.   The U.S. was aggressively pursuing open skies negotiations with Korea.   The main concern of the Korean side in the negotiation was about 'past imbalances' in the U.S.-Korea ASA, and it was very reluctant to allow change of gauge rights (essentially seventh freedom rights).   Eventually, the open skies agreement was reached in April 1998, and signed on June 8, 1998.   The U.S.-Korea Open Skies agreements permit unrestricted air service by the airlines of both sides between and beyond the other's territory, eliminating restrictions on how often carriers can fly, the kind of aircraft they use and the prices they can charge.   The allure for Korea's airlines of fifth freedom flights into Latin America helped convince Seoul to become Washington's largest open skies partner in Asia.   Korea's Ministry of Construction and Transportation estimates Korean airlines will gain U.S.$ 100 million in savings from the accord.

In the future, Korea will want to attract more foreign carriers to route their traffic via the New Seoul (Inchon) Airport, presently under construction.   But the need to adopt a more liberal approach towards foreign carriers will clash with the current needs to look after short-term interests of its flag carriers.   To develop the Inchon airport as an Asian super-hub, Korea accepted the U.S. demand for change of gauge so that U.S. carriers can use Inchon as their mini-hub to practice so-called 'Star-Burst' operations. This will undoubtedly give U.S. carriers a substantial relative advantage, not only in intra-Asian markets, but also on the trans-Pacific flights.   Korean carriers may not realize similar advantages in North

America because the Korea-U.S. open skies agreements does not include cabotage opportunities in the U.S. market.[12]

In the Asia-Pacific multilateral fora, Korean aviation authorities appear to favour liberalization in Asia. For example, at the February 1996 Kyoto conference, attended by delegates from 13 Australasian nations, Korean delegates seemed to have the most ambitious paper. It suggested two alternatives: either consider multilateral liberalization throughout Asia; or allow the more aggressive groups to form an open skies bloc among themselves, with others free to join later. Such views were in the minority at the conference (Magnier, 1996).

China

Prior to 1980, China's airline industry was a semi-military organization with the Civil Aviation Administration of China (CAAC) as a department of the air force for many years. The CAAC fulfilled a dual role as both civil aviation administrator/regulator and operator of airlines and airports. Due to its conflicting dual roles, it was difficult for the CAAC to operate as an economic entity, and thus, it lacked an efficient mechanism to fulfill its operational and regulatory functions. There was a four-level 'chain of command' system within the CAAC: CAAC, six regional civil aviation bureaux, twenty-three provincial civil aviation bureaux, and seventy-eight civil aviation stations (Zhang 1998). The industry was regulated in every aspect of air service provisions including market entry, route entry, frequency, and even passenger eligibility for air travel.

Since the early 1980's, when the overall Chinese economic reform began in earnest, China's aviation industry has undergone dramatic administrative and regulatory reforms. The first stage of the reform, between 1980 to 1986, separated civil aviation from the air force, and re-introduced business aspects to the airline industry. In addition, the six regional civil aviation bureaux became 'profit centres',[13] and were given more autonomy in making operational decisions.

The second stage of reform separated the CAAC's role as an administrator/regulator from that of an operator. The CAAC assumed a purely administrative/regulatory role from 1987.[14] A system of six state-owned semi-autonomous trunk carriers was established to provide domestic and international services.[15] Second-stage reforms also separated airport operations from airline operations, and established the 'airport decentralization' policy.[16] In addition, independent local/regional carriers, funded by local governments or large enterprises, were encouraged to enter the market.

From May 1994, foreign investors were allowed to invest in China's aviation industry, including equity stakes in airlines and airports. This was motivated by China's desire to achieve international air transport standards so that Chinese airlines could compete in global markets, as well as meet domestic demands (Lee, 1993). Foreign air transport enterprises are permitted to form joint ventures with a Chinese air transport enterprise and invest in China (Bowman, 1994). In fact, airport projects with overseas involvement are given priority in allocation of state resources and approvals.[17] In 1995, Hainan Airlines, a third tier carrier, emerged as China's first aviation enterprise to adopt the joint ownership system when a U.S. investor bought a 25 percent stake through private placement. In January 1997, China Eastern became the first Chinese airline to be listed on New York and Hong Kong Stock markets. China Southern has also listed its stocks in New York and Hong Kong since then. Air China is considering to do the same.

Although China has opened its aviation sector to foreign investments, it has been cautious in liberalizing its aviation sector, particularly in the international markets, it does not want to open its market too fast (Magnier, 1996). As the regulator of China's civil aviation, CAAC is responsible for negotiating bilateral air services agreements with foreign countries. CAAC has adopted a very restrictive view on international air transport. Here, we identify three aspects of the CAAC's approach to bilateral negotiation which limit competition in China's international air transport markets. First, in bilateral negotiations for third and fourth freedoms, the reciprocity principle was typically based on the actual market shares between Chinese and foreign carriers, not on the capacity provisions. It was claimed, for example, that on the Shanghai-Hong Kong route, the route capacity between China Eastern and Dragonair used to be a 2-1 division, i.e. for every one Dragonair flight, China Eastern could provide two flights. This is because, as argued by the Chinese side, the capacity allocation should be based on the realized market share which was 50/50 on the route even though it was a 2/1 capacity allocation. Second, no fifth freedom right is granted in any of China's bilaterals.[18] Third, generally, only one Chinese carrier is designated on a specific route, despite provisions in bilateral agreements allowing for the designation of multiple carriers.

China's restrictive policy in international air transport reflects the state of development of China's aviation industry. The policy is intended to protect China's uncompetitive carriers. On routes served by both Chinese and foreign carriers, travellers appear to prefer foreign carriers despite the lower prices and more flights offered by Chinese carriers.[19] The policy also attempts to alleviate some pressure on the capacity constraints in domestic airports and other infrastructures. China has little experience in liberal international airline market. Both CAAC and Chinese flag carriers are very cautious in increasing flight capacity. As a result, capacity growth has been incremental rather than major in nature. CAAC takes a slightly more liberal approach in dealing with charter services and scheduled international services to/from a growing number of secondary Chinese cities. China is gradually liberalizing foreign carrier access. In recent years, China has signed dozens of new air service agreements, many of which allow for dual designation and optimistic capacity increases. By 1997, China has signed air services agreement with 78 countries and has direct flights to over 40 countries. However, CAAC has closely monitored international capacity growth in fear of Chinese carriers losing out to their foreign counterparts.

An agreement signed with the U.S. in January 1996 opened the first non-stop direct flight from the U.S. to Beijing. One of the most important aspects of the agreement is that it opens the door for codesharing between Chinese and U.S. carriers. The agreement gives China the right to begin codesharing immediately. U.S. carriers can begin codesharing three years from the date Chinese codesharing commences[20]. Consequently, American Airlines and China Eastern Airlines signed a memorandum of understanding in February 1997 for a cooperative service agreement for reciprocal code sharing between U.S. cities served by American and Chinese gateways of Beijing and Shanghai served by China Eastern.[21] Since then, Air China has become the first Chinese airline to fully enter into an international alliance with Northwest Airlines and its partners Continental Airlines, Alaska Airlines and America West, while China Southern has established code-sharing operations with Delta Air Lines. Recently, Australia's Qantas Airways and China Eastern Airlines have signed a commercial agreement for a codesharing partnership (Ionides, 1999).[22] In addition, starting January 1, 1999, the Chinese government is not to interfere with the operations of Air China and its alliance with Northwest, allowing the airline to be responsible for its own profits and losses, and giving the company more freedom.

In April 1999, China signed a new aviation agreement with the U.S. which is expected to significantly expand commercial air service between the two nations.[23] Under the new agreement, scheduled flights will double, growing from 27 to 54 per week for each country's carriers. Eight of the new flights will be available immediately, nine on April 1, 2000, and 10 on

April 1, 2001. An additional carrier from each country will be able to serve the market on April 1, 2001, raising the total to four per country. U.S. carriers will have unlimited freedom to choose the city of origin in the United States. By April 1, 2002, U.S. airlines will be able to serve 20 additional Chinese cities through code-share agreements with Chinese partners, and Chinese carriers will be able to serve 30 U.S. cities with U.S. code-share partners. Both U.S. and Chinese carriers will be allowed to serve two additional cities in the other country. Further negotiations will be held within a year on such issues as additional carriers in the market, code sharing between same-country and third-country airlines, charter operations and establishing U.S. carrier ticket offices in China. However, the U.S. government understands that neither Chinese aviation authorities nor its air carriers are ready to agree on anything close to an open skies bilateral.

Hong Kong

Relations with China Hong Kong is now a Special Administrative Region (SAR) of China. The Basic Law of the Hong Kong SAR provides for Hong Kong to govern its own affairs for the next 50 years under the one-country two-system framework. Aviation is covered under the Basic Law's aviation annex (Section 4, attached in the appendix to this chapter). This allows for Hong Kong and China to negotiate their own air service agreements separately. For international services to, from or through Hong Kong, which do not operate to, from or through mainland China, Hong Kong can negotiate its own air services agreements and arrangements, subject to final approval by China. As of June 1997, 21 bilateral Air Services Agreements (ASA's) were signed.[24] These ASA's, signed with full approval by China, provide a firm legal framework for the operation of air services in Hong Kong beyond 1997. Hong Kong shall maintain its status as a centre of international and regional aviation, continue the previous system of civil aviation management, and keep its own aircraft register.[25]

Despite the Sino-British Joint Declaration, there are clear signs that the Chinese authorities will slowly participate in Hong Kong's aviation affairs. Several airline experts in Asia predict that China will use a two-pronged approach to intervene in Hong Kong's aviation affairs. A recent turn of events has led some to anticipate the following scenario for Hong Kong's aviation. First, China will use the CNAC (China National Aviation Corp), a subsidiary of China's airline regulator (CAAC), to control flying rights into the Chinese market. CNAC can indirectly control what occurs in Hong Kong's airline industry through its ownership of Dragonair, Air Macao, and possibly Cathay Pacific.[26] In fact, in April 1996, China-backed CITIC Pacific raised its stake in Cathay from 10 percent to 25 percent, reducing Swire's majority ownership to less than 44 percent. In a related deal, CNAC acquired 36 percent of Dragonair,[27] effectively ending Cathay's control over Dragonair. CNAC was expected to use Dragonair as the vehicle for development of its aviation interests in Hong Kong. Second, China will indirectly discipline Hong Kong by expanding international services and routes to Mainland China from Macao and Guangzhou. For example, China Southern launched direct services between Guangzhou and Los Angeles in July 1997.

There are eight Chinese carriers flying into Hong Kong on scheduled or charter services. Just over 10 percent of all flights out of Hong Kong are bound for China. This accounts for 45 of about 440 daily flights, of which 33 are mainland carriers. Dragonair has six or seven flights a day to the mainland. It is also noteworthy that from July 1, 1997, CAAC has the right to authorize any Chinese airlines to serve international routes via Hong Kong.[28] This means that potentially, many carriers in China can compete with Cathay Pacific and Dragonair in overseas travel to/from Hong Kong.

In sum, it is our view that the Chinese government, through CAAC, has enough means to intervene with Hong Kong's commercial aviation affairs if it wishes.

Relations with Other Bilateral Partners   Major air service agreements (ASA) between Hong Kong, and the U.S., the UK (which is related to PRC-UK bilateral), Japan, Singapore, and Australia as well as the special agreement between Hong Kong and Taiwan, highlight the importance of Hong Kong in an Asian or global aviation context. Airlines from those countries consider their Hong Kong operations fundamental to their future global and Asian growth strategies, and have thus fought hard to expand their Hong Kong operations.

U.S. demands for liberalization have caused friction with Hong Kong in the past. The U.S. previously requested increased cargo rights beyond Hong Kong, as well as the right to develop more services from other points in Asia. In exchange, the U.S. was extremely willing to increase Hong Kong's access to the U.S. and grant fifth freedom rights. However, Hong Kong carriers, chiefly Cathay Pacific, had no overwhelming ambitions in the U.S. and beyond (Jennings, 1992). Finally, in September 1995, an aviation accord was reached between the U.S. and Hong Kong, culminating eight years of negotiations. The accord significantly expands U.S. carriers' rights to Hong Kong, and importantly, protects those rights after the return of Hong Kong to Chinese sovereignty in July 1997. This deal was the first stand-alone accord with Hong Kong. The previous bilateral agreement had been negotiated between the U.S. and Britain, and would have become null once Hong Kong returns to China (Burgess, 1995a).

The new agreement allows U.S. carriers, for the first time, to carry both cargo and passengers from Hong Kong to third countries (fifth-freedom rights). The accord granted U.S. carriers a total of 14 combination flights per week (direct from U.S. cities or via Japan) and a total of eight fifth-freedom all cargo flights each week to Hong Kong. The cargo rights were a critical benefit for time-sensitive cargo carriers such as Fed Ex and UPS (Burgess, 1995b), helping boost their business in the burgeoning air cargo market in the Pacific Rim. In exchange, the agreement increased the number of U.S. gateways to Hong Kong from seven to ten. The deal permits Cathay to expand its U.S. service. Previously, Cathay launched an all-cargo service to Toronto because the old bilateral did not permit it to go to Chicago, its preferred destination.

In 1995, a series of talks took place to negotiate renewal of an accord regarding the lucrative Hong Kong-Taiwan route. A new agreement was finally reached in June 1996 with China's approval. This new agreement ended the monopoly on the Hong Kong-Taiwan route formerly held by Cathay Pacific and China Airlines. EVA won rights to 16 passenger flights per week between Hong Kong and Taiwan. Dragonair is allowed to operate three-times daily services to Kaohsiung, Taiwan's second largest city. In addition, Dragonair is authorised to operate same-plane service between Mainland China and Taiwan via Hong Kong, as long as it switches flight numbers in Hong Kong.[29]

Hong Kong has negotiated more liberal arrangements with a large number of its bilateral partners on the basis of exchange of balanced and reciprocal rights. However, one of Hong Kong's major concerns is in respect to fifth freedoms. Since Hong Kong's airlines do not have a protected domestic market, they have to compete in international markets. Opening up fifth freedoms to one partner would directly impact Hong Kong airlines' third and fourth freedom service markets. Hong Kong is only willing to grant fifth freedoms if realized benefits will compensate for losses on third and fourth freedom rights.

Hong Kong Government's Announced Position   The government of Hong Kong's announced position is that, 'to allow maximum scope for market competition, it is Hong Kong's policy to regulate only when market forces are not operating sufficiently to protect consumers' best interests and to promote the necessary degree of economic efficiency.'[30]   Competition is seen as the best means for ensuring that consumers get quality services at reasonable prices. Accordingly, Hong Kong practices and encourages competition in the provision and development of transportation services.

Despite this announced pro-competitive position, Hong Kong's aviation policy has been largely guided by protection of carriers, and thus, the exchange of balanced and reciprocal traffic rights.

Under Article 130 of the Basic Law, 'The Hong Kong Special Administrative Region shall be responsible on its own for matters of routine business and technical management of civil aviation, including the management of airports, the provision of air traffic services within the flight information region of the Hong Kong Special Administrative Region, and the discharge of other responsibilities allocated to it under the regional air navigation procedures of the International Civil Aviation Organization.' While the government will avoid direct intervention in the provision of aviation services, it is committed to ensuring that Hong Kong's airport and aviation services continue to match the growth in demand, and to maintain Hong Kong's position as a major international and regional aviation centre.

Taiwan

Prior to 1987, airlines in Taiwan were constrained to provide services only in their designated markets: China Airlines to provide international services, China Airlines and Far Eastern Air Transport to provide domestic inland services, and Formosa Airlines and Taiwan Airlines to provide domestic off-shore island services. The movement toward liberalization in Taiwan began in 1987 with the lifting of martial law.[31] Taiwan now permits more of its airlines to fly internationally, but it imposes strict requirements for international licenses. Carriers must first operate satisfactorily for three years in domestic markets, and they must use all new equipment. In recent years, EVA Airways and Mandarin Airlines have entered international scheduled air services, and a number of carriers are entitled to operate international charter flights. EVA Airways was instrumental in Taiwan's adoption of an open skies policy.

Taiwan's international expansion is hampered by Taiwan's lack of diplomatic relations with many countries, as ASAs are usually negotiated at the state level. In addition, China often puts pressure on countries that grant aviation rights to Taiwan. For example, South Korea suspended its aviation accord with Taiwan in 1992 following Seoul's diplomatic switch to Beijing. This move costs Korean air carriers millions of dollars of foregone profits a year.[32]

Since Taiwan is Asia's second largest generator of tourists after Japan, its airline industry has tremendous potential. To circumvent its political/diplomatic difficulties, Taiwan uses inter-company, such as the commercial agreement between China Airlines and Cathay Pacific, rather than inter-country agreements. In addition, both Taiwan and foreign airlines have created subsidiaries to avoid conflict with China. For example, Japan Asia Airways services Taiwan while its parent company, Japan Airlines, services China. Mandarin Airlines, a subsidiary of China Airlines, services New Zealand, Australia, and Canada, which all have official aviation agreements with China.

On April 25, 1996, American Airlines and China Airlines signed a code-sharing agreement.[33] Under the agreement, American can place its code on China Airlines flights between Taipei and both Los Angeles and San Francisco. And China Airlines can put its code on American flights between Los Angeles and both Dallas/Fort Worth and New York's Kennedy airport.

In February 1997, Taiwan and the United States reached an open skies agreement, the U.S.' third open skies agreements in the Asia-Pacific region. The agreement permits airlines of Taiwan and the United States to operate U.S.-Taiwan air services without restriction.[34] The agreement is similar to those signed by the United States with 12 European countries. Currently, two Taiwan carriers (China Airlines and Eva Airways) and three U.S. carriers (Northwest, United, and Continental Micronesia) fly between Taiwan and the United States.

Recently, Taiwan and Malaysia have finalized details on an open skies accord to liberalize bilateral air traffic.[35] This move is expected to inspire other member countries of the ASEAN to follow suit. Taiwan is actively seeking to sign similar open skies accords with more countries to help boost its civil aviation market and to improve the island's prospects of becoming an Asia-Pacific air trans-shipment hub.

Taiwan's political rifts with Mainland China still remain. Although Taiwan permits its citizens to travel to the mainland, it does not recognize the PRC government as legitimate. It has imposed a ban on direct air links with the mainland since 1949. Consequently, a traveller seeking transportation to China must go through Hong Kong or some other gateway, deplane, identify his luggage and have it re-tagged for the China destination (Baum, 1995). However, starting November 1995, Taiwan made an exception for *Air Macau* to provide same plane services between Taiwan and Mainland China. Moreover, under the new 5-year air service agreement between Taiwan and Hong Kong, Dragonair is authorized to operate same-plane service between mainland China and Taiwan as long as it switches flight numbers in Hong Kong (Shon, Chang, and Lin, 1999). In another development, China Airlines (CAL), Taiwan's national carrier, underwent a corporate make-over by removing Taiwan's flag from its planes. One of the most compelling reasons for the make-over was CAL's desire to retain access to Hong Kong after 1997. This should also make it easier for CAL to realize its goal of flying to the mainland. Chinese officials have hinted that CAL could lose access to the highly lucrative Hong Kong route if Taiwan does not open up direct air links to the Chinese mainland (Baum, 1995).

There is widespread speculation that limited direct air links between China and Taiwan may soon be restored in the wake of restoration of direct shipping links between Taiwan and the mainland in April 1997. Industry analysts have noted that the mainland and Taiwanese aviation industry are increasingly ready for direct links.[36] These speculations are further fuelled by the move, in late 1996, by Taipei-based China Airlines, to establish a Beijing office to handle ticketing arrangements (Knibb, 1997b), and by a series of direct high-level contacts among senior industry officials (Tabakoff, 1997). Taiwan's transport ministry has also drafted a plan to ease Chinese visits to Taiwan, starting with government officials, then business visitors, and finally all citizens. This plan awaits final approval, but the very fact that the ministry is proposing something that would not have been considered several years ago illustrates the shift in attitude. China's quick return of a hijacked Taiwanese aircraft in early 1997 has also led Taipei to renew calls for cross-strait talks[37] (Knibb 1997).

5.3 Other Asian and Oceanian Countries' Approaches to Bilateral Agreements

Singapore

Singapore has the most liberal aviation policies in Asia with many liberal bilateral agreements. It is linked to 119 cities in 53 countries by 64 airlines. In April 1997, it became the first country in the region to sign an open skies accord with the United States under the U.S. Asian Open Skies Initiative.[38] Singapore has always promoted open skies air transportation, both in bilateral negotiations and in multilateral fora such as APEC, WTO, ICAO, etc. Obviously, as a city state with a small aviation market, the gateway function of Singapore's aviation industry would be enhanced in an open aviation regime than in a restrictive regime. Its current position is economically rational. Also, the fact that Singapore Airlines is very competitive and highly efficient is consistent with Singapore government's promotion of open skies policy.

Thailand

The airline industry in Thailand was traditionally controlled by the Thai air force, thus fractions between the air force and civilians were a constant problem. Civilian executives had control of the airlines for a brief two-year period in 1992-94, before air force officers regained control. Seven percent of Thai Airways' shares are owned by the public, with remaining shares held by the government. Further privatization is expected in the near future. Thailand reached a new aviation agreement with the United States in January 1996 which significantly expanded passenger, cargo, and charter services between the two countries (Burgess, 1996). It is reported that Thailand's Department of Aviation (DOA) is working on a partial open-skies policy to enable airlines to compete on domestic and international routes. Under the plan, the government would set up an independent regulatory agency similar to the FAA in the United States, while DOA will be privatized and remain responsible for all airline operations.[39] However, it is not clear when the plan would be ready and implemented. Recently, Malaysia, Thailand and Indonesia have signed an open-skies agreement, the first among Asian countries.[40] The agreement covers the northern states of West Malaysia (Perak, Penang and Kedah), Southern Thailand and Western Indonesia. The move, initiated by Malaysian Prime Minister Mahathir Mohamed, paves the way for airlines of the three countries to mount services within their respective boundaries with no restriction on capacity or frequency. The pact, which takes effect immediately, aims to promote tourism and trade. The ultimate objective is to issue border passes to tourists and business travellers instead of passports for easier movement within the three countries.

Malaysia

Malaysia used to have a rather restrictive air policy. However, since 1993, the government has allowed smaller airlines to seriously compete in the market. In 1994, the national carrier, Malaysia Airlines (MAS), was privatized. Malaysia has also adopted a rather liberal policy towards foreign carriers. It negotiated and signed an open skies agreement with the United States in June 1997. Malaysia also has a similar accord with Australia. In a recent Asia Pacific Regional Aviation conference, Malaysia's Transport Minister Dr Ling Liong Sik said that Malaysia will continue to pursue its liberalization policy to enhance accessibility by actively establishing more liberal air services agreements and traffic rights arrangements with other countries. Malaysia would also continue to lay emphasis on the development of facilities and infrastructure necessary to support the growth of the air transport industry.[41]

In a bid to attract more airlines to Kuala Lumpur International Airport (KLIA), Malaysia signed an open skies agreement with New Zealand in June 1998, and has recently finalized details on open skies accords with Taiwan and India.[42] It plans to sign open skies agreements with a number of other Asia Pacific countries as well. Negotiations with several European countries are also in progress. The airlines of these countries will be free to operate into all or any of the country's six international airports with no restriction on capacity, aircraft type or frequency. The six are KLIA, Penang Airport, Kota Kinabalu Airport, Kuching Airport, Langkawi Airport, and Senai Airport in Johor Baru. The Malaysian government is disappointed that despite the low landing and aircraft parking charges, KLIA has not been able to attract more foreign carriers. Malaysia has agreements with 52 countries but currently only 31 airlines operate into KLIA.

Philippines

Like many of its Asian counterparts, Philippines' flag carrier, Philippines Airlines (PAL), used to enjoy a monopolistic position in its international market. PAL operated as a private firm until 1977, when the government of the Philippines took a 99.7 percent share. Just as the airline re-equipped, traffic fell and the second oil shock hit, leading to continuing setbacks in the airline's operations. By the 1990's, the airline had accumulated losses of U.S.$300 million and there was mounting criticism of PAL's poor service, lack of capacity, and bloated bureaucracy in both international and domestic operations. In 1992, the airline was partially privatized through the sale of 67 percent of its equity to the PR Holdings consortium. However, PAL continued to have financial troubles, and was forced to seek bankruptcy protection in September, 1998 after a bitter dispute with its pilots.

In a bid to boost efficiency and service in the aviation industry, the Ramos government issued a landmark executive order in January 1995, allowing competition in the sector. Grand Air began flying to Hong Kong from mid-1996, and has plans to fly to Taipei, Tokyo, Beijing, Vietnam, Brunei, Jakarta, Singapore, Kuala Lumpur and Bangkok. Cebu Air and Air Philippines also announced their international ambitions. The privatization of PAL and the new entrants, vying for domestic and international markets, began a new competitive regime in the Philippines.

The Ramos administration pursued a very liberal international air services policy which includes double disapproval pricing scheme, liberal charter flight approvals, and liberal cargo rights regime and open code sharing. The policy allows foreign airlines to operate to and from beyond a sovereign nation with unrestricted route/traffic rights regime. The collapse of PAL in 1998 led the current government to declare a partial open skies, allowing initially five airports to accept flights from any foreign airline, excluding Manila's Ninoy Aquino Airport, to solve the problem of the lack of flights. Of the five airports, only Cebu is qualified to handle a fully loaded 747-400. There has been strong opposition from the industry against the open skies policy, claiming that the unfair competition between foreign airlines and local airlines hampers the growth and development of local airlines. At the same time, there are many people seeking further open skies, citing competition would give customers more opportunity to choose among the best. President Estrada has been reluctant to adopt a full 'open skies' policy, and has said that he favours a more gradual liberalization rather than the granting of unlimited air rights to foreign airlines to boost tourism. President Estrada has recently made commitment to review the government's open skies policy on the grant of landing rights to foreign and regional airlines, to shield Philippine Airlines (PAL) from unfair competition, and to seek more landing rights for PAL in major destinations to ensure its survival and viability as a commercial enterprise.[43] Despite of President Estrada's reluctance, the Philippines' Congress has recently proposed a new house bill, the International Air Transport Liberalizing Act, seeking to deregulate the international air transport. The bill is intended to provide new entrants more opportunities to service the country or to develop new international routes, calling for the streamlining of requirements for airlines that wish to fly international routes. The bill aims to give balanced treatment for both domestic and international routes.[44]

In another development, the implementation of the 'open skies' agreement between the Philippines and the United States has been postponed to October 1, 2003 from the original October 1, 1996. At present, the U.S. essentially has unlimited fifth freedom rights from the Philippines, while the Philippine carriers' access to the U.S. market is somewhat limited, similar to that of most other Asian bilaterals with the U.S.

Indonesia

Until 1991, the national carrier, Garuda Indonesia, was the only Indonesian airline to operate jet aircraft. Since then, the government has allowed competing carriers to enter the scheduled service market. Garuda now focuses on serving lucrative international and main domestic routes. Merpati Nusantara Airlines, another state-owned airline, and private Sempati Airlines are also authorized to fly international routes. There are three independent airlines (Sempati Air, Bouraq Indonesia, Mandala Airlines and Dirgantara Air Services) competing for domestic traffic. Sempati Air, partly owned by (past) President Suharto's Humpuss Group, had grown from a small charter airline operating a few aging turbo-props into a dynamic international airline. Sempati was flying modern Fokker, Boeing and Airbus jets on domestic routes in Indonesia, a number of border-crossing routes to Malaysia and Singapore, regional routes to Perth (Australia), Taipei (Taiwan), Hong Kong, Kuming (China), and a few other international routes. However, Sempati Airlines has been forced out of business, falling victim to the economic crisis gripping the country. The other airlines are also facing serious financial problems, while Garuda Indonesia is seeking more alliances with foreign airlines.

The U.S. essentially has unlimited fifth freedom rights on routes between Indonesia and virtually all Asian countries, while Indonesia has unlimited rights to/from Guam, Honolulu and Los Angeles. Indonesia will allow foreign carriers fifth freedom rights subject to reciprocity for Indonesian carriers. Limited cabotage rights may be allowed on domestic routes when codesharing agreements are established with Indonesian carriers (Chin, 1997). Recently, the Indonesian government has signalled that it will allow foreign airlines to serve domestic routes, as long as they establish companies registered in Indonesia[45]. Under the proposed policy, for example, Qantas can set up a company registered in Indonesia, Qantas Indonesia or Lufthansa can establish Lufthansa Indonesia. These Indonesia registered airlines can serve domestic routes. The parent companies would be allowed to control 100 per cent of the stakes in the locally-registered companies. This policy is intended to help promote Indonesian tourism as the foreign airlines would promote Indonesia in their home countries in order to provide their locally registered airlines with passengers. At present, Indonesia allows foreign airlines to fly directly to some Indonesian tourist areas.

Australia and New Zealand

Australia and New Zealand have both made major changes to their aviation regulatory framework. The Australian government has completely deregulated its domestic air services and fully privatized its national airline,

Qantas. The New Zealand government has divested its ownership in flag carrier, Air New Zealand, and also opened domestic aviation to foreign competition. New Zealand has bilateral air service agreements with 30 countries/territories, and signed an open skies accord with the United States in May 1997.[46] Airports and air traffic control in New Zealand have been commercialized as well. Furthermore, under the Closer Economic Relations (CER) agreement, the governments of Australia and New Zealand have taken measures to create a single aviation market with multiple designation. However, Australia withdrew from the agreement at the last minute on the grounds that New Zealand would benefit unequally from the total liberalization of the exercise of air traffic rights between the two countries.[47]

New Zealand has signed open skies pacts with the U.S., Singapore, Malaysia, Brunei and the United Arab Emirates. Recently, the Australian government has followed recommendations by Australian Productivity Commission in adopting new policies to open regional airports to international airlines. All airports, other than the major gateways of Sydney, Melbourne, Brisbane and Perth, will be open to any international airlines under the new policy. The four largest gateways, which are key destinations for foreign travellers, will be subject to a more liberal bilateral agreement with like-minded countries such as the U.S. and Singapore. Similar moves are expected to benefit air cargo more. However, Australia's two main carriers, Qantas and Ansett, as well as its Transport Worker Union have been strongly opposing the Australian government's attempt to further open skies.

5.4   Flaws in Current Bilateral Process

In many countries, flag carriers are allowed to influence the bilateral negotiation process. This is especially true when a country has only one airline. Carrier interests are bound to dominate the bilateral negotiation process while consumer interests tend to take a back seat. In this environment, governments would not agree to increase competition to benefit consumers unless their flag carriers can also win. This definitely is one of the reasons why the countries with competitive carriers are pro-liberalization while other countries oppose liberalization. This bilateral process is, therefore, unworkable unless liberalization offers a win-win situation to the carriers of both countries involved. It is inherently flawed because increased competition usually makes some players win and some lose.

In order to make the bilateral process work, aviation should be included in the negotiations for the broader goods and services trade. This would offer a better chance for striking a compromise between the countries, and allow the theory of comparative advantage to take its course in determining winning industries of each country. It is arguable that the European countries were able to form a single European air services market because the aviation was included as a part of the whole economic integration among the EU members. It was possible to agree on a single aviation market despite the fact that some countries will eventually lose their airlines and much of the associated employment base.

There are two additional ways to improve the bilateral air negotiation process. First, as countries deregulate their domestic markets, new entrants will emerge. Sooner or later, some of these new entrants will be allowed to enter international markets. This will tend to reduce the influence of flag carriers in the bilateral negotiation process as the governments need to deal with conflicting interests between the competing carriers, and it needs to play fair with the multiple carriers. There is also strong empirical evidence that countries with multiple carriers make efforts to increase competition via multiple designation of carriers. In addition, deregulation of domestic airline markets has positive effects for increasing competition in international markets. Secondly, economic advancement tends to enhance consumer power and encourage consumer movement. This will likely add to the weight for consumer benefits of increasing competition relative to the weight given to the carrier interests.

5.5   Summary Comments

The Asia-Pacific region is comprised of countries of very different political systems and economies of varying degrees of openness. There is no Asia-Pacific body akin to the EC to provide a base forum for uniting air transport policy in the region. Liberalization is almost entirely confined to domestic skies, and multilateralism, where it exists, remains within Asia-Pacific's alluring borders. There have been movements towards liberalizing aviation among some ASEAN[48] countries, in line with the group's move towards a trading environment akin to the European Union. For example, Malaysia, Thailand and Indonesia have recently signed an open skies agreement, the first among Asian countries. The agreement covers the northern states of West Malaysia (Perak, Penang and Kedah), Southern Thailand, and Western Indonesia. The move, initiated by Malaysian Prime Minister

Mahathir Mohamed, paves the way for airlines of the three countries to mount services within their respective boundaries with no restriction on capacity or frequency.   In addition, the BIMP-EAGA (Brunei-Indonesia-Malaysia, Philippines-East Asia Growth Area), born in 1994, is hoping to become the first Asian group to forge a joint airline system.[49] Furthermore, 13 Asia-Pacific countries met in January 1996 to explore regional cooperation in aviation and greater openness in air service markets, and possibly coexistence of multilateral and bilateral approaches to liberalization.   Despite these developments, so far the effort to move towards a regional open-skies agreement has not made much progress.

Appendix V

Excerpt from the Basic Law of the Hong Kong Special Administrative Region

Section 4: Civil Aviation

Article 128
The Government of the Hong Kong Special Administrative Region shall provide conditions and take measures for the maintenance of the status of Hong Kong as a centre of international and regional aviation.

Article 129
The Hong Kong Special Administrative Region shall continue the previous system of civil aviation management in Hong Kong and keep its own aircraft register in accordance with provisions laid down by the Central People's Government concerning nationality marks and registration marks of aircraft.

Access of foreign state aircraft to the Hong Kong Special Administrative Region shall require the special permission of the Central People's Government.

Article 130
The Hong Kong Special Administrative Region shall be responsible on its own for matters of routine business and technical management of civil aviation, including the management of airports, the provision of air traffic services within the flight information region of the Hong Kong Special Administrative Region, and the discharge of other responsibilities allocated

to it under the regional air navigation procedures of the International Civil Aviation Organization.

Article 131

The Central People's Government shall, in consultation with the Government of the Hong Kong Special Administrative Region, make arrangements providing air services between the Region and other parts of the People's Republic of China for airlines incorporated in the Hong Kong Special Administrative Region and having their principal place of business in Hong Kong and other airlines of the People's Republic of China.

Article 132

All air service agreements providing air services between other parts of the People's Republic of China and other states and regions with stops at the Hong Kong Special Administrative Region and air services between the Hong Kong Special Administrative Region and other states and regions with stops at other parts of the People's Republic of China shall be concluded by the Central People's Government.

In concluding the air service agreements referred to in the first paragraph of this Article, the Central People's Government shall take account of the special conditions and economic interests of the Hong Kong Special Administrative Region and consult the government of the Region.

Representatives of the Government of the Hong Kong Special Administrative Region may, as members of the delegations of the Government of the People's Republic of China, participate in air service consultations conducted by the Central People's Government with foreign governments concerning arrangements for such services referred to in the first paragraph of this Article.

Article 133

Acting under specific authorizations from the Central People's Government, the Government of the Hong Kong Special Administrative Region may:
> (1) renew or amend air service agreements and arrangements previously in force;
> (2) negotiate and conclude new air service agreements providing routes for airlines incorporated in the Hong Kong Special

Administrative Region and having their principal place of business in Hong Kong and providing rights for over-flights and technical stops; and

(3) negotiate and conclude provisional arrangements with foreign states or regions with which no air service agreements have been concluded.

All scheduled air services to, from or through Hong Kong, which do not operate to, from or through the mainland of China shall be regulated by the air service agreements or provisional arrangements referred to in this Article.

Article 134

The Central People's Government shall give the Government of the Hong Kong Special Administrative Region the authority to:

(1) negotiate and conclude with other authorities all arrangements concerning the implementation of the air service agreements and provisional arrangements referred to in Article 133 of this Law;

(2) issue licences to airlines incorporated in the Hong Kong Special Administrative Region and having their principal place of business in Hong Kong;

(3) designate such airlines under the air service agreements and provisional arrangements referred to in Article 133 of this Law; and

(4) issue permits to foreign airlines for services other than those to, from or through the mainland of China.

Article 135

Airlines incorporated and having their principal place of business in Hong Kong and businesses related to civil aviation functioning there prior to the establishment of the Hong Kong Special Administrative Region may continue to operate.

Notes

[1] After the War, the Supreme Commander for the Allied Powers imposed a total ban on aviation of any kind in Japan (Abeyratne, 1996). The ban was in effect for 5 years.

[2] United acquired Pan Am's trans-Pacific and intra-Asia routes in 1986. U.S. carriers, including United and Northwest, are now among the world's most efficient and are

using their competitive strength to gain higher market shares in Japan and other trans-Pacific markets, where airlines are more heavily protected.

[3] *Jiji Press Ticker Service*, March 6, 1997.

[4] Naha (Okinawa) was occupied by the United States, and was returned to Japan in 1972.

[5] The carriers that were originally granted rights in 1952 (and the carriers that subsequently acquired those rights) are called 'incumbent' or 'full right' carriers. Full right carriers are authorized to increase or decrease capacity freely.

[6] See the U.S.-Japan ASA in Air Transport Association of America, *Air Service Rights in U.S. International Air Transport Agreements* (1997).

[7] U.S. carriers counter Japanese complaints by saying that they attract so many Japanese passengers because their costs are far lower than those of their Japanese competitors, 33 percent~55 percent lower.

[8] There are at least two explanations for the increased six freedom traffic from Japan via Seoul: (1) airfares via Seoul are considerably lower; and (2) because of the congestion at Japan's major airports, Japanese government had encouraged carriers to operate international routes from some secondary airports before the opening of Kansai in response to the demands by local governments and foreign carriers. However, passengers originating from these secondary airports are mostly price-sensitive non-business travellers, thus not many carriers wanted to enter these carriers. Korean carriers were the exceptions.

[9] A Japanese airline executive once mentioned to the authors that the U.S. divide and conquer approach is not likely to work in Northeast Asia because China and Japan are very large countries and threat of diversion of traffic may not work as well as in the case of Europe. This implies that Japan is counting on Korea's cooperation on this issue.

[10] On virtually all routes to/from Japan, passengers originating travel in Japan pay significantly higher air fares than those originating travel from a foreign city on the same route. For example, airfares between Japan and Korea are twice as expensive for those originating trips in Japan than those originating trips in Korea.

[11] Previously Japan Airlines was the only airline with unrestricted access to the United States.

[12] Extensive codesharing with a U.S. carrier may be able to alleviate some of the unbalance problem for Korean carriers, but it can not be a complete solution.

[13] The practice was extended to the twenty-three provincial civil aviation bureaux a year later (Zhang 1998).

[14] Aircraft acquisitions still requires approval by the CAAC. This is due to CAAC's concerns about having too many aircraft in the air. CAAC is responsible for managing airline routing, but cannot independently increase the amount of air space allotted to civil aircraft.

[15] Within China, each of these airlines has its own base, but the nation is not allocated between them. Many routes overlap and carriers compete, although demand outstrips capacity on many routes.

[16] Airport system reform has progressed as a much slower pace than airline reform. Many airports are still under CAAC's direct control and supervision.

[17] A minimum 51 percent Chinese shareholding is required in airport construction joint ventures. For air transport enterprises/ventures, there is a 35 percent cap on foreign registered capital, and a 25 percent cap on foreign voting rights (Woolward, 1995).

[18] Pakistan International Airlines and Iran National Airlines operate some services between China and Japan. However, it is not clear whether fifth freedom rights are actually included in these bilaterals.

[19] According to Chen and Zhang (1999), Chinese carriers in general, have only one third of the market share on such routes.

[20] *Asian Aviation News*, January 12, 1996.

[21] Note that the current ASA between the U.S. and China prohibits American from operating its own aircraft to China and from doing third country code-sharing.

[22] Lufthansa has been in talks with the three major Chinese airlines in a bid to extend the Star Alliance into Mainland China (Gethin, 1998).

[23] U.S. DOT News Release 52-99, April 9, 1999.

[24] A five-year commercial agreement between the airlines of Hong Kong and Taiwan was reached in June 1996.

[25] 'Key Transportation Issues in Hong Kong,' speech delivered at APEC Transportation Ministerial, Washington D.C., 12-13 June 1995.

[26] At least one expert on China's aviation affairs predicts that the CNAC will let management of these airlines operate fairly autonomously to benefit from experienced management. Thus, he does not expect major visible changes soon.

[27] CITIC owns 28.5 percent of Dragonair.

[28] In fact, the present UK-China aviation accord allows Air China to operate fifth freedom Hong Kong-London flights.

[29] *Airline Business*, August 1, 1996, p.16.

[30] 'Key Transportation Issues in Hong Kong,' APEC Speech 1995.

[31] *Aviation Week and Space Technology* 130.19 (8 May 1989): 37.

[32] *China Economic News Service*, January 23, 1996.

[33] *Airline Financial News*, Vol. 11, No. 17, April 29, 1996.

[34] U.S. DOT News 22-97.

[35] 'Malaysia Eyes Open- Skies Pacts To Boost Air Traffic', *Aviation Daily*, February 19, 1999.

[36] *Reuters North American Wire*, February 1, 1996.

[37] China has subsequently returned the hijacker to Taiwan in exchange for two Chinese hijackers.

[38] U.S. DOT News 48-97.

[39] 'Thailand Liberalization Move Includes Partial Open Skies', *Aviation Daily*, October 20, 1998.

[40] 'Three-Way Open-Skies Agreement Signed By Malaysia, Thailand, Indonesia', *Aviation Daily*, March 9, 1999.

[41] 'Malaysia to Continue to Liberalize Air Transport Sector', *Nationwide Financial News*, March 16, 1999.

[42] 'Malaysia Eyes Open Skies Pacts To Boost Air Traffic', *Aviation Daily*, February 19, 1999.

[43] 'Estrada Re-affirms Commitment to Philippines Airlines', *Asia Pulse*, June, 10, 1999.

[44] 'Philippines May Deregulate International Air Transport', *Asia Pulse*, July 5, 1999.

[45] 'Indonesia May Let Foreign Airlines Serve Domestic Routes', *ASIA ULSE*, November 17, 1998.

[46] U.S. DOT News 82-97.
[47] Some analysts speculated that the action was motivated by fears that New Zealand competition on domestic Australian routes would lower Qantas' value before its pending sale of the following year.
[48] Association of South-East Asian Nations. ASEAN includes Brunei Darussalam, Indonesia, Malaysia, Philippines, Singapore, and Thailand.
[49] 'New Group on the Bloc: Brunei-Indonesia-Malaysia-Philippines East Asia Growth Area', *Airline Business*, September, 1997, vol 12, No. 9, p.100.

6 International Aviation Reform and the U.S. Open Skies Initiatives

Aviation activities cross the boundaries of countries, enter foreign jurisdictions and operate in different legal systems. Therefore, there is a need for international standardization of procedures and practices and for unification and/or coordination of regulations on the global scale. This applies not only to the technical and operational aspects of civil aviation but also to the wide fields of facilitation, security, environmental protection, etc. The economic regulation of air transport poses a particular challenge to the creation of seamless services to customers via globalization and to the improvement of efficiency.

This chapter reviews the development of international aviation regulations and discusses the current and future issues facing the Asia Pacific air carriers and governments. In addition, this chapter will discuss the U.S. open skies initiatives towards the Asia Pacific countries, and their implications for carriers and governments.

6.1 History of International Air Services Regulation

In 1944, the delegations from 53 countries[1] at a Conference, convened by President F. D. Roosevelt in Chicago, adopted the Convention on International Civil Aviation (commonly referred to as the Chicago Convention)[2] and laid the groundwork for the regulation of international civil aviation in the post-war period. One of the most significant aspects of the Chicago Convention is the formation of the International Civil Aviation Organization (ICAO). ICAO is an inter-governmental agency, whose objectives are to develop the principles and techniques of international air navigation and to foster the planning and development of international air transport so as to meet the needs of the peoples of the world for safe, regular, efficient and economical air transport. ICAO also aims to prevent economic waste caused by unreasonable competition and to insure that the rights of contracting states are fully respected and that every contracting state has a fair and equal opportunity to operate international airlines.

Acting as a counterweight to ICAO, IATA was established in 1945 to represent the interest of airlines, and is involved in the technical and commercial aspects of aviation. IATA served as an effective industry cartel for a long time. One of its most important functions has been to set air fares and cargo rates.

Based on the principle that 'every state has complete and exclusive sovereignty over the airspace above its territory,' the Chicago Convention established multilateral agreements in some areas, mainly regarding overfly and technical stops in foreign territory, but not in areas of commercial rights. Commercial rights are left to bilateral agreements to be negotiated between the two countries involved. Bilateral agreements are negotiated based on the principle of reciprocity, an equal and fair exchange of rights between countries of different sizes and with airlines of varied strength. Bilateral agreements vary in form, but they generally specify services and routes to be operated between two countries, designate airlines and capacity to be provided by each airline, and specify conditions under which passengers may be picked up in each country and flown to a third country (so-called fifth freedom rights).

The U.S. and U.K. signed the first bilateral agreement in 1946, known as 'Bermuda I,' which has provided a framework for other bilaterals to follow (Kasper, 1988). The Bermuda I agreement had a restrictive pricing regime and liberal capacity agreements and route descriptions,[3] a compromise between the 'free market' approach of the Untied States and the somewhat more cautious and conservative approach of the United Kingdom. Many other countries followed the Bermuda model in their air services agreements for nearly thirty years. The Bermuda model contains an IATA tariff setting clause. As a result, certain multilateralism was achieved through bilateralism. One of Bermuda I's main disadvantages has been that it gave governments a basis to formulate their civil aviation policies and sometimes adopt an unduly restrictive stance on their sovereignty in airspace, leading to frequent withdrawal of air traffic rights by countries. In 1976, the UK gave notice of termination of Bermuda I, claiming that under the terms of the treaty, U.S. carriers had a disproportionate share of traffic. The U.S. was forced to sign the Bermuda II agreement in 1977, which accommodates British demands to virtually eliminate multiple carrier designations, limit capacity supplied, and give up some of the U.S. carriers' 'beyond rights' to carry traffic between Britain and other countries. It was a devastating policy setback for the U.S. (Toh, 1998).

There is, at present, an extensive network of bilateral agreements.[4] Each international airline faces a complex web of bilateral air services agreements signed by its home state. The existence of these bilateral agreements has greatly constrained the freedom of individual scheduled airlines, and limited competition in the international air transport industry (Oum and Yu, 1998).

6.2 International Development in Aviation Reform

The world has changed a great deal since Bermuda I. These changes have created constant pressures for changes in the regulatory system, particularly the bilateral system of the international airline industry. One source of pressure is from the multilateral trading system. The regulatory system in air transport clashes with many of the principles of multilateralism of the world trading system. Another source of the pressure comes from the consumers. Increasingly, consumers have been demanding better services. In addition, the deregulation of the U.S. domestic air transport markets in 1978 has demonstrated the advantages of a competitive airline system. Therefore, reform is inevitable in the international air transport industry.

US Initiatives for Liberalization

The Carter Administration initiated the movements towards liberalizing international air service regulations in 1977 when it produced guidelines on a new international aviation policy. President Carter signed a Presidential Statement on International Air Transport Negotiations on August 21, 1978. The policy was formalized through the enactment of the International Air Transport Competition Act of 1979 (IATCA).[5] The broad aim of this policy was to 'provide the greatest possible benefit to travellers and shippers' and 'maximum consumer benefits can best be achieved through the preservation and extension of competition between airlines in a fair market place.' This was to be achieved through the negotiation or renegotiation of bilateral agreements (Dresner and Tretheway, 1987). Under the guidance of this new policy, the United States negotiated and signed the 'liberal bilateral' agreements with 23 European and Asian countries over the 1977-82 period, including the Netherlands, Germany, Belgium, Israel, Singapore, Thailand[6], Korea, and the Philippines (Haanappel, 1983). These new liberal bilaterals led to dramatic expansion of the number of airlines operating, the total scheduled capacity offered in those markets, and the number of U.S. gateway points with direct services to European or Asian destinations.

The new U.S. aviation policy also directly affected IATA's price-setting activities. In June 1978, the U.S. Civil Aeronautics Board (CAB) issued an order requiring IATA and associated parties to show cause for why CAB should not withdraw its approval of, and consequently anti-trust exemption for, IATA's Traffic Conferences and other related agreements.[7] Without exemption from anti-trust legislation, airlines participating in pricing agreements would risk being taken to U.S. courts when flying to the United States. The immediate short-term effect of the Show Cause Order was the withdrawal of all U.S. airlines from IATA membership. Over 40 percent of IATA member airlines' international traffic were to and from the United States, so the potential threat to IATA was considerable. Although the Show Cause Order was subsequently abandoned amidst protests from governments worldwide, it seriously undermined IATA's influence in the industry.

In March 1992, the United States began to negotiate transborder 'open skies' agreements with all European countries. The first U.S. 'open skies' deal was signed in September 1992 between the U.S. and the Netherlands. In February 1995, Canada and the U.S. signed an open skies agreement with a three-year phase-in provision. By May 1995, the United States signed open skies agreements with 9 European countries including Switzerland, Sweden, Norway, Luxembourg, Iceland, Finland, Denmark, Belgium, and Austria.[8] In the process, the United States has made open skies a condition for approving codeshare alliances. One year later, an open skies agreement was signed between the U.S. and Germany (Kayal, 1997). The U.S. also signed a phased open skies agreement with the Czech Republic in December 1995, the first of such pact with a former Eastern bloc country.[9] By 1997, about 40 percent of Europe-U.S. traffic were flying under open skies (Hill, 1997). France and the U.S. signed a bilateral aviation agreement in June 1998[10] that largely liberalizes air service between the two countries after a five-year phase-in period of comparable, equitable rights for U.S. and French carriers.[11] The accord falls short of open skies, as fifth freedom passenger service is not included. Talks between the U.S. and UK over an 'open skies' accord are underway as a prerequisite for approval of the proposed BA-AA alliance.

Following the successes in Europe, the U.S. started to shift the focus of its international aviation policy to Asia. The U.S. Open Skies Initiative in Asia was announced in summer 1996, and by April 1997, Singapore became the first country in Asia to sign an open skies agreement with the U.S. Since then the U.S. government has accomplished open skies air service agreements (ASAs) with Brunei (January, 1997), Taiwan (February, 1997), Malaysia (June, 1997), New Zealand (June, 1997), Korea (June, 1998), and Pakistan (May, 1999)[12] (see Exhibit 6-1 for the location of these

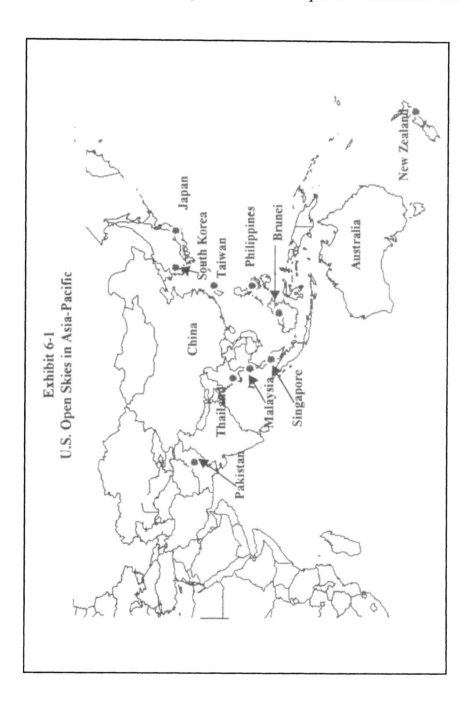

Exhibit 6-1
U.S. Open Skies in Asia-Pacific

countries). Most of these agreements allow airlines from both countries to fly between any point in the U.S. and any point in that country with no restrictions on capacity or frequency. The agreements also provide unlimited beyond traffic (5th freedom) rights to both countries' carriers. In addition, at least the agreements between the U.S. and Singapore and Brunei include seventh freedom traffic rights on cargo (hubbing rights in foreign territory). The latter provision is intended to help Federal Express and UPS set up mini-hubs in Asia. The U.S.-Korea agreement also includes change of gauge rights (change of aircraft size). This will allow the U.S. carriers that have unlimited 5th freedom rights in Korea to operate small aircraft on their intra-Asia routes to/from Seoul while taking advantage of economies of larger aircraft size in transpacific markets. By May 1999, the United States had signed 34 Open Skies agreements.[13]

Despite the denial by a senior U.S. government official,[14] the progress in Asia parallels the U.S. approach in Europe, where a series of open skies treaties with 'soft targets' eventually led Germany into signing a deal. France also signed a new liberal bilateral with the U.S. in June 1998. The U.S. is now working on the UK. In Asia, it appears that Washington's strategy includes forcing Japan to liberalize. Of course, in this approach, Korea holds a key to the U.S. policy given its proximity to Japan and somewhat liberal attitude on international air transportation matters. The new U.S. policy toward Asia has shifted away from focussing directly on Japan to working with the rest of the Asian countries because successes with them will later pressure Japan to sign a truly open skies bilateral.

Undoubtedly, the U.S. government will have open skies or nearly open skies treaties with a number of Asian countries within a few years. Since many of these open skies agreements may include extensive fifth freedom and some seventh freedom rights, U.S. carriers may be in a position to set up intra-Asian services more freely than most Asian carriers can. The reason is that bilateral agreements between Asian countries have quite restrictive 3rd/4th freedom traffic rights. For example, most of intra-Asian ASAs apply the 'equal benefits' principle for determining capacity and frequency of services while U.S. carriers could have complete freedom to set their flight frequency and prices in the same markets. Because the potential negative consequences of such an anomaly has caused enough worry to some countries, the ASEAN transport ministers have established a group to study this problem and to develop a competitive air services policy as a prelude to an eventual open skies regime in ASEAN.

European Initiatives

The European Union (EU) has been active in deregulating its internal market through the adoption of the three packages for liberalization (Tretheway, 1991, and Marin, 1995). From April 1997, the EU created a single aviation market similar to the U.S. domestic market. Any EU-registered carrier has the right to run domestic services within any of the EU's 15 member countries, as well as in Norway and Iceland. The single European aviation market thus became the world's largest aviation market with more than 370 million potential passengers. National ownership rules have been replaced by EU ownership criteria. Airlines have been given freedom to set fares, with safeguards against predatory pricing through competition rules.

So far, these changes do not apply to extra-EU agreements. Negotiations on foreign carriers' access to EU member states remain with individual members of the community. Many of its members have been pursuing liberal bilateral air services agreements with non-EU states, including open skies agreements with the U.S. (Button, 1997). However, the European Commission (EC) opposes independent negotiation by individual states, and is making efforts to negotiate air treaties on behalf of member states as a bloc. In 1996, the EU transport ministers decided to authorize the Commission to negotiate a multilateral aviation agreement with the United States (Barnard, 1996). The Commission is promoting a deal with the United States as a model for EU-wide accords with third countries. EU has urged its member countries to act collectively to forge a common open skies aviation agreement with the U.S., believing that if EU countries continue to act separately, the U.S. would continue to dominate aviation markets at European operators' expense.[15] In October 1998, the European Commission formally filed a complaint against eight European Union countries that secured bilateral agreements with the U.S. since aviation in the EU was liberalized in 1993. The Court of Justice of the European Union must decide whether bilateral air pacts between EU and third countries create an illegal competitive imbalance in Europe's single aviation market. EU Transport Commissioner Neil Kinnock said. 'The fragmented approach of EU member states toward the U.S. is placing European business at a disadvantage.'[16] The countries targeted by the EC's complaint are Austria, Belgium, Denmark, Finland, Germany, Luxembourg, Sweden and the U.K.

International Activities

The ICAO Council held a World-Wide Air Transport Colloquium in April 1992 on the theme of exploring the future of air transport regulation. ICAO took this initiative in order to re-examine the existing system of bilateral air services agreements between countries in light of the trend toward multilateral regulation on a regional basis. Other compelling factors were the increasing multilateral ownership of airlines, the development of code-sharing, and alliances and other marketing arrangements. This was the first global review of the regulation of air transport since the adoption of the Chicago Convention and subsequent efforts to develop a multilateral structure to apply to international air transport services. The primary concern of the Colloquium was air traffic rights. The colloquium discussed the strengths and weaknesses of the bilateral system; possible complementary and alternative multilateral regulatory structures; air service regulatory relationships between blocs of countries on the one hand and between individual countries and blocs of countries on the other; the applicability or inapplicability to air transport of international trade concepts such as market access, non-discrimination, transparency and increasing participation by developing countries, foreign and multinational ownership of national airlines; and nationality of aircraft and access to domestic traffic by foreign airlines.[17] At the conclusion of the colloquium, there appeared to have been the general view that caution should be applied in considering a multilateral approach to the award of air traffic rights.

ICAO strongly maintains that any external multilateral framework that sought general or limited application would need to recognize and be compatible with the existing structure of air transport. However, multilateralism in the form of a broad-based consensus on principles and guidance to countries in the conduct of their air transport activities has enjoyed renewed interest in ICAO in recent years. ICAO has continued cooperating with General Agreement on Tariffs and Trade (GATT)[18] and the Group of Negotiators on Services (GNS)[19] in their trade-in-services discussions to address the concerns and the particular features of the international air transport sector.

IATA has suggested that ICAO adopt GATT principles with regards to all aspects of the air services agreements except in the air traffic rights and frequency of operations of aircraft. This suggestion has been strongly resisted by the International Chamber of Commerce, which argues that the aviation field should retain its purity of having characteristics and attributes that are susceptible to negotiation, although air traffic rights should be negotiated under a more efficient system than the prevailing bilateral system (Abeyratne, 1996).

Emerging Trends

Recent developments in commercial aviation reflect the inclination of countries to 'club' so that they award each other with multilateral air traffic rights. The most prominent among those agreements are: the Andean Pact of May 1991, where Bolivia, Colombia, Ecuador, Peru and Venezuela awarded each other with open air traffic rights; the Policy on Airline Integration and Co-operation between All African States signed in 1988, which was intended to lead to 'open skies' in Africa; the January 1992 declaration by the six ASEAN States (Brunei, Indonesia, Malaysia, the Philippines, Thailand, and Singapore), whereby these countries endorsed a plan to establish a free trade area within fifteen years (Abeyratne, 1996); the 1995 open skies agreement between Canada and U.S.; and the establishment of a single European aviation market in 1997.

6.3 Recent Trends in Asia-Pacific Airline Industry

The Asia-Pacific region has been the fastest growing air travel market in the world during the last two decades. However, air transport deregulation and liberalization process in the region has been slower than that in North America and Europe. Countries within the region have generally been cautious and restrictive in terms of liberalization. Many countries in the region have not allowed their bilateral air services agreements to keep pace with their economies, and changes are usually reactive rather than pro-active. Protectionist attitudes still prevail among governments in their policy towards aviation regulation. Their philosophy has basically been one of 'incremental increases' based on growth and market demand justification. Bilateral agreements are generally restrictive except for liberal bilaterals or open skies agreements signed between the United States and a number of countries in the region, including Singapore, New Zealand, Taiwan, Brunei, Thailand, Philippines, Macau, South Korea, and most recently Pakistan.

The Asia Pacific region is more diverse politically, economically, and culturally than North America and Europe. There is a wide gap between countries seeking rapid liberalization, such as Singapore, and those wanting to preserve the existing bilateral systems. Monopolistic flag carriers traditionally dominate the air service market of the region. However, since the mid-1980s, some countries have started to allow second tier airlines to enter the market, although many of these smaller airlines are confined to relatively few points and are frequently excluded from long-haul high density markets. For example, Japan Airlines (JAL)'s monopoly in the international market was broken in 1986 by the designation of All Nippon Airways (ANA) and Japan Air System (JAS) as alternative Japanese carriers on some international routes. Entry to a specific route, however, is still subject to regulatory control. South Korea had a monopolistic regime until 1988 when Asiana Airlines came into existence. Since then, the South Korean government has allowed Asiana to expand into many inter-continental routes as well as intra-Asia routes. Second tier intra-Asia regional carriers were growing rapidly (Knibb, 1993), and appeared to becoming a permanent and boisterous part of Asia's aviation industry. Many second tier carriers, however, have tumbled recently as a result of the economic crisis which has caused rising currency costs and plunging traffic in the region. In addition to the emergence of second tier carriers, there has been an on-going trend towards privatization of national flag carriers. The examples include Qantas, Air New Zealand, and Malaysia Airlines.

Asian carriers have traditionally enjoyed the benefits of low input costs (Oum and Yu, 1998), particularly low labour costs. This, coupled with high traffic growth, has been able to keep many Asian carriers relatively comfortable financially. Thus, many Asian governments do not see any urgent need for regulatory reform in the international airline industry. However, input prices are rising fast in the region, especially in the newly industrialized countries. At the same time, yields have been moving downwards due to increasing competition. This puts pressures on the carriers to become more efficient, and competitive. In addition, European carriers and U.S. have been aggressively making their in-road into the region, through liberal bilaterals, open skies agreements, and alliances with carriers of a number of pro-competitive countries in the region. This poses a threat to some carriers in their own territory. Moreover, the desire of emerging secondary carriers (mostly private carriers) to expand their services in the region is hindered by existing regulatory constraints. Thus, these carriers are putting pressures on the governments to change the status quo. All these forces have been working together to push the region towards liberalization.

There has been an increasing awareness in the region to develop stronger aviation links among the countries, to encourage economic and traffic growth at a regional level. For example, Indonesia, Malaysia and Thailand have signed a somewhat limited 'Open Skies' deal as part of a package to liberalize trade and services in the Growth Triangle area. Another example is the Brunei, Indonesia, Malaysia, and Philippines

(BIMP) - East Asia Growth Area regional pact. Asian countries are increasingly willing to work more closely together. Overall, regional cooperation and global attempts to further free trade will gradually pave the way for liberalization of the air services sector.

Not very long ago, many Asian carriers had been reluctant to join alliances with major U.S. and European carriers, believing the alliances would mostly benefit the 'outside' carriers wishing to establish a stronger presence in the region. However, the recent economic crisis has brought an abrupt halt to regional growth, and caused their once booming home markets to contract. This led some airlines to seek growth opportunity beyond their traditional territories, and to define/re-define their positions in an integrated global network. As a result, we have seen more Asian carriers joining global alliances. For example, Cathay Pacific[20] became a founding member of the OneWorld alliance in September 1998. Japan Airlines has also entered into separate marketing partnerships with OneWorld leaders, American Airlines and British Airways.[21] Air New Zealand and Ansett-Australia have recently joined the Star Alliance. All Nippon Airways is expected to become a full member of the Star Alliance in October 1999. In addition, an increasing number of carriers in the region have established code-sharing and other forms of cooperation with major U.S. and European carriers. However, there is little evidence that alliances have changed the structure of the competitive environment. The majority of airport pair had the same number of airline competitors in 1998 as was in 1988 (Boeing, 1999). Nevertheless, by raising competition to the level of global route networks, alliances will be able to support higher levels of service on both high-density and thin routes.

6.4   Issues and Problems in Aviation Reform

Unbalanced Traffic Distribution

One of the most significant issues facing commercial aviation under the bilateral system of negotiation was the resulting imbalance in the distribution of international traffic. In 1993, of a total of 1000 airports in 182 countries, forty-four percent of air travellers embarked or disembarked at only twenty-five airports in seventeen countries. Fifteen airports in twelve countries accounted for fifty percent of the total amount of international cargo loaded and unloaded worldwide.[22] Thirty air carriers from twenty-five countries accounted for seventy-six percent of total international passenger-kilometres travelled by 365 air carriers. This concentration of international passenger services in a few air carriers also manifested itself in international cargo, where thirty scheduled air carriers from twenty-six countries were responsible for the carriage of seventy-five percent of the total ton-kilometres in 1993.

Disputes over unfair exercises of traffic rights are rather often. For example, Australia sought independent international arbitration in 1993 on its air services agreement with the United States and the bilateral air services agreement between the United States and Japan, claiming that the exercise of fifth freedom traffic rights by U.S. carriers between Sydney and Tokyo gave those carriers an unfair commercial advantage. Another example is the termination by Australia of the single Australasian aviation agreement between Australia and New Zealand on the grounds that New Zealand would benefit unequally from the total liberalization of the exercise of air traffic rights between the two countries.[23] Also, Japan has been constantly seeking to equalize traffic rights with the United States.

'Safety Net'

'Safety Net' is extraordinary measures to ensure a fair competition in achieving a gradual, progressive, orderly and safeguarded liberalization of the international air transport market. One proposed future regulatory arrangement would be that parties would grant each other full market access (unrestricted route, operational and traffic), rights for use by designated air carriers, with cabotage and so-called seventh freedom rights exchanges optional. Each party would have the right to impose a time-limited capacity freeze as an extraordinary measure and in response to rapid and significant decline in that party's participation in a country pair market. The latter measure is the so-called 'safety net,' and is intended to form a buffer against a swing towards favouring unregulated commercial operations of certain air carriers.

'Safety Net' would play a very important role in persuading and inducing the 'unsure' countries to participate in the liberalization process. Therefore, the 'safety net' concept requires close attention in making policy decisions. Also, it would be useful to examine the possibility of including some forms of compensation as a component of the 'safety net.'

International Alliances and Ownership

International alliances have been formed partly to circumvent restrictions imposed by air bilaterals and foreign ownership restrictions. That is, forming alliances would avoid the complications associated with fifth and seventh freedom rights and major investment in a foreign carrier. Since fifth and seventh freedom flights are perceived as aggressive actions, they tend to ring alarm bells on all sides. National governments and carriers often react strongly against the idea of a foreign carrier operating within their boundaries. Also, many countries impose a limit on the percentage of foreign ownership of airlines.

The emergence of strong airline alliances, however, could eventually break the back of the bilateral systems. The growth in cross-border investment and strategic alliances, helped by the lifting of foreign restrictions, would make the bilateral negotiation process obsolete. The growth of multinational airlines would make it hard for government negotiators to know whose interests they were supposed to represent.

Airport Capacity

Airport capacity is an important factor in the formulation of international aviation policies. Slot allocation at congested airports is a major issue in bilateral negotiations. Any movement towards liberalization means gradual lifting of frequency and capacity restrictions on point-to-point services between two countries. However, having the rights to fly, while having no place to load and unload passengers or cargo, is meaningless. Therefore, sufficient airport capacity becomes a pre-requisite for relaxing various restrictions on air services. For example, airport slot shortage is one of the main reasons that the Japanese government has been reluctant to deregulate the airline industry.

At present, most major international airports in the Asia-Pacific region are facing congestion and infrastructure problems. Committing landing slots at a congested airport in a bilateral negotiation can be a difficult task. In this regard, airport capacity constraint is not only a bottleneck for traffic growth, but also a bottleneck for movements towards liberalization. Governments' willingness to undertake major expansion or open new airports will have a direct impact on the pace of liberalization.

Carrier Competitiveness

Airline competitiveness has two aspects: yields and cost competitiveness. Asian carriers have been able to remain viable either through high yields, such as Japanese carriers, or through low costs, such as Thai Airways. Oum and Yu (1998) found that except for the Japanese carriers, other Asian airlines have unit cost advantages relative to their North American or

European competitors mainly because of their lower input prices, while their efficiencies are relatively low compared to their North American and European counterparts. With rising input prices, the carriers must improve their productivity and efficiency in order to compete effectively with U.S. and European carriers in a liberalized market. The economic crisis has amplified this point, as overall yields in the region have fallen considerably,[24] while costs have further increased. Like receding tide exposing rocks, the economic crisis has exposed many deficiencies in the airlines' operation. This is a good opportunity for the carriers to thoroughly examine all aspects of their operations and to undertake necessary reform to improve their long-term competitive position in the global airline market.

On the other hand, self perceived low competitiveness could lead to the fear of being swarmed by mega carriers from North America and Europe. This may reinforce some carriers' resistance to liberalization, and drive them to put up barriers for protections. Countries whose carriers are ill prepared and incapable to withstand competition may be reluctant to pursue liberalization. Thus, it is important to seek a gradual liberalization process that would allow these carriers to strengthen themselves to face competition under a liberalized environment.

6.5   Lessons from the Success of the U.S.-Canada Open Skies Agreement

Until WTO and/or APEC become effective multilateral fora to negotiate air services liberalization, the aviation industry is stuck with bilateral air treaty process. Liberalization between like-minded countries is probably the only option in the short run. In this case, U.S.-Canada open skies agreement, signed in February 1995, serves as a successful example with some useful lessons.

Prior to February 1995, the U.S. and Canada had one of the most restrictive bilateral air services agreements although they share the largest bilateral air services market in the world. Experts agreed that, in the event of an open skies agreement, Canadian carriers would be structurally disadvantaged as compared to the major U.S. carriers. Canada's fear was based on the following reasons. First, U.S. carriers have well developed continental services network supported by a large population and strong and defensible hubs. Second, since the majority of transborder travellers originate from or destined to eight major cities in Canada, U.S. carriers would be able to reach over 80 percent of Canadian transborder market cost-effectively by extending their spokes to these Canadian cities from their U.S. hubs. Third, Canadian carriers may not be able to access landing slots, gates and counters at some congested U.S. airports, so they may not be able to initiate new services or provide high frequency services.

Although there were disagreements on the extent of these problems, both sides agreed that these problems existed. In order to remedy the situation and create a level playing field, the two countries agreed on the following measures. First, U.S. carriers' entry into major Canadian markets (Toronto, Montreal and Vancouver) was to be relaxed gradually over a three-year phase-in period[25] while allowing Canadian carriers into the U.S. market from day 1 without any limitation. Second, the U.S. guaranteed that Canadian carriers get some additional airport slots and gate spaces at the congested U.S. airports such as Chicago and LaGuardia in New York. The three-year anniversary report published by the U.S. DOT (1998) indicates that Air Canada did outstandingly well and Canadian did very well during the first three years. The total U.S.-Canada transborder passenger traffic increased by 37.2 percent during the period.

In addition to the efforts to create the level playing field, there were several important factors that helped conclude the open skies agreement. First, both of the two major Canadian carriers (Air Canada and Canadian Airlines International) had alliance relationship with at least one major U.S. carriers. Air Canada had the alliance with United while Canadian had an equity alliance with American Airlines (Oum and Park, 1997).[26] These alliance relationships reduced some fear of Canadian carriers. Second, shortly before the open skies agreement with the U.S., Canada transferred the operating rights of four major airports (Vancouver, Montreal, Edmonton, and Calgary) to local airport authorities. These airport authorities, representing the local business interests, played an important role in lobbying vigorously for the open skies agreement. Third, the negotiation on the open skies air services was conducted taking into account the overall economic and political relationships between the two countries. These other relationships were taken into account indirectly because President Clinton and Prime Minister Chretien appointed their respective special negotiators. At this high level of negotiation, other economic and political factors played an important role at least indirectly.

The most important lesson learnt from the U.S.-Canada open skies agreement is that it is possible to create a level playing field even if the flag carriers of the two countries are not equally competitive. For example, if airlines in China feel insecure about liberalization of bilateral agreement with South Korea. South Korea may be able to offer significant concessions such as doing codesharing alliance with the Chinese flag carriers via which they could pool traffic and/or revenue. Even though these measures may be construed as an anti-competitive behaviour in western industrialized countries, the opening-up of Chinese aviation market itself increases competition and thus benefits air travellers.

6.6　Summary

The international airline industry is governed by a complex web of bilateral air services agreements. The existence of these bilateral agreements has greatly constrained the freedom of individual scheduled airlines, and limited competition in the international air transport industry. Thus, reform is inevitable. However, changes have been happening at varying paces, and taking different forms due to the differences in culture, stages of economic development, social and political structures. During the last two decades, the United States has been aggressively pushing for liberalization of the international air transport industry through liberal bilaterals and open skies agreements. In the meantime, the European Union has been active in deregulating its internal market through the adoption of the three liberalization packages, leading to the creation of a single aviation market in April 1997. However, EU has not been very successful in unifying its members' efforts in negotiating air services agreements with non-E.U. countries. Countries in the Asia Pacific region have generally been cautious in liberalizing their air transport markets. Protectionism still prevails among governments in their policy towards aviation regulation. There is a wide gap between countries seeking rapid liberalization and those wanting to preserve the existing bilateral systems. Bilateral agreements are generally restrictive except for liberal bilaterals and open skies agreements signed between the United States and a number of countries in the region. However, the emergence of secondary carriers, the trend towards privatization of national flag carriers, and gradual relaxation of various restrictions in bilateral negotiations show that the region is moving towards liberalization.

There has been an increasing awareness in the Asia Pacific region to develop stronger aviation links among the countries in the region and with 'outsiders.' This can be shown by the creation of regional pacts, such as the BIMP (Brunei, Indonesia, Malaysia, and Philippines) pact, and the increasing number of carriers in the region establishing code-sharing alliances and other forms of cooperation with major U.S. and European carriers.

Although liberalization is inevitable, there are many issues and problems needing to be addressed, including the unbalanced traffic distribution, the concept of safety net for weaker carriers, airport and infrastructure capacity constraints, varying degrees of competitiveness of the carriers in the regions, international alliances, etc. These issues have important implications for the formation of a country's international air transport policy and liberalization process.

The U.S. open skies initiatives targeted towards Asian countries appear to have two clear objectives. First, it recognizes direct benefits for the U.S. carriers of having open skies agreements with Asian economies whose aviation markets are expected to grow very rapidly in the future. Second, despite the U.S. denial, the U.S. strategy appears to include a 'divide and conquer' strategy for forcing Japan to the open skies regime. Despite Japan's repeated threat to repeal its 'unbalanced' 1952 Air Services Agreement with the U.S., it is not possible for Japan to take that course of action because of its fear of U.S. retaliation in the areas of general goods and services trade. Given the fact that Japanese international carriers are not cost competitive relative to the U.S. or other Asian carriers, the rational policy for Japan is to postpone the U.S.-led open skies initiatives as long as possible. In addition, it is premature for either the Chinese government or Chinese carriers to even consider open skies with the U.S. Therefore, the U.S. initiatives are not likely to be successful for opening the Northeast Asian market in the near future despite of the signing of the U.S. - Korea open skies agreement.

Unlike the U.S. or European carriers, none of the Asian carriers has efficient traffic collection and distribution network covering the entire Asian continent effectively. Essentially, each Asian airline has a fairly extensive network to and from its own home base, but does not have any hubs in other parts of Asia. Therefore, major U.S. or European carriers looking for Asian alliance partners have an incentive to align with more than one Asian carrier. Since these Asian carriers are mutual competitors in the Asian market, they are at a disadvantage in joining a global alliance network such as STAR Alliance. When two or more Asian carriers join a global alliance network, other senior partners in the global alliance network may be in a position to play one Asian carrier against another and thereby extract better conditions for alliance.

The recent U.S. open skies initiatives directed to Asian countries pose a major threat to Asian carriers. The U.S. wishes to negotiate for unlimited freedom for setting up hubs (star-burst operations) in Asian countries so that U.S. carriers can provide high frequency services using smaller aircraft in the intra-Asian markets while enjoying economies of larger aircraft in the trans-Pacific routes. Since most Asian countries already have far more liberal bilateral agreements with the U.S. than among themselves, if one or two countries situated in strategic locations in Asia (such as Korea, Taiwan and Hong Kong) agrees to give unlimited seventh freedom rights or change of gauge rights to the U.S., it will lead to the dismantling of the system of restrictive bilateral agreements among Asian countries. This would happen because Asian carriers would be far more constrained in their own intra-Asian markets than the U.S. carriers. Most bilaterals between Asian countries have restrictions on seat capacity and/or frequency and pricing even on the third/fourth freedom traffic.

Therefore, it is better for Asian countries to create an open skies bloc (or substantially more liberalized air transport region) before allowing the U.S. carriers to do hub (or star burst) operations in Asia in a major way. This will induce the major Asian carriers to set up an efficient multiple hub airline network covering the entire continent. This will also enhance their status in global alliance networks. In addition, Asian carriers, which are facing fast rising input prices, will be able to shift their significant cost bases to the countries that enjoy low input costs. This will help prolong the period in which Asian carriers enjoy unit cost advantage vis-à-vis the U.S. or European carriers.

Notes

[1]   There were also representatives of two governments-in-exile: Denmark and Thailand.
[2]   The conference also adopted three other agreements: the International Air Services Transit Agreement; the International Air Transport Agreement, and the Interim Agreement on International Civil Aviation.
[3]   It included no capacity limit on 3rd/4th-freedoms, multiple carrier designations, and substantial 5th freedom rights.
[4]   There are over 1800 separate bilateral agreements or treaties related to the international air transport (Abeyratne, 1996).
[5]   United States, Public Law 96-192, 1980, 94 STAT. 34.
[6]   Thailand renounced its air service agreement (ASA) with the U.S. in 1990, claiming the agreement favoured U.S. airlines. A new agreement was signed in May 1996 to open their aviation markets to each other's carriers.
[7]   United States, Civil Aeronautics Board, Order 78-6-78, June 12, 1978.
[8]   According to Air Transport Association of America (1995), the United States signed new liberal agreements or amendments with 16 countries in 1995.
[9]   It offered a similar agreement to Poland too, but still needs to work it out.
[10]   US DOT News 117-98.
[11]   The U.S. and France had not had an aviation bilateral since 1993, making the U.S.-France market the largest U.S. aviation market not governed by a bilateral agreement. France is the third most popular European destination for U.S. travelers.
[12]   US DOT News 91-99.

[13] US Transportation Secretary, R. E. Slater, 1999.

[14] Mr. Mark Gerchick, Deputy Assistant Secretary of State for Transportation, has said in his interview published in *Orient Aviation* (June/July, 1997 issue) that the U.S. government approach to Asia does not include a strategy of 'divide and conquer', designed to pressure the toughest target of all, Japan, into U.S. liberalization demands.

[15] 'European Countries Urged to Work toward Open Skies with U.S.', *Airline Industry Information*, May 14, 1999.

[16] 'EC Lodges Complaint Against EU Nations That Signed Air Accords With U.S.', *Aviation Daily*, November 2, 1998.

[17] ICAO News Release PIO 9/91.

[18] GATT is a multilateral body established in Geneva on January 1, 1948, by the General Agreement on Tariff and Trade (GATT) which was negotiated and signed by 23 countries.

[19] GATT established GNS in 1986 to conduct services negotiations.

[20] Cathay Pacific used to be rather adamant in not forming any alliance relationship.

[21] *Air Transport World*, July, 1999, Page 59.

[22] ICAO Doc. No. AT Conf/4-WP/5 (August, 1994).

[23] *The Air Letter*, Nov. 8, 1994.

[24] For example, Singapore Airlines reported a 9.5 percent decline in passenger yields and a 2.2 percent rise in cargo yields, resulting in a 5.2 percent decline in its overall yield in its 1998/99 fiscal year.

[25] In fact, a two-year phase-in period was adopted to Montreal and Vancouver while the full three-year period was used for Toronto.

[26] Air Canada also had alliance with Continental which it had 28.5 percent ownership. American owns 33.3 percent equity shares of Canadian.

7 Challenges for Airlines and Governments and Approaches to Liberalization

Government policy makers and bureaucrats regulating the airline industry would agree that their long-run objectives are essentially two-fold: to serve consumer interests (travelling public and air cargo shippers) and to ensure a strong and viable airline industry within the country. This chapter argues that liberalization of bilateral air services agreements (and perhaps the creation of a liberalized air transport bloc in Asia) will help achieve both of these long-run policy objectives. It also discusses the challenges facing Asian carriers in their journey towards liberalization and various issues Asian countries may encounter in adopting different approaches to liberalize their air transport markets.

7.1 Need for Liberalization of Intra-Asia Air Transport

Until recently, most of the national governments in the Asia-Pacific region tightly regulated civil aviation industries and restricted their citizens' overseas travels. Governments typically prohibited new entry on both international and national routes, controlled cargo and passenger prices, and determined the size and configuration of the domestic air network. In addition, until the mid-1980s the majority of major airlines in the region were state owned. Government ownership of these national 'flag' carriers often skewed policy decisions in their favour. Carrier interests regularly prevailed over consumer interests in the formulation of aviation policy, particularly as reflected by high fares and less frequency and services. Also, national governments limited foreign gateways (i.e. airports with facilities and personnel to process flights to and from foreign countries), to just a few large cities. These restrictions seemed to be acceptable when air travel was a luxury, and most of the countries in the region were struggling to catch-up with more developed western countries. However, the 1970s, 1980s and early 1990s saw dramatic economic boom in the region, and the removal of travel restrictions in some countries. Demand for air travel rose rapidly, and flying became a common means of travel. Consequently, significant traffic growth has led to the emergence of new carriers, almost all of them are privately owned. These new carriers as well as the established flag carriers have been seeking for more opportunities to grow. However, their ability to grow has often been constrained by various regulatory restrictions. This chapter argues that such restrictions will jeopardize the opportunity for major Asian carriers to become important players in the global aviation industry, as well as harm consumer interests. The main reasons are as follows:

Under a restrictive bilateral policy regime, Asian airlines will continue to serve various parts of the region in an uneven manner. Fragmented networks result due to the airlines' inability to evenly serve the entire region. U.S. and European carriers will thus continue to align themselves with several Asian carriers. As these Asian partners also compete with each other within the same alliance network, U.S. and European partners will continue to reap benefits from the situation.

Because of protection provided by bilateral restrictions, Asian carriers are less exposed to aggressive competition from more efficient carriers. This reduces incentives to become efficient and to avoid necessary, but painful restructuring, eventually making Asian carriers less efficient than would be under a liberalized regime. Oum and Yu (1998) show that Asian carriers are less efficient than their U.S. counterparts. Their study also shows that European carriers significantly improved their productive efficiency after the three packages of liberalization measures were introduced in 1987, 1989, and 1993 by the European Commission.

Regulatory protection is likely to induce faster increases in airline input prices, particularly in labour prices, for Asian carriers. The situation will be further aggravated by rising consumer power and rapidly declining average yields anticipated for Asia.[1] These factors will have further negative consequences on the cost competitiveness of Asian carriers.

Many Asian countries hope to develop their airports (many of them newly constructed, under construction or expansion) as Asian super-hubs. Successful implementation of a super-hub strategy requires drastic liberalization of air transport in Asia. But liberalization of access to a nation's airport without reciprocity from other countries may work against the interests of the nation's flag carriers, at least in the short run.

Liberalization would enable the airlines to provide services in response to the need of the market, and to a limited degree, the services would be provided by airlines with comparative advantages. However, some instability is expected during the process towards liberalization. The airlines will be facing many challenges as they adjust to a more competitive environment. These challenges are discussed in the next two sections.

7.2   External Challenge

Deregulation in the United States and many other countries[2] has fostered airline efficiency through the formation of domestic hub-and-spoke networks,[3] and created conditions for the emergence of mega-carriers (United, American, and Delta).   Oum, Taylor, and Zhang (1993) and Debbage (1994) predicted that continued liberalization of international aviation would bring similar changes in forming intercontinental networks. At the moment, the world airline industry is undergoing major structural transformations in response to increased trade and air transport liberalization and deregulation.   Over the past few years, major airlines have focussed their efforts on creating and strengthening global service networks to attract more traffic in increasingly competitive international markets.   Although international air services have been substantially liberalized over the past fifteen years or so, it is still impossible for a carrier to set up an efficient traffic collection/distribution system in a foreign territory or continent.   Therefore, most major carriers are developing global service networks, primarily by linking continental hubs of alliance partners, whose networks are concentrated in different continents.[4]   Wherever allowed,[5] *codesharing* arrangements between two partner carriers are used to enhance services and to create marketing advantages of on-line connecting services.

On the other hand, major carriers in North America and Europe are racing to create networks covering the entire continental market by creating multiple hub networks and acquiring majority or minority shares in feeder carriers.   The status of the race for creating continental networks is described below.

North America

During the 1980s, over 25 U.S. interstate airlines were consolidated into six major carriers (American, United, Delta, Northwest, Continental, US Air) through mergers. In the 1990s, consolidation has taken a different form, that is, forming alliances rather than merger. Recently, there has been a wave of alliance formation among the major carriers. In January 1998, Northwest and Continental reached an agreement to form a strategic alliance. The alliance has since been partially implemented.[6] In April 1998, American and US Airways unveiled a broad marketing alliance. In the same month, United and Delta announced plans to join in a far-reaching alliance that would blend the airlines' ticket reservations systems in a code-sharing arrangement and merge the companies' frequent-flier programs.[7]

Such consolidation is not limited only to the U.S. carriers. In 1993, American Airlines (AA) purchased a major ownership stake in Canadian Airlines International (CAI) to strengthen its North American market coverage, with the additional benefit of expanding access to Asia through CAI's Pacific route rights.[8] In 1991, Air Canada and Air Partners (a non-airline investment company based in Texas) together acquired a 55 percent share of Continental Airlines (CO). Through this equity alliance, Air Canada (AC) sought to secure coverage of the North American market. However, Air Canada has since decided to divest its equity in Continental while still maintaining commercial cooperation with CO for the time being.[9] As predicted by Oum and Taylor (1995), when the government of Canada was considering AA's investment in CAI, Air Canada and United agreed to expand their broad commercial alliance whereby the airlines mutually feed traffic to each other, cooperate on frequent flyer programs, and operate code-shared flights. This allows United to secure effective coverage of the entire North American market, including Canada. In the long run, each of the Canadian affiliates is likely to assume the role of a feeder network supporting the larger U.S. network.

Europe

Major European carriers are also attempting to strengthen continental market coverage. For example, British Airways (BA) merged with its rival, British Caledonian, acquired 100 percent of Danair and Brymon, a 49 percent stake in Deutsche BA, and a 49.9 percent equity in Transport Aerien Trans-Regional (TAT) France, with options on the rest (Doganis, 1994). BA is reportedly creating a multiple hub network in the European market. Similarly, Air France acquired 100 percent of UTA, 73 percent of Air Inter, and attempted to embrace Sabena Belgian Airlines.[10] And SAS owns 40 percent of British Midland. The failed *Alcazar* attempt to establish an alliance between KLM, SAS, Swissair, and Austrian Air vividly demonstrated the importance for mid-size European carriers to establish a multiple hub system for effective coverage of the European market. In March 1998, a truly European alliance group was formed, the Qualiflyer. The Qualiflyer Group includes eleven airlines from seven countries: Swissair, Austrian Airlines, Sabena, TAP Air Portugal, Turkish Airlines, AOM French Airlines, Crossair, Lauda Air, Tyrolean Airways, Air Litoral and Air Europe. The partner airlines operate as a coordinated multi-hub system in Europe, with numerous connections to the entire world. Together they serve over 190 destinations in Europe, and over 300 destinations worldwide.[11] Although it is too early to predict the outcome of the changes taking place in Europe, it is clear that major carriers are actively strengthening continent-wide market coverage. This process is being expedited by the open transborder air policy among EU nations, which began in January 1993, and is strengthened by the formation of a single European aviation market on April 1, 1997. Already, 'Fortress Europe' is creating considerable concern in parts of Asia. Europe is feared by some airline executives as an 'impenetrable fortress.'[12]

Inter-Continental Alliance[13]

Because European and North American markets are regarded as single continental markets, major carriers are creating alliance networks by selecting a partner carrier in each continent. Since 1993, Lufthansa (LH) and United (UA) have formed a broad and deep commercial alliance.[14] To solidify their relationship, both LH and UA discontinued minor alliances with carriers that competed with their respective partner. This alliance initially put UA in a strategic dilemma because UA had been using Heathrow as their European mini-hub, from which they operated many 5th freedom intra-European flights. United now appears to have reduced intra-Europe 5th freedom flights to/from Heathrow and replaced them with UA-LH code-shared flights. UA-LH now have anti-trust immunity from the U.S. Department of Justice, which will immensely help these carriers link their respective networks in Europe and the U.S.. Furthermore, United and Lufthansa, together with three other airlines, launched the 'Star Alliance' in May 1997. The other participating carriers include SAS, Thai Airways, Air Canada, Varig, Air New Zealand, Ansett-Australia and South Africa Airlines. All Nippon Airways is expected to become a full member in October 1999.

Similar to the United-Lufthansa alliance, KLM and Northwest Airlines have created a strong trans-Atlantic partnership in order to provide 'seamless services' to North Atlantic passengers by linking KLM's Amsterdam hub to Northwest's U.S. hubs.[15]   Despite some temporary difficulties in their relationship, the KLM-NW alliance is expanding due to their permanent right for extensive codesharing operations, which effectively links the two carriers' networks. This right was granted as a result of an open-skies agreement signed by the U.S. and Dutch governments in 1992. So far, evidence shows that KLM and Northwest are operating as equal partners.   KLM discontinued the (aborted) *Alcazar* alliance project to strengthen the KLM-Northwest equity alliance.

British Airways had a 19.9 percent share in US Air, securing its access to the U.S.   The U.S.-UK bilateral agreement, revised in 1995, provides BA-US Air with extensive codesharing linkages (70 additional cities in the U.S.).[16]   Due to the US Air's repeated financial losses[17] and some other factors, BA started to seek a partnership with one of the stronger U.S. mega-carriers.   In June 1996, BA and American Airlines announced their intention to form a strategic alliance to create the largest global network.[18]   Also, British Airways and America West have a number of code-share routes connecting to/from the London Gatwick-Phoenix service.   In creating its global network, BA had attempted to form a series of alliances with major foreign carriers that were weaker than itself, and which provided network complementarity.[19]   BA has insisted on operating the international alliance routes with 'BA standards.'   Until recently, BA appeared to take an anchor carrier approach in the global alliance network it was creating.   The U.S. government was not happy because it found that most benefits accrued to BA.[20]

Growing Power of Global Alliance Networks

As discussed early, strategic alliances have been formed to create networks linking respective continental networks in Europe, North America, and to a lesser extent, in Asia.   According to Boston Consulting Group,[21] there were about 500 airline alliances operating in 1998.   In the recent years, there has been a shift of focus from 'bilateral' alliances to global alliance networks. The two largest global alliance networks, Star Alliance and OneWorld, currently include 16 carriers,[22] and accounted for 37 percent of the world available seat kilometres in 1998 (Exhibit 7-1).   The Northwest-KLM anchored Wing alliance network accounted for another 9 percent. Recently, Delta and Air France reached an exclusive 10-year marketing agreement (Thurston, 1999).   The two carriers expect to add more partners by the end of 1999, creating a new global alliance network to challenge those already formed by rivals.[23]   These global alliance networks have been more

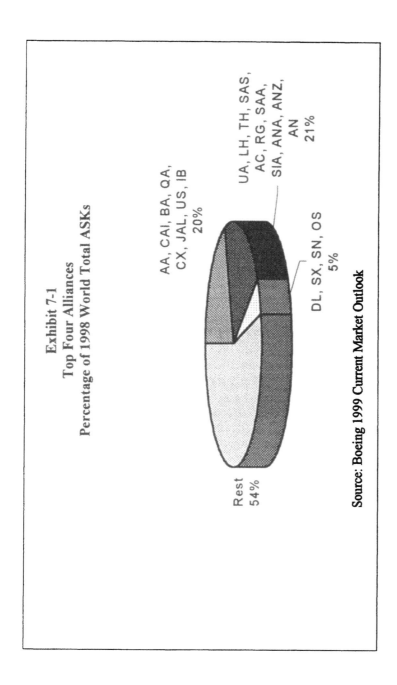

Exhibit 7-1
Top Four Alliances
Percentage of 1998 World Total ASKs

AA, CAI, BA, QA,
CX, JAL, US, IB
20%

UA, LH, TH, SAS,
AC, RG, SAA,
SIA, ANA, ANZ,
AN
21%

DL, SX, SN, OS
5%

Rest
54%

Source: Boeing 1999 Current Market Outlook

successful than originally anticipated and have been effective at redirecting traffic to benefit member airlines. Carriers have begun to realize tremendous financial benefits from the alliances, especially in operations and joint purchasing. For example, SAS expects to reap as much as a $200 million impact on its bottom line from the Star Alliance. United has already seen that amount in the incremental revenues from the same alliance network.[24]

A Strategic Challenge for Asian Carriers

For historical and political reasons, most major Asian carriers have one-hub networks centred at a home country's airport. As a result, carriers serve parts of Asia unevenly.[25] A foreign carrier, when seeking to expand its global network, would need to align with more than one Asian carrier to effectively cover the entire Asia continent. Since Asian carriers compete with one another on intra-Asia trunk routes and for intercontinental routes, competition among Asian carriers within a global alliance family would allow the non-Asian partner to exploit their stronger position when negotiating and executing alliance agreements. In other words, the U.S. and European carriers benefit when dealing with several competing Asian partners. Furthermore, U.S. carriers may be able to exploit the situation more effectively because bilateral agreements between Asian countries are far more restrictive than those between each Asian country and the U.S.. If U.S. carriers start to take full advantage of the open skies agreements in Asia, and set up efficient intra-Asian network, the Asian carriers would not be able to compete effectively with the U.S. carriers in their own continent because their capability is limited by the restrictive bilateral agreements with their Asian neighbours. For example, U.S. carriers may be able to take away a significant portion of the Japan's international travellers from the Japanese carriers by routing them via Seoul, taking advantage of the U.S.-Korea open skies agreement.

While complex and restrictive bilateral air treaties existing among Asian countries may help protect flag carriers in the short run, in the long run, they collectively hamper the growth of Asian carriers, provide incumbents with room for being less efficient, and allow major foreign carriers to exploit Asian carriers. These will eventually hurt Asian carriers.

7.3 Can Asian Carriers Maintain Cost Advantages Relative to Other Carriers?

Currently, major Asian carriers (except Japanese carriers) enjoy unit cost advantages relative to North American and European carriers, mainly due to lower input prices, particularly labour prices. Oum and Yu (1998) showed that after removing the effects of stage length and output mix on costs, Korean Air, Singapore Airlines, Thai Airways, and Cathay Pacific enjoyed 23 percent, 16 percent, 9 percent, and 4 percent unit cost advantages, respectively, relative to American Airlines (AA) in 1993 (see Exhibit 7-2). They also showed that input price differentials alone should have given these four Asian carriers, respectively, 24 percent, 20 percent, 52 percent and 6 percent lower unit costs than AA. This implies that if these carriers pay the same input prices as AA, they would have 1 percent, 4 percent, 43 percent and 2 percent higher unit costs than AA because they were producing airline services less efficiently. In general, most U.S. carriers, including AA, UA and Delta, have achieved higher productive efficiencies than Asian carriers (Oum and Yu, 1998). U.S. carriers were able to improve their productive efficiencies and marketing advantages via formation of efficient multiple hub collection/distribution networks.

Input price advantages enjoyed by Asian carriers rapidly diminished during the 1980s (Exhibit 7-3). They are likely to soon disappear for Cathay Pacific, and in the next five to ten years for Singapore Airlines. This is mainly because that airline input prices are expected to increase faster in Asian NICs than in the U.S. or other industrialized countries; and increasing global sourcing will further reduce the input price differentials.

Since June 1997, Asian currencies have been subject to varying degree of devaluation. For example, between June 1997 and December 1998 the currencies of Indonesia, Malaysia, Philippines, Thailand and Korea are devalued by 76 percent, 34 percent, 32 percent, 31 percent and 27 percent, respectively. The immediate effect of these currency devaluation is to increase unit cost advantages of the Asian carriers. Although aircraft financing cost and fuel prices are not likely to change in U.S. dollar terms, labour and purchased materials and services prices in terms of U.S. dollar are likely to decrease due to the currency devaluation. In the medium to long term, it is clear that currencies of these Asian countries are likely to be revalued to their previous levels while inflationary pressure following their economic recovery will increase labour and other input prices in those countries. This implies that, unless the carriers improve productivity in the medium to long term, cost competitiveness for

Exhibit 7-2
Unit Cost Competitiveness

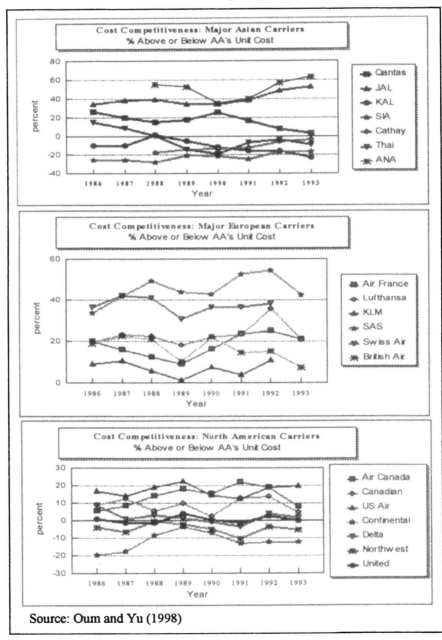

Source: Oum and Yu (1998)

Exhibit 7-3
Effects of Inputs Prices on Cost Competitiveness

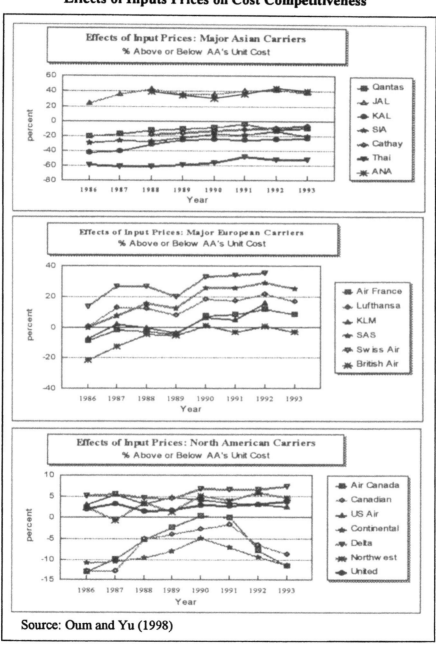

Source: Oum and Yu (1998)

these carriers are not likely to improve beyond the levels they enjoyed prior to the economic crisis.

In the next decade, when input price differentials diminish, Asian carriers will be challenged to become cost competitive vis-à-vis efficient U.S. carriers. The necessity of effective cost cutting is highlighted by the economic crisis, which exposed much inefficiency in the Asian carriers' operation once hidden behind high traffic growth. Asian carriers must improve productive efficiency by removing regulatory restrictions and increasing competition. In addition, since Asia comprises of countries at varying stages of economic development, an open air transport system in Asia would provide airlines in Japan and the NICs with greater opportunity and flexibility to increase regional sourcing of cheap inputs (labour, maintenance, supplies, services, etc.). This would help moderate the rising input prices.

7.4   Internal Challenges Generated from Within Each Country

Consumer Power and Rapidly Declining Average Yields

Average air fares for travel to, from, and within Asia are significantly higher than those to, from and within North America. Both IATA and Boeing predict that average airline yield will decrease by an average rate of 1.1 percent per year between 1995 and 2010. However, because current average yields for Asian markets are considerably higher than in other advanced markets, these yields will decrease much faster compared to other markets. The recent economic crisis has created additional downward pressures on the yield.

Currently, many Asian governments do not sufficiently consider user benefits when making decisions on domestic or international air transport issues. That is, governments promote their flag carriers, but at the expense of their own consumers. Virtually all economic studies on the airline industry indicate that user benefits (consumer surplus) are a much larger component of national benefits than producer surplus (airline profits). As the society becomes increasingly democratic, consumer powers are bound to rise. National air policies will thus need to reckon with this reality. This will also increase competition and put pressure on airline yields.

Asian carriers will be challenged to continue expanding market shares while dealing with rising demands for liberalization, competition, and rapidly declining yields. The protective and inward looking policies of some countries, including Japan, harm not only consumers, but also, in the long run, flag carriers relying on regulatory protection. The result is inefficient and uncompetitive airlines.

In the long run, airlines and governments have no choice but to respond to growing competitive pressures. The current restrictive bilateral system cannot protect inefficient and high cost airlines from their losses. Protection worsens a situation by merely postponing the inevitable (i.e., aggravating inefficient and high cost carriers to the point of no salvation).

Need To Develop a Super-Hub Airport

Many major Asian airports have recently been expanded, or are currently being constructed. Singapore (Changi), Osaka (Kansai), Tokyo (Narita), Nagoya (Chubu), Seoul (New Seoul Int'l), Shanghai (Pudong), Hong Kong[26] (Chek Lap Kok), Bangkok, Kuala Lumpur, Macao, Hanoi, and Manila are such examples. Virtually all governments in Asia plan to develop their new or expanded airports as continental super-hubs for Asia.

> *Southeast Asia*: Singapore, Kuala Lumpur, Bangkok, Jakarta, Manila.

> *Northeast Asia*: Seoul, Osaka, Tokyo, Beijing, Shanghai, Hong Kong, Taipei.

Under the current restrictive bilateral regime, these airports can only expect 'gateway' status for their national carriers. The bilateral system does not provide carriers with sufficient rights to set up mini-hubs outside their home countries. Therefore, restrictive Asian air policies severely limit the ability of countries to develop 'super hubs.'

Formation of a substantial liberalized air transport or open skies bloc in Asia would turn competition into a positive-sum game for airports and airlines. The ability for a carrier to establish mini-hubs in neighbouring countries will allow new and expanded airports to play an important role. That is, an airport cannot become a super-hub unless access to that airport is open to many carriers, as is in the U.S. and Europe. Although many countries would like to develop super-hubs, their aspirations are impossible without creating virtual open skies. In the short run, policy makers must balance the interests of flag carriers (who want less competition from foreign carriers) and airports (who want to attract more foreign carriers). Policy makers must convince flag carriers that an open system benefits flag carriers in the long run as well as helps to establish an efficient traffic collection/distribution network, where several Asian countries open their markets reciprocally.

Emergence of New International Carriers

Since the 1980s, many Asian countries have allowed entry of second tier carriers to compete with incumbent flag carriers on international routes:

Japan: ANA, Japan Air System, Air Nippon, Nippon Cargo Air Lines vs. JAL

China: China Eastern, China Southern, China Northern vs. Air China;

Korea: Asiana vs. Korean Air

Taiwan: EVA Airways, Mandarin Airlines and Trans-Asia Airlines vs. China Airlines

Hong Kong: Dragonair vs. Cathay Pacific

Philippines: GrandAir International, PEAC Airlines vs. Philippine Airlines

The emergence of new international carriers will alter each country's approach in bilateral negotiations, mainly for the following reasons. First, existence of multiple international carriers makes it necessary for governments to consider international route allocation problems. This means that governments may be more liberal in terms of carrier designation. For example, most of Korea's bilateral agreements signed after the advent of Asiana Airlines have 'multiple designation' as a standard feature. Secondly, second tier carriers can exert substantial influence on the power structure of bilateral negotiations by asserting their right to grow in international markets. Often new carriers have substantial economic and political power within the nation (e.g., Asiana is owned by the powerful Kumho Business Group of Korea, EVA Airlines is owned by the powerful Evergreen Group of Taiwan). For these reasons, airline policy makers and bureaucrats must take a more liberal stance in bilateral negotiations and international route allocations.

While a small, new local competitor may have little initial impact on the market, the trend towards multiple designation in air bilateral agreements means that existing carriers will face new competition on many of their routes. On routes from South Korea to Australia, for instance, Korean Air competes not only against Qantas, but also Asiana, Ansett, and Air New Zealand. If this trend is duplicated across an airline's network, the impact becomes increasingly serious. In addition, new operators may be looking for commercial alliances with large airlines from other parts of the world, given government approval, in order to increase their competitiveness. Sempati in Indonesia, which has an agreement with British Airways, is already one example.

7.5 Impediments to Liberalization in Asia

From discussions in previous sections, it is clear that substantial liberalization of commercial airline markets in Asia are needed not only to increase consumer welfare, but also to make Asian carriers efficient and competitive (by reducing x-inefficiency and forming efficient networks), and thus, ensure their future in the globalizing airline industry. This section discusses major impediments to achieving a liberalized air transport system in Asia.

Differential Capability of Airlines in Different Countries

There are significant differences in size and capability among airlines in different countries. As a result, countries with weak airlines fear that their carriers would lose out in a competitive system if international air transport were liberalized. Those countries and their airlines thus take a protective and inward looking approach in bilateral and multilateral negotiations. For the time being, it is difficult, if not impossible, to expect Asian countries to agree to a substantially liberalized air transport bloc without some guarantee of equitable gain-sharing among the nations involved. The principle of *'balance of opportunities (market access),'* which is advocated by countries with strong airlines, is not acceptable to countries with weak airlines. In the short run, the **'balance of the outcomes (results)'** with key incentives for carriers to become efficient and competitive is the way to liberalize air transport in Asia. Therefore, a major joint study by countries involved could be used to clearly measure the benefits and costs of a liberalized or open-skies air transport bloc, and to study mutually acceptable gain-sharing rules under a competitive airline system. Such a study would help Asian governments design a mutually agreeable liberalization package by reducing fears and uncertainties.

Weak Consumer Power

In many Asian countries, consumer power is weak as compared to in North America and Europe. As a result, governments pay less attention to consumer interests when making air transport policy decisions. Some governments do not even consider consumer welfare in debating pros and cons of alternative international air policies! In addition, in some countries, such as Japan, consumer organizations tend to be closely associated with labour interests (unions), thus they may not truly represent consumer interests. This lack of consumer power gives governments and airlines a free hand. However, there are signs that consumers and their organizations are becoming increasingly vocal. In the future, increasing consumer power may become the unifying force for liberalization of international air transport.

Different Political Systems and Military Use of Air-Space and Airports

Unlike in North America and Europe, Asia has countries with very different political systems and economies with varying degrees of openness. This makes it difficult and costly to predict parameters for negotiation and anticipate responses. Furthermore, military use of air-space and airports can be used as an excuse to restrict foreign carriers' access and to increase rival carriers' costs.[27]

Japan Has High Cost Airlines

Japan is the most economically advanced country in Asia. However, its airlines are not cost competitive in international markets, due mainly to high input prices (see Oum and Yu, 1998). Japanese airlines have been losing market shares in Asia. On the other hand, Japan enjoys huge trade surpluses with its Asian neighbours. Japan thus takes a schizophrenic view on air transport matters with its Asian neighbours. The lack of Japanese leadership in air transport certainly slows liberalization of Asian air transport markets. When negotiating bilateral agreements, the Japanese government, like many other Asian countries, fails to look beyond its flag carriers' short term interests.

Uncompetitive Chinese Carriers

Geographically and population wise, China holds the key for shaping Asian air transport networks. But China does not have strong carriers. Even the top three carriers are small by global standards. China Southern and China Eastern have been pro-active in developing international routes, but they still need to build their size and reputation in international markets. Partly due to their uncompetitive carriers, the Chinese authority has taken a very restrictive approach in international air transport. China does not even grant foreign carriers the right to overfly Chinese territory (the first freedom right in international aviation).[28] This has significantly slowed progress of Asian air transport liberalization.

7.6 Approaches to Liberalization

Liberalization of the international air transport industry is inevitable. How to achieve liberalization, however, is not a simple matter. This is especially true in the Asia Pacific region where countries and their air transport systems are at different stages of development.

Bilateral vs. Multilateral Approach

The benefits of free trade in goods and services to the world's economy have been proved beyond a doubt. Each country can expect to benefit from free trade by focusing on the supply of goods and services in which the country has a comparative advantage (Daniels and Radebaugh, 1995). This is the main reason why the WTO (formerly GATT) was created, and WTO member countries have agreed on the GATT (General Agreement on Tariffs and Trade) and the GATS (General Agreement on Trade in Services).

International trade in civil aviation services is constrained by a complicated and outdated system of bilateral agreements, which govern every aspect of the airline business: market entry and exit, carrier designation, capacity, frequency, type of aircraft used, prices, and other business conditions. Civil aviation has never been covered by the GATT, nor is it included in the new GATS of the Uruguay Round. Because it is not included as a part of the trade negotiation package for all goods and services, the benefit of trade based on the comparative advantage of each nation does not provide an effective argument for free trade in air services. Were it included in the general trade negotiation package, it would be possible to convince some countries (e.g., Japan) to give up the airline business and focus on businesses such as automobiles and electronics in which they have comparative advantages over many other nations. Therefore, in order to pursue free trade in air services, each nation will have to gain from liberalization of international air services. Unless all nations can be convinced that there are gains from free trade in air services, change is unlikely to occur. For this reason, the multilateral approach involving many countries will not be effective in reaching a free trade agreement on air transportation, in isolation from other international trade issues (Findlay, Hufbauer and Jaffi, 1996).

Even on the regional front, the Asia-Pacific region does not include air services in a trade package. The European Union was able to liberalize European air transport and eventually create a single European air transport market mainly because air services were included in a trade package with other goods and services. Once it was established that the Treaty of Rome applied to air transport within the Union, nations found it in their own self-interest to adopt free trade in air services.   The Asia Pacific region, however, has no equivalent to the Treaty of Rome.   Trade in air transport services is not linked in any other good and service (Tretheway, 1995). The Asia Pacific Economic Cooperation (APEC) forum is attempting to include air and other transportation matters as part of a general trade package.   However, APEC has not been effective in bringing about any concrete agreements on liberalization.   In fact, APEC appears to be making a mistake by creating a Transport Ministers' conference, which encourages negotiation of transport issues separately from the general trade issues.

In summary, until air transport matters are included as a part of general trade negotiations with other goods and services, multilateral (international or regional) fora are not likely to bring about a free trade agreement in air transport services.   There are some issues for which multilateral fora such as APEC, WTO or ICAO may be an effective place to debate, including overfly rights involving Flight Information Regions (FIR), cooperative arrangements for anti-hijacking and safe operation, and air navigation and air traffic control issues requiring international cooperation.   Under the current institutional framework for international trade and air transportation, bilateral negotiations between two countries are likely to be more effective in bringing about liberalization or open skies than multilateral negotiations.

With this background knowledge, we are going to examine the approaches Asian countries need to take to liberalize air services trade with their Asian neighbours.

7.7   Approaches to Bilateral Negotiation

China, Hong Kong and Taiwan

China plays a key role in determining the pattern of airline networks for Asian carriers. In order for other Asian carriers to develop an efficient Asian network, it is important to secure liberal access to China, Hong Kong and Taiwan.   Since the government of China has declared a gradual liberalization policy to equally share international markets between designated Chinese and foreign carriers, other Asian carriers should plan to grow together with their Chinese counterparts.

Since Chinese carriers are not up to speed in running and marketing their airline services, more advanced countries, such as Japan, Singapore and Korea, may consider the U.S. approach. That is, to implement a phase-in approach to expand their carriers' presence in China, and to use codesharing arrangements with Chinese carriers involving both Chinese domestic markets and their own carriers' international markets. For example, the 1996 U.S.-China bilateral provides Chinese carriers with a three-year head start in codeshare services to ten U.S. domestic destinations. U.S. carriers receive codeshare rights to six Chinese destinations three years after Chinese carriers have inaugurated their codeshare services. Since then, Air China, China Eastern and China Southern have signed codesharing agreements with Northwest, American and Delta, respectively.

China encourages joint venture activities, thus a joint venture with one or more winning airlines, such as China Eastern, should be considered as a way to penetrate air transport markets in China. Charter or freight services could be used to establish presence in new Chinese cities before negotiating for scheduled passenger services, as China is less restrictive towards charter services. With respects to capacity, it would be easier for the Chinese aviation authorities to come to terms with equality of traffic carried rather than equality of opportunity (seats or frequency). For example, Dragonair, a Hong Kong-based carrier, agreed to operate only half of the frequency China Eastern serve between Hong Kong and Shanghai. But, Dragonair carries about 50 percent of total passengers on that route. Also, until China's airlines become reasonably competitive, gain-sharing arrangements with Chinese air carriers are inevitable for liberalizing foreign carrier access to China.

Japan

Japan is the largest air traffic generator in the Asia Pacific region, while its carriers are the least cost competitive. Since Japan's major airports are severely congested, the availability of airport slots in Tokyo tends to become a bottleneck in bilateral negotiations with Japan. Therefore, countries wishing to make a real progress with Japan may consider initiating services to some secondary cities in Japan, and thereby, to attract not only the local O-D traffic, but also 6th freedom traffic to and from Japan. Similarly in the future, Japanese carriers may wish to develop 6th freedom traffic markets by linking with some secondary cities in other

Asian countries, such as Pusan, Cheju, Taegu, Kwangju and Taejon in Korea, and many cities in China.

Countries who currently enjoy traffic advantages over Japan, such as Korea, should consider approaching Japan with an open skies proposal to be phased in over a number of years. Japan may feel it necessary to create a liberalized Asian bloc before accepting U.S. proposal for open skies.

Other Asian Countries

For carriers that are facing diminishing cost competitiveness, such as those in Hong Kong, Singapore, and Korean, it is important for them to seize their window of opportunity to set up efficient traffic collection and distribution systems with a few mini-hubs in other countries in Asia before their input cost advantage disappears entirely. In order to assist those carriers, their governments should take the initiative to create a liberal or open skies Asian bloc. This may be accomplished via a series of liberalized bilateral agreements with like-minded countries having substantial domestic markets, such as Taiwan, the Philippines, Thailand, Indonesia, etc. If necessary, a phase-in approach for liberalization of various aspects of airline business (route and carrier designation, capacity and frequency, pricing, and other doing business conditions) could be proposed. In any case, it is important to set a time table for eventual open skies with various countries as early as possible so that the carriers can plan for the transition to a competitive regime.

The Singapore government has the most liberal approach, primarily because it does not have a domestic market beyond Singapore, thus has virtually nothing to lose and everything to gain in an open skies environment. In addition, Singapore Airlines is one of the most competitive airlines in the world. Although Singapore itself does not have a large domestic market it can use a far more liberal approach in giving out 5th freedom rights to foreign carriers in order to pursuade other countries to liberalize.

7.8 Approaches to Multilateral Fora

When trade negotiations are confined to a single good or service, the principle of comparative advantage, by definition, cannot be exploited. Linking trade in air services to trade in other goods and services is important to successfully form a free trade bloc. This increases opportunity for compromise because each country may find gains in most industries while making sacrifices in certain industries through a packaged deal. Regional economic fora that pursue free trade as a package of all goods and services, such as APEC and ASEAN, would be a good avenue for negotiating free trade in commercial air services. The key point is that free trade in air transport should be dealt within a package of goods and services, rather than treating it separately. This may require a significant change in institutional structure of governments involved. Currently, in most countries the Ministry of Transport personnel are the main people who control negotiation process for air bilaterals. This should be changed accordingly if trade-offs between air transport and other goods and services trade matters are to be made.

The APEC Transport Ministers' conference and Transport Working Group Meetings can deal with detailed analysis and preliminary negotiations. But air transport liberalization issues must be treated at APEC Summit Meetings as packaged free trade in all goods and services. For the same reason, the WTO could be an effective forum to discuss liberalization of air transport markets as a package of trade in goods and services. However, both the WTO and APEC are perhaps too large and diverse in membership to accomplish substantial liberalization within a short period of time. Therefore, it may be useful to form an East Asian Economic Forum where trade matters for all goods and services, including air transport, can be negotiated.

Any attempt to discuss air transport liberalization under ICAO will not accomplish anything, because ICAO cannot provide any opportunity to deal with air transport as a package of trade in all goods and services. It will be impossible to reach any substantial liberalization of air transport services because some members will always lose out while others gain.

In sum, we suggest that Asian countries attempt to make an effort to include air transport liberalization issues in a trade negotiation package on a regional basis, such as among ASEAN countries, or among the East Asian countries. A regional forum, such as Korea-Japan-China, would be able to discuss the aviation liberalization issues among themselves. However, for such measures to work it would be easier to agree within a total trade package rather than just on air transportation.

7.9   Practical Measures for Liberalization

Ideally, open skies should occur first among the Asian countries, and then, with countries outside of Asia. However, it is also important to set a date for full competition with U.S. carriers, which will end up dismantling restrictive bilateral agreements among Asian countries, so that their carriers may prepare for the eventual full competition with the U.S. and European carriers.

The governments should thus become proactive in liberalizing its bilateral agreements with their Asian neighbours, and if necessary, persuade their bilateral partners to compete in the eventual open skies environment. The following specific measures should be taken in stages.

Capacity for the 3rd/4th freedom flights   Restrictions on flight frequency and aircraft size should be removed on all 3rd/4th freedom routes. For reluctant partners, proactive countries might want to negotiate a phase-in period (3~4 years), within which the $3^{rd}/4^{th}$ freedom capacity is gradually expanded before the complete removal of restrictions on capacity and frequency. It is also appropriate to consider giving a head start rights to the countries with weaker carriers such as China.

Price regulation   All 'double approval' provisions should be changed to 'double disapproval' regime, and then eventually move to complete pricing freedom, subject to application of anti-predatory pricing regulation.

Route designations   In order for carriers to set up efficient service networks, complete freedom of access to all routes should be eventually allowed. However, as a transitional measure, it is possible to negotiate access to a number of cities.

Carrier designation   Although the eventual goal is open entry by any certified carrier of either country, a transitional measure such as moving from single designation to dual designation, and then to multiple designation could be used.

Sixth freedom rights   Immediate complete removal of any restrictions is desirable.

Fifth freedom rights   Eventual goal would be to move to complete removal of restrictions on beyond and intermediate points. But as a transitional measure, it is possible to negotiate for a limited number of beyond and/or intermediate points. Since *Change of gauge* dramatically increases the value of fifth freedom rights, in principle, this should be negotiated always as part of fifth freedom rights.

Codesharing rights As the U.S. is doing, proactive countries may want to use codesharing rights of foreign carriers when negotiating its bilateral agreements. These countries should study effects of granting unlimited codesharing rights to carriers of countries willing to sign open skies agreements with them. Where fifth freedoms are controversial to negotiate, codesharing allowances (along with block seat sale provisions) could be used as a substitute or complement to limited fifth freedom rights.

Seventh freedom rights In order for carriers to set up truly efficient cross-border mini-hubs at a foreign airport, unlimited seventh freedom rights need to be negotiated with select countries where the carriers would like to set up a min-hub.

Dealing with Protective Countries

For countries cautious in opening up their markets, proactive countries might consider first negotiating open access for the following services.

Open charter markets Charter services could play an increasingly important role in Asia, given the fast growth of leisure traffic and tight regulations on scheduled services. Most countries tend to be more flexible towards charter services than scheduled services. For example, the U.S., Canada, Australia, and many European nations deregulated their charter markets first.[29] Opening of charter markets first helped deregulate scheduled service markets by allowing all participants (consumers, carriers and policy makers) to experience the benefits and costs of deregulation. That is, lessons about deregulation were learned from the charter market. Therefore, it is a good idea to attempt to open charter markets first in the region.

Open freight markets The rapidly growing air freight sector could benefit significantly from deregulation. For example, given the severe directional traffic imbalance in air freight movements, deregulation of this sector would improve efficiency by allowing carriers to use back-haul space more efficiently than under the regulated system. Since most countries are more flexible towards freight than for passenger issues, attempts to open freight markets first is likely to be successful.

Open secondary airports The current regime could be retained for hub airports and a more open system could be adopted for secondary airports.

Countries may be more agreeable to opening routes to and from secondary airports than their main airports. This also helps alleviate congestion at hub airports.

Compensating for differential competitiveness of carriers If carriers in a certain country are less efficient or structurally disadvantaged than other countries' carriers, it may be desirable to devise a method of compensating those carriers. For example, Chinese carriers are less competitive than other major Asian carriers such as Singapore or Korean Air. It is possible for Singapore or Korea Air to compensate the Chinese carriers in such a way that the benefits from the liberalized markets be shared fairly with Chinese carriers[30]. Another way of compensating the disadvantaged carriers is to adopt some safeguard measures to protect those carriers for some time. For example, when the U.S.-Canada open skies agreement was signed, the U.S. carriers were allowed in the three major Canadian cities on a gradual basis (3-year phase-in) while Canadian carriers were allowed in the U.S. market unlimited from Day 1.

In the long run, creation of an open-skies Asian bloc, with liberalized inter-continental markets, is essential for both carriers and consumers. The liberalization of the intra-Asian market or creation of an open skies bloc would increase competition among several, but strong carriers, and thus induce them to improve efficiency of the air transport system. This is important for airlines to secure multiple hub networks in Asia, and allow airlines to become major players in globalizing alliance networks. Consumer welfare would naturally increase in such a competitive system.

7.10 Summary and Conclusions

This chapter discussed major challenges that Asian carriers face in the increasingly competitive international airline markets and various issues with regards to different approaches to liberalization. The important points of the discussions can be summarized as follows.

> The fragmented airline markets in Asia, where each carrier has a single hub network concentrated at a home country's gateway airport, are seriously hindering Asian carriers in their strategic positioning for future profit and growth.

> In order to become a major player in the global airline industry, each major Asian carrier needs to develop a multiple hub network effectively covering the entire continent.

In order to facilitate the development of multiple hub networks in Asia, it is essential to create a substantially liberalized or open skies air transport bloc in Asia.

Japan and China's aviation policies are to play an important role in determining pattern of networks Asian carriers can set up in the future.

Until air transport matters are included as a part of general trade package with other goods and services, multilateral forum is not likely to bring about a free trade agreement in air transport services. Thus Asian countries should make an effort to include air transport liberalization issues in a trade negotiation package on a regional basis.

It is desirable for Asian countries to establish open skies or near open skies agreements with their neighbours before granting U.S. carriers total freedom. It is important to set a date for total dismantling of restrictive bilateral agreements among Asian countries, so that their carriers may prepare for the eventual full competition with the U.S. and European carriers.

In dealing with protective countries, proactive countries might consider a gradual process which first negotiate open access for some markets such as charter services, freight services, and open secondary airports.

Since it is impossible for all or a majority of Asian countries to agree on liberalization of air transport markets, it may be more effective to begin making an effort to create an open skies market among a few *like-minded countries*. Such examples of open skies can demonstrate the benefits of liberalized air transport and *the threat of traffic diversion*. This may eventually lead to an open skies bloc in Asia. Long term policy goals discussed in this chapter also include relaxation or removal of foreign ownership rules (particularly, working towards creating a community or continental ownership concept, and away from national ownership), and liberalization of bilaterals with countries outside the region. For the world community to reap maximum benefits from the airline industry, it is necessary to work toward adopting the non-discrimination principle being promoted by the WTO.

Notes

1   Overall airline yield has been considerably reduced by the economic downturn, while costs have been going up. The declining trend for yields is expected to continue after the recovery from the current economic downturn.

2   The effects of deregulation or liberalization on the domestic airline markets of the U.S., Canada, Australia, New Zealand, Chile, and Europe have been summarized by many authors (see, for instance, Morrison and Winston (1986), Oum, Stanbury, and Tretheway (1991), Bureau of Transport and Communications Economics (BTCE, 1993) and Button and Swann (1991)).

3   Hub-and-spoke networks enable an airline to cover a large number of origin-destination markets including small and medium size cities with a relatively small number of routes, providing high frequency service (see Oum and Tretheway (1990)) and improved efficiency of airline operations (McShane and Windle (1989)). Such networks also benefit the carrier by conferring a 'strategic advantage' by altering future terms of inter-firm rivalry in its favour (see Oum, Zhang, and Zhang (1995)).

4   Undoubtedly, these networks will also offer point-to-point direct services between major population centres which are not hubs.

5   In most countries, codesharing is allowed only between the two cities where the foreign carrier has its operating authority.   However, U.S. Department of Transportation (DOT) has recently allowed British Airways and Lufthansa to operate codeshared flight.

6   The initial plan includes a substantial equity investment in Continental by Northwest, which is in dispute with the U.S. Justice Department. The Justice Department filed a complaint in October 1998 against Northwest, challenging Northwest's proposal to assume a controlling interest in Continental (*Aviation Daily*, October, 26, 1998).

7   The code-sharing plan was forced to be dropped because of the opposition from Delta's pilots union.   However, the airlines have started to link up their frequent-flier programs.

8   AMR, the parent of AA, invested US$190 million in CAI for 33.3 percent ownership, but only exercises 25 percent voting rights to meet Canada's foreign ownership limitation.   AMR also made CAI switch its CRS internal host system from Gemini (joint with Air Canada) to AA's Sabre as well as allow AMR to provide key management services to CAI for 20 years.

9   In May, 1996, Air Canada sold 2.2 million of its Class B common shares in Continental, and gained C$129 million investment earnings.   It now holds 2.8 million Class B common shares (10 percent) in Continental.

10   Air France acquired 37.5 percent equity stake in Sabena. However, it had to give up its shares due to irreconcilable differences between the two carriers.   Later, Swissair acquired a major stake in Sabena.

11   A number of other airlines also participate in the Qualiflyer frequent flyer programme, including Aero Mexico, Air One, All Nippon Airways, Austrian Air transport, Cathay Pacific Airways, Delta Air Lines, Finnair, Malaysia Airlines, Nationwide Airlines, Singapore Airlines, Ukraine International Airlines and US Airways.

[12] 'Asia: An Asia Divided over EC Block Air Rights Negotiations Strategy,' *Airline Business* 1 August 1990.

[13] A comprehensive treatment of airline alliances and their economic effects is available in Oum, Park and Zhang (2000).

[14] US-German liberal bilateral agreement signed on 24 September 1993.

[15] In the early stage of the alliance, KLM owned 49 percent of Northwest's equity shares.

[16] See *Aviation Daily*, June 3, 1995.

[17] BA's cooperation with US Airways ended in March 1997 (Gallacher 1997).

[18] US Airways is suing BA for compensation in the wake of BA's switch to American (Gallacher 1997).

[19] BA also acquired 25 percent ownership in Qantas and 31 percent ownership in Air Russia, a new airline to operate flights from Moscow to Western Europe, North America and Asia.

[20] See 'A Study of International Airline Code sharing' released by the U.S. Department of Transportation in December 1994.

[21] *Airline Industry Information*, March 5, 1999.

[22] ANA is expected to join the Star Alliance in October 1999. While Singapore Airlines is not officially a member of the Star Alliance, it has separate agreements with Lufthansa, SAS, Air New Zealand, Ansett, and United. Singapore has also signed Memorandum of Understanding to form alliances with South Africa Airlines and Air Canada.

[23] Swissair and Sabena, two Delta's long time partners in Europe, have agreed to be American Airlines' marketing partner on a handful of trans-Atlantic routes, in reaction to the announcement of the Delta-Air France alliance. Both carriers will continue to cooperate with Delta on routes where they already cooperate, but they will not likely to join the Delta-Air France alliance since they compete too directly with Air France to be its partner (Reed, 1999).

[24] *Airline Financial News*, October 12, 1998.

[25] The Asian airline industry has experienced minimal consolidation as most Asian countries have only one major airline and restrictive laws governing foreign ownership of carriers. Although Cathay Pacific acquired Dragonair to participate in China's growing air travel market, Cathay recently had to give up its majority stake in Dragonair to appease Chinese authorities.

[26] The second run-way at Hong Kong International Airport has recently opened for daily operation.

[27] There are legitimate cases where military use of air space and airports limit civilian use of these facilities.

[28] Recently China selectively allowed some foreign carriers to overfly its territory. But China is reportedly charging steep fees for the overfly rights.

[29] See, for example, Oum and Tretheway (1984) for the discussion about how the deregulation of charter services made inevitable for Canada to deregulate scheduled services later on.

[30] Some may argue against the idea of using the balance of benefits approach for liberalizing Chinese aviation markets as being anti-competitive. However, we believe that the overall benefits of opening Chinese markets are far greater than the negative effects of anti-competitive consequences. It may even speed up

modernizing airline management for Chinese carriers via cooperating with foreign carriers.

8 Infrastructure and Logistics Hub Development

Transportation systems in the Asia Pacific region face challenges as providers try to keep pace with the fast growing economies. The rapid increase in passenger and freight traffic is causing congestion problems in many parts of the region's transportation system. Without significant expansion and/or improved efficiency of transportation infrastructure, congestion in the movement of passengers and freight may impede regional economic growth.

Transportation bottlenecks are already pronounced at the airports, air traffic control systems, and marine terminals that serve as transportation and logistics hubs in the region. Meeting the challenges of transportation infrastructure development will require enormous capital investment. Increasingly, private capital and ownership are accepted as part of the solution for overcoming infrastructure capacity problems. In order to induce private capital for infrastructure capacity expansion and to enhance the efficiency of investment, operations and management, the Asia Pacific economies must offer facilitating institutional, regulatory and administrative environments.

While investments in airports and air traffic control systems are necessary, the efficient use of the existing and new infrastructure is equally important if the transportation system is to serve the future economic growth of the region effectively. The scale of investments and extent of trade relationships are affected by the level of co-ordination of regulatory policies between economies and regions. Further, an integrated logistics system not only requires efficient operation of passenger and cargo terminals, but also demands a closer co-ordination among air transport systems, governmental procedures (customs, immigrations and duty free light manufacturing, etc.) and surface transportation.

The purpose of this chapter is to discuss the issues of capacity and operational efficiency of airports and air traffic control systems in the context of liberalizing air transport systems in the region, and in the context of building efficient passenger and cargo hubs.

8.1 Airport Constraints

It is well known that air traffic grows faster than the general economy. Given the rapid economic growth in the Asia Pacific region, it is not surprising that air transport infrastructure has been strained. At present, the region has a large number of busy airports, with 16 recording traffic levels in excess of 10 million passengers in 1998 despite significant traffic decline due to the economic crisis. Nine of those airports were ranked among the top 50 in the world in terms of passenger volume (Gill, 1999). Exhibit 8-1 lists passenger volumes and flight frequencies of the top ten airports in the region.

Exhibit 8-1
Top Ten Asia Pacific Airports in 1998

City	Airport	Passenger	Freight	Frequencies per day		
		000'	000' ton	Number	Domestic	Int'l
Tokyo	Haneda	51,241	693	718	98.8%	1.2%
Seoul	Kimpo	29,429	1,425	609	60.8%	39.2%
Hong Kong	Int'l	27,828	1,663	488	0.0%	100%
Bangkok	Bangkok	25,624	719	500	31.4%	68.6%
Tokyo	Narita	24,441	1,638	400	5.1%	94.9%
Singapore	Changi	23,803	1,306	501	0.0%	100%
Sydney	Kingsford Smith	21,207	519	888	86.3%	13.7%
Osaka	Kansai	19,224	767	349	47.1%	52.9%
Beijing	Capital	17,319	361	424	78.7%	21.3%
Taipei	Chiang Kai Shek	15,725	917	324	6.2%	93.8%

Source: *Airline Business*, June 1999

Before the Asian economic crisis, many airports were experiencing severe capacity shortages of various dimensions; some are identified in Exhibit 8-2. Many of these cities are attempting to deal with the capacity shortage by constructing new airports or expanding capacity of the existing airports.

Exhibit 8-2
Asia Pacific Airports Experiencing Severe Capacity Shortages

City	Airport	Capacity Shortages
Tokyo	Narita	Runway slots
Seoul	Kimpo	Runway slots and, landside access
Bangkok	Bangkok	Terminal capacity, apron aircraft Parking capacity and runway slots
Bali, Indonesia	Denpasar-Ngurah Rai Airport	Apron aircraft parking, international Terminal and landside access
Sydney	Kingsford Smith	Runway capacity, gate capacity during Peak hours and noise concerns
Beijing	Capital	Runway slots and passenger processing capacity
Taipei	Chiang Kai Shek	Terminal capacity (passenger and cargo), Apron facilities; runway capacity problem due to the runway being parallel to nearby military base

Seoul (Inchon): new airport under construction, due to open in year 2000

Bangkok: a second international airport to be completed by 2004

Tokyo (Narita): new runway under construction

Osaka (Kansai): new runway under construction, to open in year 2008

Taipei (CKS International Airport): new terminal under construction

Singapore (Changi): new terminal 3 to be completed by year 2012

Sydney: planning to build a second international airport

Beijing (Capital): new terminal to open in October 1999

India: India is planning to spend US$ 812 million on airport development in the country during the 1997-2002 period

Despite the recent economic crises in Asia, both the International Air Transport Association (IATA) and Boeing forecast that high air traffic growth would resume within a few years.[1] The rapid growth of air passenger and freight traffic is expected to bring back the serious congestion problems for airports and air traffic control systems experienced in the past, especially at the major hubs and gateways. ICAO expects that about $ US200 billion will be spent in the Asia Pacific region to build new airports and other aviation-related infrastructure to meet the projected air passenger and cargo traffic growth in the region.[2] Substantial investment in airport capacity has been carried out in the region recently, including the opening of new Kansai International Airport in Osaka Bay in1994, and the opening of the Hong Kong Airport (Chep Lok Kok), and Sepang International Airport near Kuala Lumpur in 1998, and the scheduled opening of Pudong International Airport in Shanghai in October, 1999.

There is still concern that the airport capacity may not be sufficient in the Asia Pacific region, especially at the major intercontinental hubs, despite the level of airport capacity expansion. For example, the first phase of Hong Kong's new airport (with two parallel runways) provides an average movement capacity of 40 per hour. This capacity is expected to be reached very soon. The Tokyo area will continue to have a shortage of runway capacity. Since there is a long lead time for constructing new airports or expanding capacity, capacity expansion needs to be planned far in advance of the needs. For example, Singapore is already planning for constructing Terminal 3 to be completed in the year 2012. This type of early planning is especially needed for the construction of a new airport or the addition of new runways to an existing airport because delays occur almost inevitably in the processes of environmental review, financing and land acquisition.

Peak-hour congestion is an important issue. The curfews in force at Narita (Tokyo) and Kimpo (Seoul), and at major airports in Europe and North America, lead to highly accentuated peaks at Narita and Kimpo due to the limited scheduling windows available. While some peaked operations are inevitable, they have been aggravated by pricing policies and regulations. Peak period pricing is important because it will allocate the existing capacity to those who value scarce capacity the most, i.e., it is an efficient method of demand management. While there are limits on airline scheduling flexibility, it is important to get the most efficient use of expensive airport capacity.

It is also important to recognize the importance of landside access to airports: e.g., severe road congestion is experienced to/from airports in

Bangkok and Seoul, which may also constrain the growth of an airport as a regional hub.

8.2 Air Space Congestion

Air space congestion has been identified as a major issue of concern to the international carriers and the most serious threat to the growth of traffic movement in the region. The increasing air traffic leads to congestion in air space, and strains the ATC system. The problem is especially serious in two flight corridors: (a) the group of airports centred in the North Pacific which includes the two Tokyo airports, the two Osaka airports, Seoul, Cheju, Pusan, Sapporo, Nagaya and Fukuoka; and (b) the sub-region of the South China Sea comprising Hong Kong, Bangkok, Singapore, Manila, Jakarta, Taipei, Guangzhou and Kuala Lumpur. In particular, the air space congestion is most severe in the Pearl River Delta area where airports in Hong Kong, Shenzhen, Macau and Zhuhai are located. Airspace congestion in this area and in the South China Sea area has caused frequent delays of aircraft departures. The South China Sea is a comparatively small area with a large number of air space jurisdictions: Thailand, Vietnam, China, Singapore, Hong Kong, Chinese Taipei, and the Philippines. As illustrated in Exhibit 8-3, these two flight corridors in which most of Pacific Asia and North Pacific traffic are routed are rarely more than 200 miles (O'Conner and Dempsey, 1996). The significance of these two corridors is reinforced by its great circle connections with the North American cities. There is a need for close co-ordination and cooperation among countries along these corridors and the need to upgrade to high-tech communications, navigation and surveillance (CNS) and ATC facilities. A further complication is that there are some clashes between military use of air space and civilian air traffic control.

ICAO has concluded that, given the high growth forecast of air traffic in the Asia Pacific region, the existing CNS systems will not be able to support flight operations at acceptable safety levels. As the region is faced with a highly fragmented airspace network and a very wide variance in the sophistication of ATC systems, there must be a regional approach to the problem. Until a few years ago, the 15 minutes en-route separation requirements of Myanmar, India, Pakistan and Iran has caused frequent departure delays for aircraft leaving Hong Kong, Bangkok and Singapore (other economies in the region use a 10 minute en-route separation). For example, Hong Kong experiences aircraft delays on departures to Europe

Exhibit 8-3
Asia Pacific's Main Flight Corridors

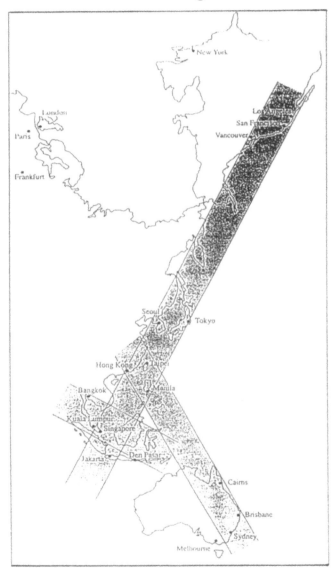

Source: O' Connor and Dempsey, 1996

overflying Myanmar because Hong Kong must regulate departures to meet Myanmar's 15-minute separation requirements. Also, airspace congestion delay is responsible for common delays of up to 20 minutes on Singapore-Hong Kong traffic.

The introduction of the advanced satellite-based CNS/ATM system called FANS (Future Air Navigation Systems), which is being strongly recommended by ICAO to the global aviation community, will allow a significant reduction of en-route separation in the long term, thus increasing air space capacity. The successful implementation of the FANS requires close cooperation involving all Asia Pacific economies, ICAO, IATA, aircraft manufacturers, communications service providers, and international organizations for satellite services. The technologies implemented must be able to link and interact flawlessly and seamlessly.[3] The Asia Pacific economies need to work on this issue closely.

In recent years, the lack of airport landing/take-off slots, and congestion in air space have constrained the speed and extent of bilateral air transport liberalization. In many cases, relaxation of bilateral air treaties to allow more carriers to enter the markets and/or increase frequency of services of the incumbent carriers would not be effective if the carriers in question cannot get their needed airport slots, gates and other facilities. Asian economies have had limited experience in looking beyond the local concern and engaging and solving the problem at a regional level (O'Connor and Dempsey, 1996). For example, Japan and Hong Kong have expressed regularly the lack of airport slots, and/or air space congestion (thus increase the separation times between two successive aircraft movements) as one of the key reasons for refusing to let more carrier to enter their markets.

8.3 Development of Airports and Continental Logistics Hubs in Asia

Transportation networks have been evolving into hub and spoke systems for some time, especially during the last 20 years. Rather than carry most traffic direct from the point of origin to the point of destination, loads are consolidated and taken to a convenient intermediate point where people or goods are transferred and consolidated once again to continue to their final destination. Hub and spoke systems achieve a number of economies in operation (higher load factors and utilization of equipment and facilities), and provide better service because service frequency is higher than would be possible with direct point to point service. By implication, traffic concentrates at a limited number of busy hubs. These hubs generate substantial economic spinoffs and employment, hence cities and regions compete to become major hubs. Hubs may also serve as a 'gateway' linking a domestic economy with other nations or economic regions.

Virtually, every economy in Asia has plans to turn at least one of its airports (usually an airport serving the capital city) into a passenger and freight logistics hub for the region. This is one of the key reasons why they invest heavily on building new airports or expanding existing airports. The substantial economic benefits to the economy mean that different countries and/or cities within a country may compete to become the dominant transportation hub or gateway for the region. The appropriate question to ask is whether or not any of the airports in Asia can become a truly integrated passenger/freight logistics hub in the current regulatory and political environment. In order to answer this question, it is necessary to examine the key characteristics and factors in developing successful hubs.

Competition between Hubs

The development of air transport hubs and gateways has distinct benefits. First, air carriers become more efficient due to economies of scope. Serving multiple markets through a consolidation point is more efficient and offers higher level of service than is possible with direct point to point services. Second, air transport becomes cheaper and more convenient than in a linear airline network due to co-ordinated flight connections and high frequency services. Third, cheaper and convenient air transport facilitates international commerce, investment and trade.

There is rivalry among potential sites to establish hubs because of the economic benefits associated with successful hubs. This rivalry takes place between nations and among alternate sites within a country. For example, competition among the North American West Coast airports has been heating up since early the 1990s. Vancouver, Seattle, San Francisco, Portland, and Los Angeles all compete to attract airlines to use their cities as the gateway to North America from Asia or to Asia from North America (see Exhibit 8-4 for the top ten North American airports to Asia Pacific in 1998).

In Northeast Asia, competition has been intensifying among Japan (Narita and Kansai), South Korea (Seoul), China (Shanghai), Taiwan and Hong Kong to become intercontinental gateways (Exhibit 8-5 lists the top ten Asia Pacific airports to North America in1998). Each economy or major city may have a strategic plan to commit a large amount of investments in airport and/or seaport capacity. Some of these plans are strategically

Exhibit 8-4
Top Ten North American Airports to Asia Pacific 1998

Rank*	City	Airport	Flights/day to Asia Pacific
1	Los Angeles	International	88
2	Honolulu	International	58
3	San Francisco	International	43
4	Vancouver	International	26
5	New York	Kennedy	15
6	Seattle/Tacoma	International	13
7	Chicago	O'Hare Int'l	13
8	Detroit	Wayne County	8
9	Portland	Portland	7
10	Dallas/Fort Worth	International	5

* Ranked by passenger volume
Source: *Airline Business*, June 1999

motivated to become inter-continental transport/logistics hubs. This could lead to over-capacity in the region, although, given the rapid growth forecast for both freight and passenger traffic in the region, it would be difficult to imagine that over-investment would go under-utilized for very long.

Exhibit 8-5
Top Ten Asia Pacific Airports to North America 1998

Rank*	City	Airport	Flights/day to Asia Pacific
1	Tokyo	Narita	140
2	Taipei	Chiang Kai Shek	42
3	Osaka	Kansai	36
4	Seoul	Kimpo	48
5	Hong Kong	International	28
6	Sydney	Kingsford Smith	15
7	Beijing	Capital	7
8	Manila	Ninoy Aquino	4
9	Shanghai	Hongqiao	4
10	Guangzhou	Guangzhou	1

* Ranked by passenger volume
Source: *Airline Business*, June 1999

Building Transportation and Logistics Hubs

Efficient and effective logistics systems facilitate inter- and intra-regional trade, encourage economic development, and influence the spatial patterns of economic activity. Although an efficient intermodal transportation system is a prerequisite for a logistics hub, logistics systems involve more than just transportation. Logistics systems also involve product storage and handling, packaging and labelling, documentation, and communications and information management. Logistics activities create substantial economic activities associated with warehouses, distribution centres, packaging and light manufacturing, service facilities for shippers, terminal and maintenance facilities for carriers. In order to develop an integrated logistics hub, all of these activities need to be co-ordinated efficiently.

Competition to become a logistics hub is, in general, beneficial to international trade and transportation. However, a successful hub is more than investing in transport and related facilities. We can learn from the success of economies that have been particularly successful in hub activities. Singapore and the Netherlands have clearly succeeded in this competition. Their success can be used as a guide to what is needed to develop a successful integrated logistics hub (see Oum and Tretheway, 1990, Singh and Li, 1997).

Base traffic level at the hub   In order to make an airport a successful hub, there needs to be substantial traffic generated from and destined to the airport's catchment area. Therefore, the city has to have a large population base and/or a certain level of business activities. Also, the catchment area for an airport can be expanded by improving surface access modes (convenient, frequent and fast train and bus/trucking services) to the airports from outlying cities and regions. The large traffic originating from and destined to the airport allows the hubbing carriers to take advantage of economies of traffic density.

Number of potential spoke cities within two to three hours of flying time   It is important that there are many medium to large size cities within two to three hours of flying time which could become spoke cities. This allows the hubbing carriers to economize joint cost advantages (economies of scope of serving various spoke and trunk routes).

Liberalized air transport regime and bilateral agreements   For developing a logistics hub involving an airport, it is essential to have deregulated domestic air transport markets and fairly liberal bilateral agreements with foreign countries, especially neighbouring countries. Attracting more services provides greater access and fosters experimentation and innovation of services. This will allow the hubbing carriers to set up efficient traffic collection and distribution system using the hub-and-spoke model.

Competitive carriers Since air transport is an important component of a logistics hub, competitive carriers are essential to the success of hub building. Singapore and Netherlands are again good examples: both SIA and KLM are among the most competitive carriers in the world.

Airport capacity Since efficient passenger and freight hubbing require arrival and departure banks of flights to be concentrated within a narrow time band, it is important that the airport has enough capacity to allow hubbing carriers the flexibility to do such operations.

Intermodal co-ordination Careful co-ordination of capacity and operational plans is needed for facilitating fully integrated intermodal operations between sea/air and surface transportation modes. Liberalization and deregulation of surface transportation modes are important as well.

Pro-business environment The business environment must be one that supports free movement of goods and services. Deregulation of the transportation industry is particularly important for developing a logistics hub because it fosters innovation to serve the diverse requirements of shippers and travellers as markets expand.

Information and communications technology Information is the key to an effective management of the total logistics chain. Therefore, cheap, convenient and state-of-the-art communications and information management technology plays an important role for enhancing the effectiveness of an integrated logistics hub. The development of EDI standards and subsequent inter-firm and inter-agency EDI activities and deregulation of telecommunication and information technology (IT) industries are key to improve efficiency of the logistics activities involving ports and airports.

Third-party logistics providers Development of capable and hi-tech oriented third party logistics service providers (to multinational corporations) appears to be one of the key success factors for an integrated logistics hub. Singapore and the Netherlands (Rotterdam and Amsterdam) are the cases in point. Third party logistics firms can be far more efficient and cheaper for foreign firms to use because of their ability to exploit economies of specialization and local knowledge. The use of third party logistics firms also allows the client (international) firms to concentrate on their core business. However, third party logistics service providers can flourish only under non-regulated, non-bureaucratic, pro-business environments.

Government commitment   Commitment by government agencies to remove red-tape and to provide world class hi-tech infrastructure such as airports, seaports, and telecommunications and IT systems is essential. In addition, a commitment to provide a steady flow of manpower trained in logistics by the public school systems and/or private sector educational and training centres would also contribute to hub building.

Free trade zones   Establishment of Free Trade Zones (FTZ) is also a contributing factor. For example, there are 7 FTZs in Singapore (6 to serve the seaports and 1 to serve the airport). Faster customs clearance and documentation have been instrumental in reducing processing time and enhancing distribution efficiency.

Building Transportation and Logistics Hubs in Asia

All of the above factors will contribute to building a successful integrated logistics hub. However, the most important factor is air carriers' freedom to build efficient traffic (passenger and freight) collection and distribution route networks at the hub city. This is perhaps the most important role a government can play in hub building.

For a carrier to be able to set up an efficient domestic traffic distribution and collection system, the government must deregulate its domestic air transport market and remove bureaucratic control of the airlines and management. However, since domestic markets of most Asian countries are small (except China) relative to the U.S. or European Union, there is a limitation on what the domestic deregulation alone can achieve.

Therefore, a carrier needs not only the liberal regulatory environment in its domestic market, but also needs liberalized international markets. Under the current regulatory regime, bilateral reciprocity is necessary for any two countries to deregulate the markets between them. This means that a country that wishes to develop its airport as an integrated logistics hub must negotiate open skies or very liberalized bilateral air service agreements with many countries in the continent. In the process, such a country will inevitably need to make a choice between protecting its flag carriers and developing the integrated logistics continental hub. This happens because unless a country gives up protecting the short term interests of its own flag carriers, it cannot get open skies or nearly open skies agreements with its Asian neighbours. In the long run the decision does not need to be a trade-off. When a country gives foreign carriers access to its own market in exchange for similar rights for its own carriers in the foreign markets, its flag carrier must improve efficiency in order to stay competitive with foreign carriers. Also, since they have free access to neighbouring countries' markets, these carriers will be able to set up efficient traffic collection/distribution systems encompassing both the domestic and foreign markets in neighbouring countries. In theory, it would be like the U.S. carriers who are free to choose any airports as their hubs or spoke cities. This will also improve productivity and cost efficiency of the domestic carriers. As a result, in terms of long term perspectives, there is no trade-off to be made between the flag carriers' interests and the integrated logistics hub development by fully opening up the domestic and foreign markets for all carriers.

Furthermore, in a liberalized continental air transport regime, different airlines will be setting their hubs in different locations to serve essentially the same market. Therefore, most of the medium size cities are likely to receive multiple carrier services from different hubs, much the same way as in the U.S. For example, Pusan may be a spoke city from Seoul (Korean Air and Asiana), Kansai (Japan Airlines, ANA), Tokyo (JAL, ANA), Shanghai (China Eastern), Taipei (China Airlines or Eva) and Hong Kong (Cathay, Dragonair). Also, each major airline in Asia Pacific is likely to have several hubs throughout the region. This situation is not only good for consumers but also good for air carriers in the region because they are given the opportunity to develop region-wide multiple hub networks much the same way as the U.S. carriers have done and the major European carriers are beginning to do.

8.4 Summary and Conclusions

Despite the recent economic crisis, the Asian economies are likely to resume high growth within a few years. As a result, air passenger and freight traffic will also resume their high growth. This will bring back congestion and capacity shortage problems in many of the major airports in Asia Pacific in the near future. This implies that the capacity investment programs for airports and air navigation and traffic control systems which have been put on hold since the beginning of the economic crises should be implemented as soon as possible. There is a need to induce private capital for such capacity investment projects both for securing the necessary funds and for injecting private sector efficiency into the construction, operation, and management of the infrastructure service business. However, in order to induce private capital, the governments must offer facilitating institutional, regulatory and administrative environments.

In recent years, the lack of airport slots and serious air space congestion have been the constraining factors for the speed and extent of bilateral air transport liberalization. This problem will need to be solved by expanding capacity and/or increasing effective capacity of given facilities through efficient pricing and management.

Because of the anticipated economic benefits of having a successful passenger and freight logistics hub, every country in the Asia Pacific wishes to develop one or more continental logistics hubs to dominate the region. In order to achieve this goal, many economies in the region have completed major investments, or are in the process of construction, or have plans to expand airport capacity. However, capacity expansion alone is not sufficient to make an airport a successful integrated logistics hub.

In order to succeed as an integrated logistics hub, in addition to providing the needed capacity for airports and related facilities, the governments and business communities must work together to achieve the following in order to gain advantages over competing hub locations:

> Deregulation of domestic air transport industry and market
> Liberalization or open skies regime for bilateral air service agreements with as many neighbouring countries as possible.
> Creation of pro-business and pro-consumer environment.
> Enhancing international competitiveness of carriers.
> Providing cheap and efficient information and telecommunications technology and services.
> Attracting many integrated logistics firms to locate their bases
> Government's strong commitment to remove red-tapes, hidden costs, and bureaucratic delays as well as streamline customs and immigration procedures and simplify documentation for freight clearance.
> Establishment of free trade zones for light assembly, labeling, and transshipment
> Ensuring that educational and training systems are in place to provide quality manpower needed by the industry

'Customer-oriented re-engineering' of the operational systems for airports related facilities, customs and immigration and other regulatory functions.

Most countries in Asia Pacific appear to realize these needs and are making good progress to deal with these issues. However, many countries are torn between their interests in establishing successful logistics hubs and their flag carriers' interests when considering liberalizing or negotiating open skies agreements with neighbouring countries.

The plain fact of matter is that unless your country is willing to open up your own markets to foreign airlines, there will not be open skies or liberalized agreements with your neighbours. If a country focuses its attention only on the short run effects, they are making a choice for protecting its flag carriers overdeveloping the integrated logistics continental hub. However, in the long run the decision does not require a trade-off. In fact, the long term competitiveness of the flag carriers would be enhanced by opening markets for competition because they must improve efficiency in order to stay competitive with foreign carriers. Also, since they have free access to neighbouring markets, these carriers would be able to set up efficient traffic collection/distribution systems encompassing both the domestic markets and its neighbouring countries. This would also improve productivity and cost efficiency of the domestic carriers. As a result, in terms of long term perspectives, there is no trade-off to be made between the flag carriers' interests and the integrated logistics hub development by fully opening the domestic and foreign markets for all carriers.

Notes

[1] See Chapter 9 for details on the impacts of the recent Asian economic crises on air traffic forecast.

[2] 'ICAO Sees US$200 Billion Spending on Airports in Asia Pacific', *Asia Pulse*, March 8, 1998.

[3] *Congestion Points Study III* vol. 1, Air Transport, p.12-13.

9 Asian Economic Crisis and its Impact on Air Transport [1]

In 1992-93, eight of the world's 15 most profitable airlines were from Asia, and their low input prices, especially for labour and 'purchased services and materials,' gave them a competitive advantage. The prospects for the aviation sector appeared to be excellent, and airlines and airports were full of confidence and embarked on ambitious expansion plans. 'Growth' was the driving force, setting the agenda for policy makers and governments to allow the private sector to participate in aviation in a broader scope through privatization and to allow new airlines to enter the industry and new markets.

Nevertheless, there were some emerging problems for the airlines. Yields were falling in highly competitive markets where capacity grew more quickly than demand, and profits were being squeezed by rising costs. Currency appreciation eroded competitive advantage, especially for Japan (see Oum and Yu, 1998). A host of new challenges emerged early in 1997. The predicted 'bubble' in the demand for travel to Hong Kong prior to the hand-over did not materialize. Concerns about the arrival of the Peoples Liberation Army in Hong Kong and possible changes to freedoms and liberties once under Chinese rule, were beginning to have an impact. The bird flu scare, in particular, deterred tourists, and the Hong Kong travel market began to decline from June 1997. Smog from the forest fires in Indonesia affected tourism demand throughout Southeast Asia, but the main factor affecting demand was that the Japanese market had lost its momentum.

Then came the events of the second half of 1997 that led to the currency crisis and the need for International Monetary Fund (IMF) assistance in Thailand, Indonesia and South Korea. Collectively, the Asian economies had accumulated over US$240 billion in short-term debts. When the Government of Thailand could no longer afford to support its currency against the attacks of speculators it floated the Baht on 2 July 1997. The ensuing crash reverberated through the Philippines, Indonesia and Malaysia. Confidence was undermined, as the extent of non-performing loans became clear. Within a very short period of time, large amounts of capital flowed out of the region, and Asia's wealth fell sharply.

The IMF provided US$1 billion emergency assistance to Thailand on July 19, 1997 and followed up with another US$17.2 billion on August 11, but the contagion continued to spread and there were sharp falls on stock exchanges late in October. The IMF offered US$40 billion in a bailout package to Indonesia on October 31 and then negotiated a record amount of assistance (US$58 billion) to South Korea on December 3. Some major corporations and conglomerates were in serious financial difficulty, governments were adopting austere economic measures, unemployment was rising and job security was threatened. Even a fiscal stimulus of US$128 billion introduced by the Government of Japan to its own economy failed to satisfy financial markets and the downward pressure on the Yen continued.

With the resulting drop in consumer confidence and fall in international purchasing power, Asia's travel markets slumped. In Japan, young office workers who previously made up an important segment of the travel market became the targets of corporations' plans to reduce cost. The crisis of confidence in South Korea was sudden and deep, and airline traffic fell by as much as 80 percent on some routes in the month following the IMF bailout package. As a result, some important players in the travel sales and distribution systems have gone out of business and it will take time and resources to rebuild these systems.

The airlines were highly exposed with commitments to purchase aircraft and spares in hard currency. The value of their debt escalated rapidly, interest rates and fuel costs (expressed in domestic currencies) increased, and traffic fell sharply. Profit projections for the region's carriers were written down immediately and some incurred losses of several hundreds of millions of dollars (US) during 1997/98. The newer carriers that relied on domestic and intra-Asian business have been the worst affected. Some airlines have gone out of business or have suspended their operations. Others responded by selling aircraft, partly to reduce capacity and partly to finance deliveries of new aircraft. Sale-and-leaseback deals have been common and aircraft orders are being deferred where possible. Airlines are reallocating capacity to stronger routes connecting Asia with Europe and North America.

The currency devaluation ultimately should help stimulate travel demand of the foreign tourists coming to Asia-Pacific countries, and there will be winners and losers as destinations compete for their share of a smaller market. Also, as some airlines pull out of routes the remaining carriers have opportunities to increase their revenue. Depending on the ability of the airlines to maintain their yields, Asian carriers will keep their attention firmly on reducing their costs and on re-financing their fleets.

However, the restructuring process has been and will continue to be painful even under the most optimistic scenarios. There is speculation that some airlines will merge in order to create one or more mega carriers in Asia and that major European and North American carriers may become part owners of some Asian carriers.

This chapter examines the impact of the Asian economic crisis on the airlines and the responses being pursued by airline management and governments. Given the trend towards liberalization, an important question is whether the current circumstances are likely to lead to a return to more protectionist attitudes. The temptation to shield carriers from competition is being balanced against the need to open up markets, to forge alliances and to attract investments. Though we illustrate the impact of the economic crisis with examples of recent developments, our focus is on long-term impacts of the Asian economic crisis on cost competitiveness of Asian carriers and on the regulatory environment.

9.1   The Impact of the Economic Crisis on Air Traffic Levels

Informal business networks, close relationships between financial institutions and their borrowers, and low interest policy loans backed by governments were mechanisms that facilitated rapid growth in Asia, but the financial sector became exposed to risky investments. A lack of control over lending practices and inadequate disclosure and reporting requirements have been pinpointed as fundamental weaknesses of the Asian economies. When the weaknesses of the financial sector began to emerge, currencies began to enter a free-fall. Exhibit 9-1 shows that the Thai Baht fell to almost half of its value against the US dollar in the second half of 1997, although it has regained some of its value during 1998.

Were the price of an overseas holiday to be set in US dollars, the Thai consumer now would have to pay 44 percent more in terms of Bahts. The Indonesian Rupiah became so unstable that trade in it was suspended and the Indonesian consumer has to offer almost 4.5 times as many Rupiah in December, 1998 to purchase goods and services sold in US dollars compared to a year and half early. Clearly, the affordability of overseas travel outside of Asia has suffered.

Exhibit 9-1
Changes in Exchange Rates for Selected Asian Economies
(local currency per U.S. dollar)

Economy	Currency	June 97	Dec. 97	June 98	Dec 98	% devalue
China	Yuan	8.3	8.3	8.3	8.3	0%
Hong Kong	Dollar	7.8	7.8	7.8	7.8	0%
Indonesia	Rupiah	2,600	5,450	9,800	11,000	76%
Japan	Yen	114	139	146	116	2%
Malaysia	Ringgit	2.5	3.9	3.9	3.8	34%
Philippines	Peso	26.4	39.5	38.4	38.8	32%
Singapore	Dollar	1.43	1.65	1.69	1.66	14%
South Korea	Won	881	1,695	1,383	1,206	27%
Taiwan	Dollar	27.8	32.2	34.5	32.2	14%
Thailand	Baht	25	47	40	36	31%

Source: Chin, Hooper and Oum (1999)

To make matters worse, Asia's wealth devalued overnight through sharp falls in property prices and share values. Exhibit 9-2 illustrates the extent of this effect. A consumer in Malaysia, South Korea or Thailand who had invested in shares in June 1997 would be able to sell them for less than half of their previous value in June 1998. Coupled with this, the list of business failures included merchant banks through to steel producers. All businesses have been seeking to reduce their labour costs, and consumer confidence has slumped with the loss of job security. Domestic demand and imports fell by more than 20 percent in real terms in 1998 in Indonesia, Malaysia, South Korea and Thailand (Camdessus, 1999). The lower exchange rates improved international competitiveness and the Philippines, South Korea and Thailand all succeeded in selling more exports. Overall, Indonesia fared the worst, with its GDP declining by 15 percent in real terms in 1998 (IMF estimate). In the same year, the economies of Malaysia, South Korea and Thailand contracted by 6-8 percent.

Exhibit 9-2
Changes in Share Price Indices for Selected Asian Economies
(June 1997, December 1997, and June 1998)

Economy	Share Price Index			Loss in value relative to period 6 months before (%)	
	Jun 97	Dec 97	Jun 98	Dec 97	Jun 98
China - Shanghai	2,743	2,971	3,220	-8%	-17%
China - Shenzhen	4,550	3,963	3,864	13%	15%
Hong Kong	15,056	10,723	8,543	29%	43%
Indonesia	732	402	446	45%	39%
Japan	20,176	15,259	15,830	24%	22%
Malaysia	1,079	594	456	45%	58%
Philippines	2,816	1869	1,760	34%	38%
South Korea	758	376	298	50%	61%
Taiwan	8,997	8187	7,549	9%	16%
Thailand	569	373	267	34%	53%

Source: Chin, Hooper and Oum (1999)

Immediate Effects on Traffic Levels

The economic recession in several major Asian countries including Japan and South Korea had a major impact on air travel demand. Airports Council International (Gill, 1999) reports that the overall number of passenger movements for all of Asia's main airports fell by 6 percent in 1998, while cargo fell by nearly 4 percent. Among the worst hit countries, Indonesia's main hub at Jakarta saw passenger numbers collapse by nearly 40 percent as the country struggled with its economic and political traumas. Seoul Kimpo was not far behind with a near 20 percent fall, as South Korea continued its efforts to rebuild.

Boeing (Boeing, 1999) reports that air traffic in the Asia Pacific region declined by 7.6 percent in 1998 as compared to1997, while during the 1997, air traffic grew by a modest 4 percent over 1996. These figures are compared with 6.1 percent and 3.0 percent growth in the total worldwide air traffic in 1997 and 1998, respectively. Exhibit 9-3 lists the air traffic growth rates in 1997 and 1998 by regions of the world.

Exhibit 9-3
Traffic Growth by Region

Region	Annual Growth, %	
	1997	1998
North America	4.6	2.3
Europe	8.9	8.8
Asia-Pacific	4.0	-7.6
North Atlantic	8.9	8.7
Transpacific	6.7	0.5
Europe-Asia-Pacific	10.5	2.6
North America - Latin America	5.8	8.2
Europe - Latin America	8.6	12.0
Latin America	8.6	11.0
World Total	**6.1**	**3.0**

Source: *Boeing Current Market Outlook 1999*

The severity of the economic crisis faced by each country varies, so is its effect on air traffic. For example, over 90 percent of international travellers to Australia are of non-business purposes, thus it is useful to look at how the visitor volumes to Australia forecasted before and after the Asian economic crisis have changed. Australia's Tourism Forecasting Council (TFC) produced a set of long-term forecast of international visitor arrivals for Australia in November 1996 (TFC', 1996).   Like most forecasting agencies, the TFC did not anticipate the economic crisis that was to occur in the very next year, and it quickly issued a bulletin in December 1997 to revise its predictions. The new forecast took account of currency devaluation up to 31 October 1997. However, as shown in Exhibit 9-1, conditions continued to deteriorate for some countries after October 1997. Further revisions were issued in June 1998.

Exhibit 9-4 shows the TFC forecasts for the years 2000 and 2005. Actual visitor numbers to Australia are presented for each Asia Pacific market in the first column. The November 1996 forecasts and subsequent revisions are also reported in the Exhibit. However, the revisions to the November 1996 forecast are given as an index relative to the initial November 1996 forecast volumes. For example, the index of 103 for New Zealand in the year 2000 indicates a revision upwards of 3 percent in the forecast. Exhibit 9-4 also shows a similar relativity index for the most

Exhibit 9-4
Forecasts of Visitors to Australia
(Recent revisions by the Tourism Forecasting Council)

Country	Actual	Forecasts for Year 2000			Forecasts for Year 2005		
	Visitors (thousand)	Visitors	Index Showing Relativity to Nov-96		Visitors	Index Showing Relativity to Nov-96	
	1997	Nov-96	Dec-97	Jun-98	Nov-96	Dec-97	Jun-98
New Zealand	686	713	103	107	758	103	104
Indonesia	160	336	53	12	624	53	17
Malaysia	144	199	66	52	378	49	52
Singapore	239	310	78	93	416	69	88
Thailand	69	210	32	24	422	31	23
China	66	109	80	159	281	57	176
Hong Kong	152	219	85	67	348	82	67
Japan	814	1,187	83	66	1568	70	75
Korea	234	386	68	19	547	48	34
Taiwan	153	283	52	55	460	43	44
North America	394	482	100	111	617	95	95
Europe	874	1,107	102	99	1615	92	90
All regions	**4,318**	**6,013**	**79**	**77**	**8767**	**72**	**73**

Note: The Index for December 1997 is the average for the three scenarios examined by the TFC.
Source: Tourism Forecasting Council (1996, 1997,1998)

recent forecasts (June 1998). Notably, the forecast of visitors from New Zealand to Australia has been increased. One reason is that Qantas Airways and Air New Zealand are increasing the number of flights between the two countries as part of a strategy to re-deploy capacity to stronger markets. However, recent political tensions in Indonesia and the weakness of the nation's currency have led to a downgrading of the forecast of arrivals to only 12 percent of the amount forecasted just prior to the economic crisis. The severe economic crisis of South Korea has also led to a downgrading of the forecast arrival of Koreans to just 19 percent of the amount forecasted prior to the Korea's economic crisis. Other markets expected to deteriorate are Thailand, Hong Kong, Japan, and Taiwan.

Consumers in those economies that remained relatively strong, or those in countries with fixed exchange rates, were able to afford more travel. For example, the number of visitors to Singapore from Australia, China and India was up by 10.6 percent, 7.2 percent and 2.6 percent, respectively, in the first quarter of 1998. However, the general pattern was one of decline. The number of arrivals in Singapore from Japan was 31 percent lower in the first quarter of 1998 compared to the same period a year before, and the total number of visitors to Singapore declined by 20 percent.

Effects on the Forecast Traffic Levels

There are signs that the market might be about to enter the recovery phase. Thai Airways, Singapore Airlines, Malaysian Airlines, Japan Airlines and ANA increased revenue passenger kilometres (RPK) marginally in 1998 as compared to 1997. The Association of Asia Pacific Airlines reported that its members had a 2.3 percent growth in passengers for the month of September in 1998 as compared to the same month in 1997 and that the average load factor increased from 68 percent to 72 percent. These positive figures have continued through to early 1999. Notably, revenue passenger kilometres increased by 4.3 percent, reflecting the greater importance to the airlines of long haul, international flights. Thailand, for example, has succeeded in attracting more tourists from outside the region, especially from Europe. It appears that the market growth is driven largely by low prices, while yields are suffering.

Prior to the financial crisis, IATA predicted that air traffic in the Asian region would grow by 7.7 percent a year to 2001, but it has revised this to 4.4 percent per annum and 5-6 percent on international routes.[2] Boeing (1999) adjusted down Asia's GDP growth forecast from 4.1 percent per year in its 1998 forecast to 0.7 percent per year for the 1998-2002 period, stating that high growth will resume after 2002. As consumer confidence returns, and as economic growth strengthens, it is clear that Asia will again be one of the main driving forces of air traffic growth globally. Airbus is similarly optimistic that growth will re-emerge in Asia's travel markets within the next five years. Boeing now predicts that over the 1999-2008 period, the worldwide air passenger traffic will grow at an average of 4.7 percent per year (adjusted down from 5 percent per year growth for the 1998-2007 period as predicted in its 1998 CMO because of the depth of the Asian economic crisis) while cargo traffic will grow at an average 6 percent per year.

Boeing's forecasts in its 1999 CMO show the following breakdown of air passenger traffic growth between Asia-Pacific and each region of the world for the 1999-2008 period:

Intra-regional:	6.6% per year
Africa:	5.8% per year
Europe:	6.3% per year
North America	5.6% per year
Middle East:	4.6% per year
Latin America	2.7% per year

In addition, the Boeing forecasts provide the average annual growth rates of air passenger traffic for each region of the world for the 1998-2017 period the Boeing forecasts show the following average annual growth rates of air passenger traffic for each region of the world (Exhibit 9-5).

Some economists point out that the fundamental strengths of Asia are its plentiful supply of labour with increasingly high skill levels, the capability to leverage growth with proven technology, government policies that support export activity and provide necessary infrastructure. A less optimistic view is that there are major political and institutional barriers in Asia inhibiting further development and that it will take time to resolve these problems (Walton, 1997).

9.2 Financial Implications of, and Airlines' Responses to, the Economic Crisis

The economic crisis immediately placed Asia's airlines under severe financial stress. Airlines that relied on domestic and intra-regional traffic were the most exposed, but several carriers were suffering losses even before July 1997. Garuda Indonesia and Korean Air (KAL), for example, had accumulated large operating losses. KAL's net loss for 1996/97 was US$280.7 million while its competitor Asiana Airlines recorded a loss of US$281.4 million. The costs of servicing loans and leases mostly were in hard currencies so that the currency devaluation escalated debt levels. Korean Air had more than 90 percent of its debt in foreign currencies and its debt rose to US$5.5 billion, more than six times its equity. Korean Air

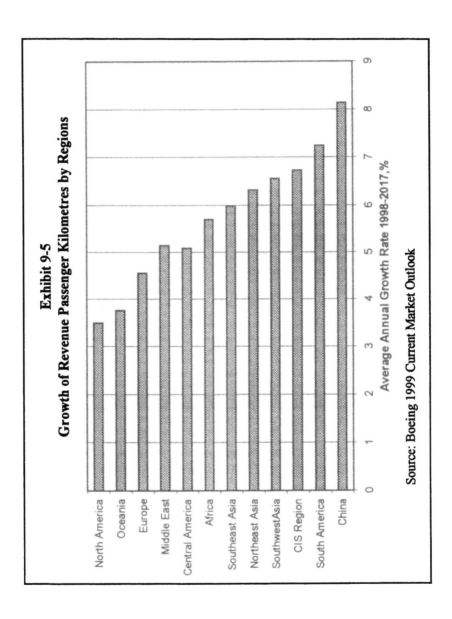

Exhibit 9-5
Growth of Revenue Passenger Kilometres by Regions

Source: Boeing 1999 Current Market Outlook

revealed in February 1998 that it had a 'paper' loss of US$900 million as a result of the devaluation of the Won, although subsequent strengthening of the Won improved the situation.

Philippine Airlines (PAL) had embarked upon a fleet renewal and expansion program prior to the onset of the economic crisis and found itself committed to financing costs of US$29 million each month. By the middle of 1998, the airline's management had decided to downsize, triggering a costly dispute with its pilots that led to 5,000 employees being laid-off. In September 1998, Philippine Airlines went into 'protected bankruptcy' after incurring a loss of US$157 million in the previous six months. In its attempts to restructure its finances, PAL attracted the interests of Northwest Airlines, Lufthansa, and EVA. The most serious proposal was by Cathay Pacific to take a 40 percent stake in PAL, but this floundered on the issue of control. PAL's rehabilitation program shifted to high gear in June, 1999 after an infusion of US$200 million in new capital by owner Lucio Tan.

Sempati Air, a second tier carrier in Indonesia, went into liquidation in June of 1998. One month later, Merpati Nusantara suspended its services. In total, 9 airlines went out of business across Asia (including South Asia) in the first twelve months of the economic crisis (Bonassies 1998). Several more carriers continue to operate with large debt burdens, but the IMF's guidelines make it difficult for governments to rescue their airlines within the strict budgetary conditions of the bailout packages. The economic crisis in Asia immediately placed other Asia Pacific's airlines under severe financial stress as well. Air New Zealand, with 13 percent of its operations in Asia, reduced its profit projection for fiscal year 1997/98 from NZ$200 million to NZ$150 million after its revenue fell by 20 percent in December 1997. Exhibit 9-6 documents some of these impacts.

Few airline managers in Asia have had to deal with falling traffic levels let alone financial problems of this magnitude. The airlines clearly needed to restructure their finances and rid themselves of excess capacity, but they also needed to develop broader strategies to take them through the remainder of this deep recession. We now turn to these strategies.

Capacity and Fleet Decisions

One of the first actions in any industry suffering a downturn in demand is to reduce capacity. This response is difficult in the airline business because cancelling flights can damage long-term marketing prospects while not resulting in significant savings. Much depends on whether capacity can be

Exhibit 9-6
Sample of Financial and Managerial Consequences
of Asian Economic Crisis

Date	Airline	Event
December 1997	Korean Airlines	Ends plans to offer shares. Employees use bonuses to buy stock to protect current management after the Government allows up to 50% foreign ownership
February 1998	Korean Airlines	US$900 million dollar foreign exchange loss due to 40% devaluation of the Won
March 1998	Air New Zealand	Announces its profits for 97/98 fiscal year to fall from prior forecast of NZ$200 million to NZ$150 million
	All Nippon Airways	Predicts loss of US$25.2 million for financial year ending 31 March 1998 compared to net profit of a similar amount in previous year. Announces a 3-year plan to restructure the airline and reduce costs. Salaries of pilots and managers reduced by 3% and staffing levels to be cut by 1,000 over the 3 years. Airline faced subsequent strike action.
	Bouraq Air	Suspends 300 staff on extended leave on 50% pay and announces plans to suspend another 900 employees
	Cathay Pacific Airways	Revealed profits for calendar year 1997, were US$217 million, 56% lower than the previous year after load factors declined from 74% to 68%. Cathay announces intention to sell 7 B747-200 aircraft to reduce capacity and lays off 40 flight engineers in 1998. Lays off 760 ground staff on January 19
	Garuda Indonesia	Announces it is selling non-core businesses (hotels, travel agencies and spare parts) and is selling up to 25% of its fleet to reduce its capacity
	Japan Airlines	Writes off US$1.2 billion of losses by reducing the value of shareholdings and loans to subsidiaries and by reducing shareholder equity
	Seaega Airlines	Malaysian start-up suspended its operations after preparing to operate to several Asian and Australian airport

Exhibit 9-6
Sample of Financial and Managerial Consequences
of Asian Economic Crisis (continued...)

Date	Airline	Event
	Sempati Air	Staff levels reduced by 60% (1,400) and 2 of its 4 A300-B4's impounded in Malaysia for failing to meet lease and maintenance payments
	Thai	Cutting costs by 6 million Baht
	Japan Air System	To cease employing ground staff and plan to reduce staff by 500 over 3 years. Wage rates and managers salaries to be held constant while flight times for cockpit crews to be reduced
	Vietnam Airlines	Government rejects proposal to increase fares and calls for a strategy to improve performance
April 1998	Air New Zealand	Downgraded its profit projection for the current fiscal year by 25%
	All Nippon Airways	Pilots pursue industrial action in opposition to 15% cut in salaries and ANA cancels services to the U.S., Hong Kong and Europe
	Korean Air	Announces record loss of US$246 million for 1996/97 and intends to raise US$640 million through the sale of and lease-back of aircraft and aircraft-secured loans, but still has orders for 11 new deliveries in 1998
	Thai Airways	Record loss of US$578.3 million in quarter ending December 1997 due mostly to currency devaluation
June 1998	Ansett Australia	Announces a US$9 million loss in the March quarter and attributes this to the Asian economic crisis
	Singapore Airlines	Announces interest in bidding for a share of Thai Airways International if (when) it is privatised. Other airlines expressing interest include BA, UA, Air France, Qantas Airways
July 1998	Sempati Air	Enters into liquidation and ceases operations
	Cathay	Plans to reduce staff by 1,500 in 1998
	Merpati	Closes down
August 1998	Philippine Airlines	Attempts to downsize led to a strike by 600 pilots sacked after striking for higher pay. Airline close to bankruptcy and severely reduces network and services. Plans to reduce workforce by 14,000

Source: Chin, Hooper and Oum (1999)

allocated elsewhere on the airline's network or whether aircraft can be leased or sold to other airlines. In any case, labour costs are difficult to adjust in the short-run and airlines have to be ready to resume services once the market improves. In addition, the share of labour costs in total cost is relatively small, 10-20 percent, for most of the Asian airlines, and as such, any further cutback would not likely improve their unit costs very much. If the service involves a congested airport, airlines also are concerned about losing access to valuable slots.

Most airline costs cannot be avoided once the schedule is set and, since this tends to occur twice a year, the scope for managerial action is limited for a period of up to six months. Under 'normal' circumstances, the typical response to a temporary fall in traffic is to increase marketing expenditure and to use promotional prices more aggressively. For example, Qantas and British Airways have offered deep discounts of up to two-thirds off their fares to London, Frankfurt or Rome. Qantas provided an additional bonus of a free domestic round-trip to any one of 10 Australian cities. Singapore Airlines gave its passengers the first night's accommodation on a stopover in Singapore for US$1, and additional nights have been priced as low as US$30.

In the current situation, demand has fallen by as much as 80 percent in some markets and the prospects of a quick recovery are poor. The airlines have no alternative but to reduce their services on the worst-affected routes and to pull out of some routes completely, relying on code-share partnerships to maintain a presence. Where possible, the capacity is being diverted to other routes, but those airlines that are most exposed to intra-Asian routes recognized that they needed to reduce the size of their fleets.

The most immediate decision has been to defer deliveries of new aircraft. In March 1998, the airlines in Asia Pacific had orders for 179 narrow-bodied aircraft valued at US$7.5 billion and 254 wide-bodied aircraft valued at US$33 billion. Korean Air and Asiana alone had orders for 76 new aircraft. Taking into account the orders placed by leasing companies that are attributable to Asia, it was estimated that the Asian carriers were accountable for one-quarter of all orders for wide-bodied aircraft in 1998 (Williamson 1998). Close to half of all orders for B747-400 and B777 aircraft have been made by Asian carriers. Boeing indicated that the Asian economic crisis would have an impact on deliveries of 150 aircraft, including 60 wide-bodied aircraft.

Those airlines in the most difficult situations have put aircraft up for sale either to reduce capacity or to make way for deliveries of new aircraft. In many cases, the sale of older aircraft has helped to provide the necessary funds to pay for new aircraft, while in others the sale-and-leaseback option has been necessary to reduce debt levels. Exhibit 9-7 illustrates the breadth and depth of airline activities in this regard. In total, 91 aircraft were sold or leased by Asia's airlines to outside Asia during 1998, but seat capacity increased by 1.3 percent overall as 140 new aircraft were delivered.[3] The prediction is that net capacity will increase by another 1 percent in 1999. Even with the depressed market conditions, it seems likely that capacity growth will fall behind demand. Since load factors are already high on many routes, this will give airlines the opportunity to improve their yields.

Forming Alliances and Using Alliance Partners

Alliance formation can be a tactical response or it can be part of a longer-term strategy. Since the onset of the Asian economic crisis, there has been widespread alliance activity. For example, when Qantas Airways ceased operation to Seoul, it turned to its code-share partner, Asiana Airlines, to carry its passengers. As Qantas enters the Australia-Argentina market, it intends to use its own aircraft while benefiting from its code-share agreement with Aerolineas Argentinas. This provides Qantas with an opportunity to use its capacity while also benefiting Aerolineas Argentinas as the latter can use the aircraft released from the Australian market to meet a growing demand for the Argentina-Europe services. Exhibit 9-8 lists alliance development involving Asian Carriers during the 1997-98 period.

While the economic crisis in Asia has placed the carriers based in the region under financial stress, the process of globalisation of the airline industry has taken a major step forward. The Star Alliance, built around United Airlines and Lufthansa, has gained momentum with the addition of Air Canada, Varig, Thai Airways, Air New Zealand, All Nippon, and Ansett Airlines with a likelihood that Singapore Airlines will become a full member of Star soon.

The formation of OneWorld between American Airlines, British Airways, Cathay Pacific, Canadian Airlines, Iberia and Qantas in September of 1998 was presented as a brand name for a global network. Among other measures, the partners have code share agreements with each other and share frequent flier plans. Cathay's dominance at the new Chek Lap Kok Airport in Hong Kong gives OneWorld a strong position in Asia. Asiana code shares with Qantas to Cairns and with American to Los Angeles, New York, San Francisco and Seattle.

Exhibit 9-7
Fleet Decisions in the Wake of the Asian Economic Crisis

Date	Airline	Decision
December 1997	Garuda Indonesia	Fails to pay US$8 million on A330 leases. Government provides sovereign guarantees so that airline can take delivery of 17 B737's
February 1998	Asiana Airlines	Sold 4 B767s plus one other aircraft in a leaseback deal and deferred plans to buy 5 new aircraft in 1998
	Korean Airlines	Already had sold 4 A300s and a B747-400 to its creditors under a nine-year leaseback arrangement. It also sold a B747-200 freighter and was arranging the sale of 3 more aircraft
March 1998	All Nippon Airways	Adding 10 aircraft in next financial year (to 31 March 1999) and selling 6 with 5.7% increase in ASK's. Its new aircraft will be its first 4 B777-300s, 2 B777-200s, 2 B747-400s and 2 A321s
	Asiana Airlines	Defers delivery of 2 B777. Cancels plans to order 5 more aircraft in 1998, sells some of existing fleet and leases them back. Selling 3 B767-300ER and 2 B747-400
	Cathay Pacific Airways	Defers options on 16 Boeing and 9 Airbus aircraft and places 7 B747-200's up for sale to reduce capacity
	Garuda Indonesia	Attempting to sell 4 DC-10, 4 B747 and 5 A300B4 after failing to pay US$8 million on A330 lease payments
	Korean Air	Sells some of its fleet and leases them back. Replacing its F100 and MD82 fleets used on domestic and regional routes with B737 -800 and -900 aircraft in expectation of growing regional market
	Malaysia Airlines	Sells a DC-10, an A300B4 and 6 737-500 to finance deliveries. Negotiating with Delta to take over commitments to buy 4 B777s.
	Philippine Airlines	Delaying aircraft deliveries and cancelling 6 B747-400 orders, and delaying 3 of its 8 A320s orders by one to two years. Said to be Asia's first default on an order
	Saega Airlines	Cancels orders for 5 A320 aircraft in suspending operations because of the state of the Malaysian economy
	Thai Airways	Delaying deliveries of 17 Airbus and Boeing aircraft and intends to sell 3 DC-10s and 5 BAe. Followed this within the month by ordering 5 A300-600Rs, 3 A330-300s and one B777-300 and one B747-400 for deliveries in 1999-2000

Exhibit 9-7
Fleet Decisions in the Wake of the Asian Economic Crisis
(continued...)

Date	Airline	Decision
April 1998	Asiana Airlines	Defers deliveries of A330-200s to 1999 or later. By May it has put all of its aircraft up for sale. Air Europe purchased 2 B767-300s, Delta one B767-300, QF one B747-400 and UPS a B767 freighter
	Bouraq Air	Returns 2 B737-200s to lessors
	Cathay Pacific	Intends to take delivery of 12 new aircraft but will sell 5 B747-200s. However, the lack of buyers has resulted in a decision to lease the aircraft
	Garuda Indonesia	Sells 4 B747-200s and 5 A300s and then leases them back. Planned to sell 5 DC-10-30s, 4 B747-200s, 5 A300B4s and 5 Fokker-28s. Withdrew DC-10-30s from market after failing to attract offers at its going price.
	Malaysian Airlines	Continuing to negotiate delivery swaps and refinancing for 11 B777-200s and –300s and 9 B747-400s. Outcome is deferral of 5 B747-400, cancellation of one B777-300 and delayed deliveries of B777-200s
April 1998	Philippine Airlines	To sell 9 A300B4s and 11 B737-300s. Deferred 6 B747-400 (3 of which were due in 1998) and 3 A320 deliveries. Intends to reduce its fleet from 54 to 21 aircraft
	Sempati Air	By March, Sempati had only 5 of its 25 aircraft in operation. Returns 4 A300s and 7 Fokker-100s to lessors prior to ceasing operations in June
	Singapore Airlines	Defers deliveries of 3 B777s and one B747-400. These actions are part of a re-adjustment of orders. Announces plans to increase capacity over next 3 years at 4% per annum. Orders 3 B747-400s and 2 B767-300s, and buys 3 B747-400s from other airlines, plus another new B767-300. Leases B747 Classic and plans to sell 4 A300s as part of a plan to confine fleet to B737, B767 and B747. Argues 300-seat aircraft (B777 and A340) have no place in its strategy.

Exhibit 9-7
Fleet Decisions in the Wake of the Asian Economic Crisis
(continued...)

Date	Airline	Decision
May 1998	Qantas Airways	Announces plans to increase capacity over next 3 years at 4% per annum. Orders 3 B747-400s and 2 B767-300s, and buys 3 B747-400s from other airlines, plus another new B767-300. Leases B747 Classic and plans to sell 4 A300s as part of a plan to confine fleet to B737, B767 and B747. Argues 300-seat aircraft (B777 and A340) have no place in its strategy.
July 1998	Air Macau	Leases one A320 to TAP Air Portugal for six months with an option to continue the lease
	Asiana	Sells one B747-400 and 3 B767-300s and considering sale of B767F
	Cathay Pacific	Leases 2 B747-300s to Virgin Atlantic but unable to lease 3 more
	Dragonair	Delayed delivery of one A320 to mid-2000
	EVA Air	Delays delivery of two B747-400s in 1999 and three in 2000
	Garuda Indonesia	Continues to cancel leases and has re-negotiated leases with Boeing for 6 MD-11s and is discussing a similar plan with Airbus in relation to 6 A330s
	Merpati Nusantara	Returns 11 leased aircraft and plans to return 2 more A310s and suspends operations
	Philippine Airlines	Plans to sell 13 aircraft as a part of a wider plan to dispose of 40 aircraft out of its current fleet of 54 planes. 27 aircraft appear likely to be sent back to lessees
	Thai Airways	Unable to finance deliveries for 5 A300s, one B747 and one B777 due in 1998
September 1998	Air New Zealand	Arranges to sell 5 B747-200 aircraft to Virgin over next few years (replacement capacity not announced)
	Ansett	Announces that B743s will be returned to SIA in 1999
	Asiana	Returns B767s to GECAS. Sells one B744 to QF
	Cathay	Plans to retire 7 B747-200s
	Garuda	Returns MD11s and A330s to lessor
	Korean Air	By the end of 1998, will have returned most aircraft on operating lease to lessors; Refinancing assistance from GECAS and Boeing - new B737 deal completed

Source: Chin, Hooper and Oum (1999)

Exhibit 9-8
Alliance Developments Involving Asian Carriers 1997-1998

Airline	Decision
Air Philippines and U-Land (Taiwan)	Air Philippines leases 3 MD82's from U-Land to meet an increase in demand following the pilots' strike at PAL. U-Land reported to be considering a 35% stake in Air Philippines
All Nippon Airways, Lufthansa & United Airlines	ANA enters code share agreement with Lufthansa and UA in preliminary move to join Star Alliance
Ansett Australia, Air New Zealand & Singapore Airlines	Code share agreement between Ansett and Singapore Airlines was approved by Australia's Competition and Consumer Commission. Approval granted for joint marketing and pricing along with code sharing to and from Australia.
Asiana Airlines & American Airlines	Formed a 'strategic business alliance' involving code sharing and shared frequent flyer programme
Cathay Pacific Airways	Becomes a founding member of OneWorld Alliance
China Airlines & Singapore Airlines	SIA purchasing up to 10% of CAL's shares along with code share and frequent flyer programme initiatives. Cooperation will include cargo operations, ground handling, fleet planning and training of crews.
China Eastern Airlines	Enters code share agreement with American Airlines
Japan Airlines & American Airlines	Code sharing on routes between Japan and U.S.
EVA & Continental	Code share and shared frequent flyer programmes
China Airlines & American	Code share and shared frequent flyer programs
Malaysian Airlines & Swissair	Alliance on 3 weekly flights from Kuala Lumpur to Zurich
Qantas Airways	Enters code share agreement with Aerolineas Argentinas as part of a strategy to re-deploy capacity from Asia
Singapore Airlines, Delta & Swissair	Alliance breaks down as Singapore Airlines moves closer to Star Alliance. MOU signed in Dec. 1997
Thai Airways	Air France, British Airways, Lufthansa, Qantas & Singapore Airlines bidding for 25% share of Thai
Philippine Airlines	Northwest Airlines evaluating an investment in PAL
Air China	Enters code share with Northwest Airlines between Beijing and Detroit

Source: Chin, Hooper and Oum (1999)

A third major global group has coalesced around KLM, Northwest Airlines and Continental Airlines and includes Malaysian Airlines. Key members of these global groups have been active in signing up partners in Asia. Korean Air is linked to Delta Air Lines, which, in turn, is allied with Air France, Austrian, Sabena and Swissair.

Some of these alliances will help the Asian carriers in the short-term, in some cases, with the injections of new capital, through sharing the use of resources, by consolidating traffic and improving utilisation of aircraft and by strengthening market positions. However, they clearly have long-term significance. For example, Thai Airways is a member of the Star Alliance, but Singapore Airlines' realignment with Star led to an announcement by Lufthansa that it would shift its South East Asian focus from Bangkok to Singapore. The subsequent decision by the Government of Thailand to privatise Thai Airways has attracted major world airlines as potential bidders. The current wave of alliance formation in Asia will help the region's airlines rationalise services, to consolidate traffic and to improve their finances, but they will also play a role in deciding the competitive strength of the major global alliances at key Asian hubs.

Decisions Involving Exit from Markets and Flight Frequency

The key service decisions that managers have made are to change frequencies, to suspend services and to withdraw from routes. Exhibit 9-9 shows the nature and extent of the key decisions being made by airlines about service in Asia in the wake of the Asian economic crisis. Other dimensions of service are difficult to target at particular routes in the short and medium term. For example, Indonesia's airlines made an application to increase domestic fares from 11 to 16 cents (US) per seat kilometre. When the Minister for Transport and Communications refused to grant permission, Sempati Air immediately cancelled services on 10 domestic and 4 regional routes (including to Taiwan). The Minister intervened to stop Merpati Nusantara, a stated owned airline, from taking similar actions on 80 of its routes. Instead, the Minister agreed it could phase out routes with load factors under 30 percent. Garuda Indonesia then cut its international flights by 30 percent and domestic flights by 26 percent.

Exhibit 9-9
Service Level Changes Resulting from the Asian Economic Crisis

Airline	Decision
Air New Zealand	Reduces services between New Zealand and Indonesia, Thailand and Malaysia and cancels services between New Zealand and South Korea. In February it announces plan to reduce capacity on Asian routes and redeployment to Australia-New Zealand market. Add more non-stop flights from Australia to the U.S.
Air Philippines	Granted international rights in June 1997 but announces it is concentrating on domestic routes
All Nippon Airways	Ceases flights to Australia as it rationalises the use of its slots at Narita Airport to increase flights to the U.S. following new air services agreement between Japan and the U.S.
Ansett International	Cancels services between Australia and South Korea and ceases daily flights from Sydney to Kuala Lumpur via Jakarta after the load factor and yields fell
Asiana Airlines	Ceases 15 flights on 6 international routes
Astro Airlines	Taiwanese new entrant to launch services to 3 cities in the Philippines
British Airways	Withdraws direct services to South Korea. Reduces Hong Kong services form 16 to 14 per week
Cathay Pacific Airways	Plans to increase frequency to Australia, UK, Europe and North America
Continental Airlines	The first foreign carrier to suspend services to Seoul (Seoul to Guam and Saipan)
EVA Air	Adds regional routes (Osaka and Phnom Penh, plus 2 European ports) and closes loss-making routes (Bangkok and Kuala Lumpur), expands cargo operations and attempts to build a sub-hub at Kaohsiung
Garuda Indonesia	Ceasing services from Jakarta to Manila, Bangkok and Canton and from Medan to Kuala Lumpur and Singapore as international flights are cut by 30% and domestic flights by 26%
Harlequin Air	Affiliate of Japan Air System plans to commence DC-10 charters from Fukuoka to Australia and add Hawaii, Bali, Kathmandu and others from mid-February 1998
Korean Airlines	Dropped 48 flights on 21 international routes

Exhibit 9-9
Service Level Changes Resulting from the Asian Economic Crisis
(continued...)

Airline	Decision
Merpati Air	Terminated services on 63 of its 423 domestic routes in February after earlier being refused permission to cease operations on 80 routes
Northwest Airlines	Increasing its Tokyo-Los Angeles flights from 7 per week to 10 to connect with onward services to other parts of Asia
Orient Thai Airlines	Ceasing suspends all domestic flights until permitted to fly to major cities
Philippine Airlines	Drastically cuts services after sacking 600 pilots. Number of domestic and international airports served reduced to 22
Qantas Airways	Cancels services between Australia and South Korea. Reduces services between Australia and Indonesia, Thailand and Malaysia. Adds more non-stop flights from New Zealand to the U.S.. Developing route to Argentina as part of a strategy to re-deploy capacity from Asia. Further reductions in services in June 1998 to Japan, Vietnam, Thailand and Indonesia (Jakarta) and redeployment of capacity to the U.S., India, Singapore, Indonesia (Bali) and New Zealand. Introduces B747 services on some long haul, domestic routes in peak season. Operates charter services in Europe for Princess Cruises (P&O).
Sempati Airways	Ceased services on 10 domestic routes and 4 regional routes (including Taiwan) in September 1997 after rupiah devalued by 10% in one month. By March it has contracted to only 10 routes, before ceasing in June
Singapore Airlines	Reduced flights to Bangkok, Jakarta, Surabaya, Kuala Lumpur and Seoul and increased flights to Australia, Europe, India and the U.S. Uses smaller aircraft on flights to Bangkok and planning similar action for Hong Kong and Seoul.
Swissair	Ceases services to Seoul after load factor falls below 30%
Turkish Airlines	After commencing an Istanbul – Seoul service two months earlier, Turkish Airlines cancelled the service late in 1997
Thai Airways International	Reduces frequencies on routes to South Korea and on other badly affected routes

Source: Chin, Hooper and Oum (1999)

Qantas Airways, Ansett International and Air New Zealand were among a number of airlines to suspend services to South Korea early in 1998 when the number of Korean residents travelling abroad fell sharply. Asiana Airlines ceased 15 flights on 6 international routes, including services on unprofitable long-haul routes to Frankfurt, Brussels, Vienna and Istanbul, and the routes to Honolulu and Macau, as well as a cargo flight to Delhi. Korean Air also dropped 48 flights on 21 international routes.

Airlines have also been seeking opportunities to re-deploy their capacity. Singapore Airlines and Cathay Pacific Airways both implemented plans to increase the frequency of flights to Australia. All Nippon Airways was quick to take advantage of its improved access to the U.S. market under the new Japan-US air services agreement reached early in 1998. After South Korea entered an open skies agreement with the U.S., Korean Air was able to increase its frequency to San Francisco, Chicago and Los Angeles.

9.3   Regulatory Responses to the Economic Crisis

The airlines clearly are realigning their capacity while setting themselves up to take best advantage of global airline groups and to pursue sustainable productivity improvements. Nevertheless, the impacts of the economic crisis are so great that there will be a temptation for at least some governments to provide their airlines with direct financial support and to protect them from competition. It seems likely that some of the financiers backing the airlines in their sale-and-leaseback deals believe that, ultimately, the governments of Asia will ensure that their airlines remain solvent (Williamson, 1998). In addition, equipment suppliers and their governments will be supportive of distressed airlines as shown by the success Korean Air has had in securing a low interest loan of US$254 million (Mann, 1998). The Government of Indonesia already has given sovereign guarantees in order for Garuda Indonesia to complete its purchases of aircraft, and has injected $US1.2 million for Merpati Nusantara Airlines to buy aircraft spare parts, ensuring its continued operations in remote areas in eastern Indonesia.

Governments could also step in to protect their airlines from competition, setting back the pace of liberalisation in Asia. However, there are good reasons to believe these options will not be favoured and that the pressure to liberalise will grow even stronger. One force working in this direction is that the governments of Asia have larger problems to solve and their ability to support airlines making large, on-going losses is limited. For Indonesia, Thailand and South Korea, the International Monetary Fund has imposed conditions on its support programmes that further constrain such actions. For example, one of the IMF conditions is to privatize Thai Airways. The IMF's prescription is to open up markets, to allow foreign investment and to privatise government business undertakings. Furthermore, as airlines are eager to gain access to stronger markets in Europe and North America, they need injections of funds, and they want to take part in global alliances.

Exhibit 9-10 documents recent regulatory responses in Asia. Though the airlines continue to suffer financial stress, the emerging picture is that the governments of Asia are accelerating regulatory reform in the direction of liberalisation. For example, South Korea signed an open skies agreement with the U.S. in June 1998. South Korea was looking to expand access for its airlines in the U.S.-Korea market, but it also valued the greater access to beyond flights to Latin America. The U.S.-Korea agreement with change-of-gauge options for the U.S. carriers will also place pressure on Japan to proceed further down the liberalisation path.

At the same time, the Government of Thailand decided to allow private airlines to fly on domestic routes without limitations and to liberalize its international markets progressively. In June 1998, the Government of Thailand amended the 1954 Aviation Act to allow for up to 49 percent ownership of Thai carriers by foreign investors. The Government of South Korea also lifted the restriction on foreign ownership of its airlines to 50 percent. Many other countries in Asia have been active in renegotiating air service agreements in order to give their airlines flexibility to adjust their networks.

Governments in the region have become concerned about safety standards in the wake of the economic crisis. In June 1997, a Boeing 737 operated by China Southern Airlines crashed at Shenzhen killing 35 passengers. Sempati Air had a crash in the next month with 30 fatalities. In August 1997, a Korean Air B747 crashed into a mountain-side in Guam with 228 people losing their lives and, in the next month, a Garuda Indonesia A300 crashed at Medan due to poor visibility associated with forest fires. In that case, 234 people died, and this was followed in December by another 104 fatalities with another airline crash in Sumatra. This time it was Silk Air. February was a difficult period with crashes

Exhibit 9-10
Regulatory Responses in Asia Pacific 1997-1998

Economy	Decision
China	Considering raising the limit on foreign ownership of airlines to 40% from 35% equity and 25% voting rights in an attempt to attract more capital
China & Malaysia	Memorandum of Understanding to allow Malaysian Airlines and any other Malaysian carriers to operate 64 flights each week to six cities in China and Chinese airlines can fly 64 flights a week to 3 Malaysian cities
China & Philippines	Memorandum of Understanding to allow airlines from Philippines to fly to Guanghzhou and Shenzhen in addition to Beijing, Shanghai and Xiamen. China's airlines now permitted to fly to Manila and one other airport
China & South Korea	Agreement for increase from 42 flights each week on 11 routes to 111 flights on 27 routes to take effect in first half of 1998
Japan & Taiwan	Agreement on increased airline services after 10 years of negotiation, increasing capacity and access to Osaka for EVA Airways
Japan & U.S.	Agrees to a liberalized air service agreement with the U.S. to give ANA greater access to the U.S.
Japan	Continues to deregulate its domestic airline industry in the first half of 1998. Restrictions on pricing removed and new entrants given slots at Haneda Airport
New Zealand & Singapore	Enter a liberal open skies agreement with no foreign ownership restrictions and free capacity on fifth freedom
Pakistan	Announces a new limited open skies policy and a restructuring of Pakistan International Airlines

Exhibit 9-10
Regulatory Responses in Asia Pacific 1997-1998 (continued...)

Economy	Decision
South Korea & the U.S.	Open skies agreement allows airlines U.S. carriers to change gauge; gives fifth freedom flights beyond Seoul provided they originate in or terminate in the U.S.. Gives Korea's airlines access to Latin America via the U.S.; Korea increases the foreign ownership of airlines to 50%
Taiwan	Civil Aeronautics Administration puts pressure on airlines to merge to achieve greater stability and improvement in safety
Taiwan & the U.S.	Open skies agreement gives greater access to the U.S. and beyond for China Airlines and EVA and alliances emerging with American and Continental
Thailand	Transport and Communications Minister announces new policy to deregulate domestic market and to allow multiple designation on international routes, commencing with regional services (e.g. Indonesia). Restrictions on charter flights by Thai and foreign airlines to be lifted
Thailand	Government increases foreign ownership limit in Thai by 10% to 30% and announces intention to reduce its own stake in Thai Airways from 79.5% to 49% or lower (pressures from IMF)

Source: Chin, Hooper and Oum (1999)

involving Cebu Pacific (104 dead) and China Airlines (205 dead). The recent Korean Air's freighter crash in Shanghai in April 1999 invoked serious concerns by regulators not only in South Korea but also in many parts of the world. The government in Taiwan has taken measures to encourage its airlines to merge to improve their economic and safety positions.   In the Philippines, the Government suspended Grand Air's operating licence after repeated violations of the regulations, and indicated it was increasing its surveillance on all carriers, including Philippine Airlines. The exact causes of some of these crashes still are unknown and it would be unreasonable to attribute them all to economic factors, but the publicity given to safety has posed further challenges for the airlines and regulators alike.

9.4 The Asian Economic Crisis and Cost Competitiveness of Asian Carriers

What impact does the current economic crisis have on the Asian airlines' cost competitiveness? In order to answer this question properly, it is necessary to discuss the factors determining cost competitiveness. Airline cost competitiveness depends on input price levels and productive efficiency - lower input prices and/or improved efficiency enhance cost competitiveness. Oum and Yu (1998) found that except for the Japanese carriers, Asian airlines have enjoyed unit cost advantages relative to their North American or European competitors. Most of this unit cost advantage comes from the lower labour and other purchased materials and services input prices in terms of international currencies.

In particular, before the Asian economic crisis, Singapore Airlines and Korean Air had unit cost advantages relative to American Airlines by about 16 percent and 23 percent, respectively, although both of these Asian carriers have slightly lower productive efficiency than American Airlines. Thai Airways had only about a 9 percent unit cost advantage relative to American Airlines although they enjoy extremely low input prices. This is because Thai Airways' productive efficiency is very low. Cathay Pacific has lost its unit cost advantage because it no longer enjoys any input price advantage relative to those in the U.S.

As shown in Exhibit 9-1, since June 1997, Asian currencies were subject to varying degrees of devaluation. For example, between June, 1997 and December, 1998 the currencies of Indonesia, Malaysia, Philippines, Thailand and South Korea were devalued by 76 percent, 34 percent, 32 percent, 31 percent and 27 percent, respectively. The immediate effect of this currency devaluation was to increase the unit cost advantages of the Asian carriers. Although aircraft financing cost and fuel prices are not likely to change in U.S. dollar terms, labour and purchased materials and services prices in U.S. dollar, are likely to decrease due to the currency devaluation. As stated earlier, because of the currency devaluations and the depressed travel demands in Asia, the Asian carriers have lowered their air fares substantially in terms of U.S. currency. For example, Japan Airlines filed an application with the Transport Ministry in May 1998 to reduce fares by up to 50 percent on round trip flights from the U.S. to Japan.[4] In the medium to long term, it is clear that currencies of these Asian countries are likely to be re-valued to their previous levels. Inflationary pressure, which will follow their economic recovery, will increase labour and other input prices in those countries. Thus, unless the carriers improve productivity, cost competitiveness in the medium to long term for these carriers are not likely to improve beyond the levels they enjoyed prior to the economic crisis.

However, the current economic crisis has been and will continue to force Asian airlines to restructure their networks and operations for improved efficiency while forcing their governments to open up markets for competition as discussed in previous section. These changes are likely to bring two positive outcomes to Asia's air transport industry. First, the pro-competitive changes are likely to induce Asian carriers to improve productive efficiency to the level the major carriers in North America enjoy. Second, in the process of restructuring the industry, one or two mega carriers may emerge in Asia. For example, Singapore Airlines may be able to participate in the ownership of one or more major Asian carriers.

JAL, ANA, or Cathay Pacific may use this opportunity to expand their markets into one of multiple hub networks by acquiring equity stakes in other Asian carriers. Because of these positive changes anticipated in the industry (and not because of their currency devaluations), in the medium to long term, the Asian economic crisis is likely to help Asia's air transport industry. In the very short run, the sudden collapse of air travel demand in the region has severely harmed the bottom line of all Asian airlines. In the short run, the devalued Asian currencies will prolong the period in which Asian carriers enjoy unit cost competitiveness relative to the North American or European carriers. Although it will take several more years to get their economies back to the pre-crisis level, air travel demands are expected to increase rapidly once the economic recovery begins in earnest (Boeing, 1999).

9.5   Conclusions

The Asian economic crisis has generated a considerable amount of pessimism about the prospects for the region's airlines. The carriers were highly exposed to currency risks and to a slowdown in traffic growth. While the economic crisis is reducing the amount of intra-regional traffic, the currency devaluations will stimulate more trips to Asia from North America and Europe. By virtue of the reduced costs of employing labour and other local inputs, the cost competitiveness of Asia's airlines has improved. The immediate problem facing the carriers is how to refinance their debt, how to realign their services and how to match capacity with the weaker demand conditions. As this adjustment process continues, the world's mega-alliances are consolidating their positions so that Asia's airlines are faced with difficult choices from a weakened position.

It seems likely that the end result will be fundamental changes in the way Asia Pacific aviation markets operate in terms of alliances, hubs, ownership, and regulation. Given the depth of the economic crisis in some Asian economies, a desire to protect national airlines would be understandable. However, the longer-term challenge for the Asian carriers is to turn the economic crisis into an opportunity to develop strategies that give them a sustainable competitive advantage. This will be achieved through productivity improvements that would be pursued most aggressively under competitive conditions. At the same time, competitive airlines need access to new markets. Attempts to protect airlines could have negative consequences including pressure from the IMF and the international financial community.

The evidence is mounting that the airlines themselves want the flexibility to adjust capacity, to enter new routes, to enter into alliances and to attract investment from the world's major carriers. Some governments have shown a willingness to liberalize competition, to privatize and to relax foreign ownership restrictions. Far from being a flight back to protection, the Asian economic crisis appears to have shifted air transport policies of Asian governments far more to the direction of liberalization. It is our opinion that this is entirely consistent with the long term interests of Asian carriers because the increasingly competitive market place will induce them to stay cost competitive and efficient, as well as inducing them to modernize management practices.

Notes

[1]   The discussions of this chapter draw heavily from Chin, Hooper and Oum (1999).
[2]   As this book was being written, IATA released the World Air Transport Statistics, which indicates that the 1998 IATA airlines made a net profit of US$3.1 billion on total revenue of US$142.7 billion on scheduled international services, a drop of US$1.9 billion compared with 1997. Passenger and cargo traffic grew only at 2.2 percent, lower than forecast.
[3]   *Air Transport World*, December 1998 issue, page 14.
[4]   'JAL cuts fares 50 percent on U.S. to Japan routes', *Financial Post*, May 9, 1998, page 23.

10 Summary and Conclusions

In this study, we first reviewed the history, current status and future prospects of the Asia Pacific aviation markets and industry in chapter 2. Chapters 3 and 4 focused on the development of airline industry and major air carriers in specific countries in the Northeast Asia, Southeast Asia and South Pacific sub-regions. The current regulatory approaches in various Asia Pacific countries are reviewed and discussed in chapter 5. The recent trends of international aviation reform and the U.S. open skies initiatives are examined in chapter 6, while the external and internal challenges facing the Asia Pacific airlines and governments and the proposed approaches to liberalization in the Asia Pacific region are discussed in chapter 7. Chapter 8 identifies congestion problems associated with the airports and air traffic control and air navigation systems and the capacity expansion projects in various parts of the Asia Pacific region. Chapter 8 also discusses the issues associated with each nation's desire to develop one or more passenger and freight logistics super hubs. The recent Asian economic crisis and their short and long term effects on Asian carriers, markets and regulatory practices are discussed in chapter 9.

Before the recent Asian economic crisis, the Asia Pacific airline market has been growing much more rapidly than North American or European markets. Despite the temporary reduction and slowdown in the growth of markets caused by the economic crisis, experts are unanimous in that the high growth in the Asian markets will resume within a few years. This implies that it is simply a matter of time before the Asia Pacific market becomes the largest aviation market in the world. In particular, virtually all forecasting agencies agree that the Asia Pacific share of the world's total international scheduled air passenger volumes will exceed 50 percent some time between year 2010 and 2015. Total scheduled international traffic to, from and within the Asia Pacific region was 134 million passengers in 1995, and is forecasted to reach 393 million passengers by 2010. The strongest sub-regional growth for the next two decades is forecasted to be within Northeast Asia, followed by Southeast Asia.

Substantial fifth freedom rights have been granted to foreign carriers by Asian countries. These rights have mainly been granted to U.S. carriers, but some intra-Asian rights have been negotiated. Singapore and Bangkok together comprise the largest share of fifth freedom flights within Asia, accounting for 36 percent of all fifth freedom traffic. About 31 percent of the fifth freedom sectors within Asia are operated by Asian airlines while U.S. carriers operates another 30 percent. Moreover, large variations exist for 5th freedom traffic among the airports. In 1993, Kuala Lumpur handled 60,000 passengers while Tokyo dealt with 2.3 million fifth freedom passengers. Bangkok, Singapore, Seoul, Taipei and Hong Kong are the other cities that experienced strong fifth freedom traffic volume.

Despite the dramatic growth of the aviation market during the last two decades, major airlines in the Asia Pacific region are still relatively small in terms of network size, traffic volume, and operating revenue as compared to their U.S. and European counterparts. They also lag behind the U.S. carriers in terms of productivity and efficiency. With their traditional advantage of low input prices starting to diminish, carriers in the region need to explore strategic opportunities in all potential markets in order to establish their positions in the increasingly globalizing air transport market. However, many parts of the region such as China, Indonesia, and Vietnam are still in the early stage of air transport development.

Air transport market in Northeast Asia has experienced tremendous growth during the past two decades. It now accounts for 11.5 percent of the global market. International scheduled airline passenger traffic in the Northeast Asia is predicted to grow from 88.8 million passengers in 1997 to 110.6 million in 2002. The intra-regional traffic within Asia Pacific is expected to grow faster than the inter-continental traffic.

Japan has been the region's dominant travel market in the past, but its share of total Asia Pacific traffic (domestic and international travel combined) is expected to decrease from 30.8 percent in 1995 to 20 percent in 2010. China is expected to replace Japan as the leader in total scheduled air passenger volume as the combined share of China and Hong Kong in the total Asia Pacific traffic is expected to increase from 23 percent in 1995 to 32 percent in 2010.

Total international scheduled passenger traffic to and from South Korea is predicted to increase from 11.3 million passengers in 1993 to 42.8 million passengers in 2010. Taiwan is also expected to have strong growth in international traffic: 13.5 million passengers in 1993 to 56.8 million in 2010. In both South Korea and Taiwan, a large part of this growth is expected to be sustained by their residents' outgoing travel and transfer passengers at their airports.

During the 1980's and 1990's, the air transport market in the Southeast Asia and South Pacific region has experienced tremendous growth, and is expected to continue to have strong growth in the future. During the next two decades, the total international scheduled passenger traffic in Southeast Asia and South Pacific is expected to grow at an average rate of 5.3 percent and 5.1 percent, respectively. Majority of this traffic is within the Asia Pacific region.

Tourist inflow is a very important component of the air traffic in the Southeast Asia and South Pacific region. In many parts of the region such as Malaysia and Philippines, the growth in inbound visitors contributed to traffic growth more than resident outgoing traffic. On the other hand, in Thailand before the economic crisis, the resident outgoing travel and Bangkok Airport transfer traffic had increased more rapidly than the incoming air visitor arrivals. Singapore and Thailand are the dominant markets in the region at present. However, Vietnam is expected to have the strongest growth over the next two decades, followed by the Philippines and Thailand.

The Asia Pacific region hosts a number of the world's major carriers, including Japan Airlines, ANA, Singapore Airlines, Korean Air, Cathay Pacific, China Airlines, Thai Airways, Philippine Air Lines, Malaysian Airways, Garuda, Qantas, China's Big-3 carriers, Air New Zealand, etc. Singapore Airlines is one of the most efficient carriers in the world, and has been able to remain profitable even in the midst of the recent Asian economic crisis. Other carriers in the region have experienced various degrees of financial difficulties, some long before the economic crisis. For example, Garuda started to lose money heavily in the mid-1980's, and has not been able to become truly profitable since then. Philippines Airlines was forced to seek bankruptcy protection in the fall of 1998. Privatization of national flag carriers appears to be an ongoing trend in the region.

Singapore Airlines, Korean Air, Qantas, and Cathay Pacific are efficient (high productivity) carriers relative to other carriers in the region, and some European carriers. However, they are somewhat less efficient than some of the major U.S. carriers. Korean Air and Qantas achieved the most productivity improvement since the mid-1980s. Singapore Airlines and Korean Air also enjoy lower input prices, and thus, unit cost advantages relative to other major carriers in the world. Cathay Pacific appears to have lost its previous unit cost advantage relative to the U.S. carriers due to the rising input prices in Hong Kong. Japanese carriers have about 50 percent higher unit cost relative to the U.S. carriers despite the fact that they have improved productivity substantially since the mid-1980s. This is mainly due to the appreciation of Japanese currency. Although Thai Airways enjoys a huge input price advantage, the carrier is not cost competitive vis-à-vis its competitors in Asia mainly because of its inefficiency (lower productivity). Similarly, Chinese carriers enjoy huge input price advantages, but they are not competitive in the market place because of their lack of modern management expertise and bureaucratic inefficiency.

The recent economic crisis in Asia has generated a considerable amount of pessimism about the prospects for the region's airlines. While the economic crisis has reduced traffic volume originating in the region, the currency devaluations will stimulate more trips to Asia from North America and Europe. Although the short run effect of the economic crisis is to reduce or slow down air traffic growth from the previous forecast volumes, it is expected that the traffic growth at least from year 2002, will be as high as previously forecasted.

By virtue of the reduced prices of labour and other local inputs due to the Asian currency devaluations, the cost competitiveness of Asian airlines has in fact improved because of the economic crisis. The immediate problem facing the carriers is how to refinance their debt, how to realign their services, and how to match capacity with the weaker demand conditions. As these adjustments continue, the world's mega-alliances are consolidating their positions so that Asia's airlines are facing difficult choices from a weakened position.

It seems likely that the end result will be fundamental changes in the way Asia Pacific aviation markets operate in terms of alliances, hubs, ownership, and regulation. Given the depth of the economic crisis in some Asian countries, a desire to protect national airlines would be understandable. However, the longer-term challenge for the Asian carriers is to turn the economic crisis into an opportunity to develop strategies that will give them a sustainable competitive advantage. This will come about through productivity improvements that would be pursued most aggressively under competitive conditions. At the same time, competitive airlines need access to new markets in order to have a strong growth. Therefore, the attempts to protect airlines could have negative consequences.

The evidence is mounting that Asian airlines themselves want the flexibility to adjust capacity, to enter new routes, to form alliances, and to attract investment from the world's major carriers. Some governments have shown willingness to liberalize competition, to privatize and to relax foreign ownership restrictions. Far from being a flight back to protection, the Asian economic crisis appears to have shifted air transport policies of Asian governments to the direction of liberalization. It is our opinion that this is entirely consistent with the long-term interests of Asian carriers because the increasingly competitive market place will induce them to stay cost competitive and efficient, and to modernize management practices.

The Asia Pacific countries have restrictive bilateral agreements between themselves. Many of these bilateral agreements control frequency and capacity of flights, route and carrier designations, and prices in the intra-regional markets. On the other hand, U.S. and European carriers are demanding more fifth freedom traffic rights in the region. Their efforts have stirred anger among many Asian countries. U.S. bilateral relations with Japan, Hong Kong, and the Philippines were stalled over this issue. The Association of Asia Pacific Airlines (formerly Orient Airlines Association) has taken centre stage in coordinating a regional campaign against fifth freedoms to stop 'uncontrolled competition from outside', arguing that U.S. fifth freedoms within Asia are comparable to cabotage in the U.S.. However, the region's position on fifth freedom is far from being uniform. Attitudes vary by geographical locations and with nations' development strategies.

There have been movements towards liberalizing aviation among some ASEAN countries, in line with the group's move towards a trading environment akin to the European Union. For example, Malaysia, Thailand and Indonesia have recently signed an open-skies agreement, the first among Asian countries. The agreement covers the northern states of West Malaysia (Perak, Penang and Kedah), Southern Thailand, and Western Indonesia. The move, initiated by Malaysia, paves the way for airlines of the three countries to mount services within their respective boundaries with no restriction on capacity or frequency.

In addition, the BIMP-EAGA (Brunei-Indonesia-Malaysia, Philippines-East Asia Growth Area), born in 1994, is hoping to become the first Asian group to forge a joint airline system. Furthermore, 13 Asia Pacific countries met in January 1996 to explore regional cooperation in aviation and greater openness in air service markets and possibly coexistence of multilateral and bilateral approaches to liberalization.

Despite these developments to cooperate intra-regionally on air transport matters, the effort to move towards a regional open-skies agreement has not made much progress. Consequently, unlike the U.S. or European carriers, none of the Asia Pacific carriers has efficient traffic collection and distribution networks that cover the entire Asia Pacific region effectively. Essentially, each airline has a fairly extensive network to and from its home base, but does not have any hubs in other parts of Asia. Therefore, when looking for Asian alliance partners, major U.S. or European carriers have an incentive to align with more than one Asian carrier. Since these Asian carriers are mutual competitors in the Asian market, they are at disadvantage in joining a global alliance network such as STAR alliance or OneWorld alliance. When two or more Asian carriers join a global alliance network, other senior partners in the alliance may be in a position to exploit the rivalry between Asian carriers and thereby extract better conditions for the alliance.

The recent U.S. open skies initiatives directed to Asian countries pose a major threat to Asian carriers. The U.S. wishes to negotiate for unlimited freedom for setting up hubs (star-burst operations) in Asian countries so that the U.S. carriers can provide high frequency services using smaller aircraft in the intra-Asian markets while enjoying economies of larger aircraft in the trans-Pacific routes. Since most Asian countries already have far more liberal bilateral agreements with the U.S. than among themselves, if one or two countries situated in strategic locations in Asia (such as South Korea, Taiwan and Hong Kong) agrees to give unlimited seventh freedom rights or change of gauge rights to the U.S., it will lead to dismantling of the system of restrictive bilateral agreements among Asian countries. This would happen because Asian carriers would be far more constrained in their own intra-Asian markets than the U.S. carriers.

Therefore, it is desirable for Asian countries to establish open skies or near open skies agreements with their neighbours before allowing the U.S. carriers to establish major hubbing operations in Asia. This would induce the major Asian carriers to set up an efficient multiple-hub airline network that would cover the entire continent, thus enhancing their status in the global alliance networks. In addition, this would allow the Asian carriers that are based in the countries where input prices are rising fast to shift their significant cost bases to the countries which enjoy low input prices. This would help prolong the period in which Asian carriers enjoy unit cost advantage vis-à-vis the U.S. or European carriers.

Since it is difficult to achieve consensus among all Asian carriers and governments, liberalization among like-minded countries should be negotiated first. The following measures may be fruitfully applied for liberalization within Asia.

Link air bilateral negotiation with negotiations on goods and services trade issues, and thereby, increase opportunity for each country to make tradeoffs between air transport and other sectors of the economy.

Attempt to design a compensation solution for the carriers in developing countries who will be disadvantaged in an open skies environment and/or to build temporary safeguards for protecting those carriers.

Establish future timetables for achieving various liberalization stages of open skies in order to get carriers and governments prepared for the eventual open skies.

Liberalize easier items first such as freight, charter, services to/from secondary airports, foreign ownership of secondary carriers, etc.

In recent years, the lack of airport slots and serious air space congestion in the Asia Pacific region have constrained the speed and the extent of air transport liberalization. This problem will need to be solved by expanding capacity and/or increasing effective capacity of given facilities through efficient pricing and management. In particular, it is necessary to resume capacity expansion and upgrading projects for airports, air traffic control and air navigation systems, which were put on, hold by many countries because of the economic crisis.

Because of the anticipated economic benefits of having a successful passenger and freight logistics hub, every country in Asia wishes to develop one or more continental logistics hubs to dominate the region. In order to achieve this goal, many Asian economies have completed major investments, or are in the process of construction, or have plans to expand airport capacity. However, capacity expansion alone is not sufficient to make an airport a successful integrated passenger and freight logistics hub.

In order to succeed as an integrated logistics hub, in addition to providing the needed capacity for airports and related facilities, the government and business communities must work together to achieve the following:

Deregulation of domestic air transport industry and market.

Liberalization or open skies regime for bilateral air services agreements with as many neighbouring countries as possible.

Creation of pro-business and pro-consumer environment.

Enhancing international competitiveness of carriers.

Providing cheap and efficient information and telecommunications technology and services.

Attracting many integrated logistics firms and multi-national firms to locate their bases.

Government's strong commitment to remove red-tapes, hidden costs, and bureaucratic delays as well as streamline customs and immigration procedures and simplify documentation for passenger and freight clearance.

Establishment of free trade zones for light assembly, labeling, and transshipment.

Ensuring that educational and training systems are in place to provide quality manpower needed by the industry.

Most countries in Asia appear to realize these needs and are making progress to deal with these issues. However, many countries are torn between their interests in establishing successful logistics hubs and their flag carriers' interests when considering liberalization of air transport markets.

The plain fact of the matter is that unless you are willing to open your own markets, there will not be open skies or liberalized agreements with your neighbours. In the short run, liberalization may hurt inefficient flag carriers while being helpful to developing the integrated logistics hub. However, in the long run the decision does not need to involve such a trade-off. Competitiveness of the flag carriers may well be enhanced, as they must improve efficiency in order to stay alive in competition with foreign carriers. In addition, when they have free access to neighbouring markets, these carriers will be able to set up efficient traffic collection/distribution systems for the entire regional market. This will also improve productivity and cost efficiency of home carriers. A collective liberalization of air transport markets or 'open skies' in Asia is likely to create a win-win situation in the long run.

Under an open skies regime in Asia, most airlines in Asia are likeley to set up a multiple hub network, much the same way as the major U.S. carriers, by retaining and strengthening a home country airport as a super hub and building secondary hubs in other parts of the region. Therefore, in order to build a continental super-hub a country needs to attract foreign carriers to build secondary hubs in the country as well as to retain super hub bases of its own carriers. In order to accomplish this, the country will need to have open skies with Asian neighbours as well as with the countries outside of the region.

Bibliography

Abeyratne, R.I.R. (1996), *Legal and Regulatory Issues in International Aviation*, Transnational Publishers Inc. (Irvinton-on-Hudson, New York).

Ahn, J. and Z. Ahmed (1994), 'South Korea's Emerging Tourism Industry', *Cornell Hotel and Restraurant Administration Quarterly*, 35.2 (April), 84.

Air Transport Association of America (1995), *International Affairs Memoranda*, April 13, July 27, and December 8, Washington, D.C.

Bailey, M. (1993), 'Asia's new airlines,' *EIU Travel and Tourism Analyst*, No. 3, 4-18.

Ballantyne, T. (1997), 'Open Skies in Asia: Today's US Perspective', *Orient Aviation*, June/July, 22-26.

Ballantyne, T. and I. Muqbil (1994), 'Asia Close to United Front; Aviation Industry Works to Prevent Liberalization.' *Airline Business* 10.11 (November): 18.

Bangsberg, P.T. (1995), 'Hong Kong-Taiwan Air Talks Head for Wire.' *The Journal of Commerce* 24 October 1995: 3B.

Barnard, B. (1996), 'EU Wins the Right to Cut Air Deals with the US', *Journal of Commerce*, June 18, 1996, 1A.

Baum, J. (1995), 'Simplified Character.' *Far Eastern Economic Review* 158.16 (20 April 1995): 68-69.

Boeing Commercial Airplane Group (1997), *Current Market Outlook*, Seattle, Washington, March.

Boeing Commercial Airplane Group (1998), *Current Market Outlook*, Seattle, Washington, March.

Boeing Commercial Airplane Group (1999), *Current Market Outlook*, Seattle, Washington, March.

Bonassies, O. (1998), 'Asia-Pacific Jet Capacity: Strategies Revises as a Harsh Period Looms', *Avmark Aviation Economist* 15 (7), 19.

Bowman, L. (1994), 'Pumping Up the Volume', *Airfinance Journal*, July/August, 37-39.

Bowen, J.T. (1997), 'The Asia Pacific Airline Industry: Prospects for Multilateral Liberalisation', in C. Findlay, C.L. Sien and K. Singh eds. *Asia Pacific Air Transport. Challenges and Policy Reforms*, Institute of Southeast Asian Studies, Singapore, 123-153.

Bowen, J.T. and T.R. Leinbach, (1995), 'The State and Liberalization: the Airline Industry in the East Asian NIC's'. *The Association of American Geographers* 85 (3), 468-491.

Brunker, D., C. Findlay, and P. Forsyth (1989), 'Comparative Advantage in Airline Services', Australian National University, Canberra.

Bureau of Transport and Communications Economics (1993), *The Progress of Aviation Reform*, BTCE Report No. 81, Australian Government Publishing Service, Canberra, Australia.

Burgess, L. (1993), 'US, Hong Kong Reach Air Accord Favorable to American Carriers.' *The Journal of Commerce*, 2 October 1995: 3B.

Burgess, L. (1995), 'With Bilateral Agreements Secured, FedEx Plans More Hong Kong Service.' *The Journal of Commerce*, 2 October 1995: 3B.

Button, K. (1997), 'The Effects of Open Skies in the European Union', a paper presented at the *First Asia Pacific Transport Conference: International Transport Liberalization, 5-6 December, Seoul, Korea.*

Button, K, and D. Swann (1991), 'Aviation Policy in Europe', in K. Button ed. *Airline Deregulation: International Experiences*, David Fulton Publishers, London, UK, 85-123.

Camdessus, M. (1999), 'Economic and Financial Situation in Asia: Latest Developments', a paper presented at the *IMF Asia-Europe Finance Ministers' Meeting*, Frankfurt, Germany, January 1996.

Chang, Y-C, and G. Williams (1999), 'Civil Aviation Development in the Taiwan Area', a paper presented at the *3rd Air Transport Research Group Conference*, Hong Kong, June, 1999.

Chang, S.C. and S. Wu (1997), 'ROC, Malaysia to Sign Open Skies Pact' *Central News Agency*, June 24, 1997.

Chen, H., and A. Zhang (1999), 'The Prospect of Air Transport Industry and Strategies for Open Skies in China', a paper presented at the *3rd Air Transport Research Group Conference*, Hong Kong, June, 1999.

Chin, A. (1997), 'Implications of Liberalization on Airport Development and Strategy in the Asia-Pacific', *Journal of Air Transport Management*, Vol. 3, NO. 3, 125- 131.

Chin, A., P. Hooper and T.H. Oum (1999), 'The Impacts of the Asian Economic Crisis on Asian Airlines: Short Term Responses and Long-Run Effects', *Journal of Air Transport Management*, Vol. 5, No.2 (April), 87-96.

Chow, G. and T. D. Heaver (1993), 'Logistics Systems in an Age of Technological, Political, and Market Change: Implications for Spatial Development', *Regional Development Dialogue*, vol.14, No.2, 1993.

Daniels, J. D. and L. H. Rodebaugh (1995), *International Business:*

Environment and Operation, New York: Addison-Wesley Publishing Company Inc.

Davies, R.E.C. (1997), *Airlines of Asia since 1920*, Paladwr Press (McLean: VA).

De Leon, P. M. (1990) ed., *Air Transport Law and Policy in the 1990s: Controlling the Boom*, Martinus Nijhoff Publishers (Dordrecht, the Netherlands).

Debbage, K. (1994), 'The International Airline Industry: Globalization, Regulation, and Strategic Alliances', *Journal of Transport Geography*, Vol. 2, No. 3.

Doganis, R. (1994), 'The impact of liberalization on European airline strategies and operations,' *Journal of Air Transport Management*, Vol. I, No.1 15-25.

Donoghue, J.A.(1996a), 'Getting a Grip on the Gripes.' *Air Transport World*, 33.2 (February 1996): 51-53.

Donoghue, J.A. (1996b), 'And One to Grow on', *Air Transport World*, 33.4 (April 1996): 61.

Dresner, M.E. and M.W. Tretheway (1987), 'Policy Choices for Canada in International Air Transport', in Ian Gregory ed. *International Business/Gestion Internationale*, Proceedings of the Administrative Sciences Association of Canada, Vol. VIII (8), 83-94.

Dresner, M. and M.W.Tretheway (1992), 'Modelling and Testing the Effect of Market Structure on Price', *Journal of Transport Economics and Policy*, Vol. 26 (2), May, 171-184.

Edwards, A. (1995), *Asia-Pacific Travel Forecast to 2005*, London: the Economic Intelligence Unit.

Feldman, J. (1999), 'Cathay's Conservative Challenge', *Air Transport World*, April, 53-54.

Fenner, S. (1998), 'Lifting the 7th Veil', *Airline Business,* October, 1998.

Feng, C.-M. (1998), 'Recent Development of Taiwan's Regulatory Changes in International Air Transport', *Journal of Air Transport Management*, Vol. 4, No. 3, 165-167.

Findlay, C., G.C. Hufbauer, and G. Jaffi (1996), 'Aviation Reform in the Asia Pacific', in Hufbauer, G.C. and C. Findlay ed. *Flying High; Liberalizing Civil Aviation in the Asia Pacific*, Institute for international Economics, Washington D.C. November, 1996, 11-32.

Flint, P. (1989), 'Korean Air: Riding the Tiger.' *Air Transport World* 26.10 (October 1989): 24.

Flint, P. (1991), 'All Dressed Up and No Place to Go; Asiana Airlines.' *Air Transport World* 28.5 (May 1991): 22.

Gallacher, J. (1995), 'Coming Clean; Aeropolitics; US Needs to Lead the Way to Multilateral Liberalization in Air Transportation Policy.' *Airline Business* 11.3 (March 1995): 30.

Gallacher, J. (1997), 'Partners for Now: Airline Alliances', *Airline Business*, Vol. 13, No. 6, June 1997.

Gethin, G. (1998), 'Lufthansa Holds China Talks as SIA Prepares to be a Star', *Flight International,* November 11, 1998.

Gill, T. (1999), 'Jockeying for Position', *Airline Business*, June, 57-70.

Haanappel, P.P.C. (1984), *Pricing and Capacity Determination in International Air Transport*, Kluwer Law and Taxation Publishers (Deventer, The Netherlands).

Havel, B. F. (1997), *In Search of Open Skies: Law and Policy for a New Era in International Aviation*, Kluwer Law International (The Hague, the Netherlands).

Hill, L. (1997), 'Bilateral Ballistics', *Air Transport World*, 2/97, 53-61.

Holloway, N. (1996), 'Dogfight Over the Pacific.' *Far Eastern Economic Review* 159.11 (14 March 1996): 56-57.

Hooper, P. (1996), 'Airline Markets in Asia: the Domestic/International Regulatory Interface', in H. Dick ed. *Towards 'Open Skies'; Airline Deregulation in the Asia-Pacific*, Institute of Transport Studies, the University of Sydney, Australia.

Hooper, P. and C. Findlay (1998), 'Developments in Australia's Aviation Policies and Current Concerns', *Journal of Air Transport Management*, Vol. 4, No.3 169-176.

Hur, J. (1995), 'Role of the New Seoul Airport in the Northeast Asian Aviation Market,' a paper presented at the World Conference on Transportation Research (July, 1995; Sydney, Australia).

International Air Transport Association (IATA) (1995), *Asia-Pacific Air Transport Forecast 1980-2010*, Geneva, Switzerland.

IATA (1997*), Asia/Pacific Air Traffic – Growth and Constraints*, Geneva, Switzerland.

IATA (1998), *Passenger Forecast 1998-2002*, Geneva, Switzerland.

Ionides, N. (1999), 'China Codeshare', *Airline Business*, June 1999.

Jennings, M (1992), 'US-Asia Bilaterals Under Pressure; International Air Transport Liberalization.' *Airline Business*, July 1992: 24.

Jones, D (1998), 'Going Up', *Airfrance Journal*, July/August, 1998.

Julius, D. (1996), 'International Aviation and National Competitiveness', London: British Airways, June 1996.

Kasper, D.M. (1988) *Deregulation and Globalization: Liberalizing*

International Trade in Air Services. An American Enterprise Institute/Ballinger Publication.

Kayal, M. (1997a), 'US, Japan Aim for a Blueprint in Final Round of Aviation Talks', *Journal of Commerce*, April 9, 1997, 1A.

Kayal, M. (1997b), 'Britain, Japan: Formidable Head Winds to Open Skies', *Journal of Commerce*, April 14, 1997, 1A.

Kayal, M. (1997c), 'European Airlines Flying in Open Skies', *Journal of Commerce*, March 31, 1997, 1B.

Kim, J. (1996), 'The Regulation and Growth of Civil Aviation in South Korea', in Hufbauer, G.C. and C. Findlay ed. *Flying High; Liberalizing Civil Aviation in the Asia Pacific*, Institute for international Economics, Washington D.C. November, 1996, 63-77.

Kim, J. (1997), 'An Economic Effect of Duopoly Competition in Domestic Air Transport Market in Korea,' a paper presented at the Air Transport Research Group (ATRG) Conference of the WCTR Society (June, 1997; Vancouver, Canada).

Kim, J. and H-K. Ha (1998), 'Liberalization in Korea's Airline Industry and Current Concerns', *Journal of Air Transport Management*, Vol. 4, No. 3, 145-154.

Kissling, C. (1998), 'Liberal Aviation Agreements – New Zealand', *Journal of Air Transport Management*, Vol. 4, No. 3,177-180.

Knibb, D. (1993), 'Asia's Little Tigers: an Expanding Group of Regional Carriers is Taking a Greater Share of Intra-Asia Passenger Traffic as Markets Matures', *Airline Business*, October, 1993.

Knibb, D. (1994), 'Asia Pacific: the fifth dimension; the region's airlines oppose fifth freedom rights for foreign carriers', *Airline Business*, Vol. 10, No. 12, December 1994.

Knibb, D. (1997a), 'China Puts on the Squeeze: Tries to Limit International Airlines', *Airline Business*, Vol. 13, No. 1, January 1997.

Knibb, D. (1997b), 'Chinas Start Strait Talking; China and Taiwan Discuss Direct Flights between Two Countries', *Airline Business*, Vol. 12, No. 5, May 1997.

Knibb, D. (1998), 'Asians have Private Ideas', *Airline Business*, April, page 10.

La Croix, S. J. (1998), 'The Future of Civil Aviation in Northeast Asia', in *A Study on the Economic Integration of Northeast Asia*, Korea Institute for International Economic Policy, 21-39.

Lee, J. W. (1993), 'The Sky's the Limit; China's Aviation Sector,' *The China Business Review* 20.3 (May 1993): 12.

Lee, Y. H. (1997), 'The Economic Effects of Airline Deregulation and the Open Sky Policy of Korea', a paper presented at the Air Transport Research

Group (ATRG) Conference of the WCTR Society (June, 1997; Vancouver, Canada).

Li, M.Z.F. (1998), 'Air Transport in ASEAN: Recent Developments and Implications', *Journal of Air Transport Management*, Vol. 4, No. 3, 135-144.

Li, M. Z. F. (1999), 'Asia-Pacific Airlines amidst the Asian Economic Crisis', a paper presented at the *3ʳᵈ Air Transport Research Group Conference*, Hong Kong, June, 1999.

Mackey, M. (1997), 'Goodbye to the Orient', *Air Transport World*, 1/97, 54-55.

Machey, M. (1998), 'A Dragon Exposed', *Air Transport World*, January, 57-58.

Magnier, M. (1996), 'Diversity Tests Asian Air Policies', *The Journal of Commerce,* 2 February 1996: 2B.

Marin, P.L. (1995), 'Competition in European Aviation: Pricing Policy and Market Structure', *The Journal of Industrial Economics,* Vol. XLIII, No. 2, June, 141-159.

McFadyen, J. (1997), 'U.S.-Japan Civil Aviation: Prospects for Progress', Working Paper No. 97-2, Institute for International Economics, Washington, D.C.

McShane, S. and R. Windle (1989), 'The Implications of Hub and Spoke Routing for Airline Costs and Competitiveness', *Logistics and Transportation Review*, Vol. 25 No.3, 209-230.

Morrison, S. and C.Winston (1986), *The Economic Effects of Airline Deregulation*, Brookings Institution, Washington, D.C.

Murakami, H. (1997), 'Japan's Attitude toward Bilateral Agreements', an unpublished manuscript, the University of British Columbia, Vancouver, Canada.

Nagata, K. (1997), 'Initiatives for Liberalization of Asia-Pacific Aviation', a speech made at the Air Transport Research Group (ATRG) Conference, June 25-27, 1997, Vancouver, Canada.

Naveau, J. (1989), *International Air Transport in a Changing World*, Martinus Nijhoff Publishers (Dordrecht, the Netherlands).

O'Conner, K. and P. Dempsey (1996), 'Airport Capacity in Pacific Asia: Regional and Local Problems and Responses', in H. Dick ed. *Airline Deregulation in the Asia Pacific*, Institute of Transport Studies, University of Sydney, Australia.

Oum, T.H. (1997), 'Challenges and Opportunities for Asian Airlines and Governments,' in C. Findlay, C.L. Sien, and K. Singh eds. *Asia Pacific Air Transport*, published jointly by Australia-Japan Research Centre, Chartered Institute of Transport, Pacific Economic Cooperation Council

(PECC) of Singapore, 1-20.

Oum, T.H., and J.H. Park (1997), 'Airline Alliances: Current Status, Policy Issues, and Future Directions,' *Journal of Air Transport Management*, Vol. 3, No.3, 133-144.

Oum, T.H., J.H. Park, and A. Zhang (2000), *Strategic Alliances of the World's Major Airlines*, Elsevier Sciences, forthcoming.

Oum, T. H., W.T.Stanbury and M.W. Tretheway (1991), 'Airline Deregulation in Canada and its Economic Effects,' *Transportation Journal*, Vol.30, No.4 (summer, 1991), 4-22.

Oum, T. H., A.J. Taylor, and A. Zhang (1993), 'Strategic airline policy in the globalizing airline networks', *Transportation Journal*, Vol.32, No.3, 14-30.

Oum, T.H. and A.J. Taylor (1995), 'Emerging Patterns of the Intercontinental Air Linkages and Implications for International Route Allocation Policy', *Transportation Journal*, Vol.34, No.4, 5-27.

Oum, T. H. and M. W. Tretheway (1984), 'Reforming Canadian Airline Regulation', *Logistics and Transportation Review*, Vol.20, No.3, September.

Oum, T . H. and M. W. Tretheway (1990), 'Airline Hub and Spoke System,' *Journal of Transportation Research Forum*, Vol. 30, 380-393.

Oum, T. H., W.G. Waters II and J. Yong (1990), *A Survey of Recent Estimates of Price Elasticities of Demand for Transport*, The World Bank Policy Planning and Research Staff Paper, Washington, D.C., 1-56.

Oum, T.H., W.G. Waters II and J. Yong (1992), 'Concepts of Transport Demand Elasticities and the Recent Estimates: An Interpretative Survey', *Journal of Transport Economics and Policy*, Vol.26 (May, 1992), 139-54; 164-69.

Oum, T.H. and C.Yu (1995), 'A Productivity Comparison of the World's Major Airlines,' *Journal Of Air Transport Management*, Vol. 2, No.3/4, 181-195.

Oum, T.H. and C.Yu (1998), 'Cost Competitiveness of the World's Major Airlines: an International Comparison,' *Transportation Research A*, Vol. 32, No. 6, 407-422.

Oum, T.H. and C.Yu (1998), *Winning Airlines: Productivity and Cost Competitiveness of the World's Major Airlines*, Kluwer Academic Publishers (Boston, MA).

Oum, T.H., A. Zhang and Y. Zhang (1995), 'Airline Network Rivalry,' *Canadian Journal of Economics*, vol.28, December, 836-57.

PECC (Pacific Economic Cooperation Council), *Air Transport in the Asia-Pacific: Challenges, Opportunities and Options*, Conference Summary

Report, 9-11 July, 1995, Singapore.

Prasad, R. (1999), 'Privatization Hopes Survives Indian Politics', *Air Transport World*, June, page 29.

Reed, D. (1999), 'Swissair to Sell Stake in Delta Air Lines, Team with American', *Fort Worth Star-Telegram*, June 24, 1999.

Samuel, M. (1996), 'Evolution and Prospects for Asia's Airline Industry: Key Policy and Liberalisation Issues for the Future', Keynote Address delivered *at Pan-Asian Summit on Aircraft Finance & Commercial Aviation*, 27 May 1996, Hong Kong.

Shin, D.C. (1996), 'The Aviation Cooperation between the Koreas Preparing for the Reunification', an unpublished manuscript.

Shon, Z-Y, Y-H Chang, and C-C Lin (1999), 'Direct Flights across Taiwan Strait and Their Impacts on Eastern Asian Air Transportation Market', a paper presented at the *3rd Air Transport Research Group Conference*, Hong Kong, June, 1999.

Singh, K. (1996), 'The Liberalization of Civil Aviation', a speech delivered in Tokyo, May 1996.

Singh, K. and M.Z.F. Li (1997), 'The Development of Aviation Hubs in Asia-Pacific', a paper presented at *The Industry Forum of Second APEC Transportation Ministerial Meeting*, Victoria, Canada, June 24, 1997.

Tabakoff, N. (1997), 'China: Air Pact Set to Follow Strait Shipping Deal', *South China Morning Post*, February 14, 1997.

Taneja, N.K. (1976) *The Commercial Airline Industry*. Lexington Books (Lexington, MA).

Thurston, S. (1999), 'Delta Air Lines Forms Alliance with Air France', *The Atlanta Journal and Constitution*, June 23, 1999.

Toh, R.S. (1998), 'Towards an International Open Skies Regime: Advances, Impediments, and Impacts' *Journal of Air Transportation World Wide*, Vol. 3 No.1, 61-70.

Tretheway, M.W. (1991), 'European Air Transport in the 1990s: Deregulating the Internal Market and Changing Relationships with the Rest of the World', Working Paper #91-TRA-003, Faculty of Commerce and Business Administration, The University of British Columbia, Vancouver, Canada.

Tretheway, M.W. (1995), 'Institutional and Economic Impediments to Liberalization in Asia-Pacific International Aviation', a paper presented at Pacific Economic Cooperation Council, Air Transport Meeting, *Air Transport in the Asia-Pacific: Challenges, Opportunities and Options*,

Singapore, July 9-11, 1995.

US Department of Commerce (1997), *The Asia/Pacific Web Site*, International Trade Administration, July 1997.

U.S. Department of Transportation (1998), 'The Impact of the New US-Canada Aviation Agreement At Its Third Anniversary', a Report published by Office of Aviation and International Economics, February.

Woolward, P. (1995), 'Flying High: Foreign Investment Should Help China's Airline Industry Take Off', *The China Business Review*, July-August 1995, 9-11.

Yamauchi, H. and T. Ito (1996), 'Air Transport Policy in Japan,' in Hufbauer, G.C. and C. Findlay ed. *Flying High; Liberalizing Civil Aviation in the Asia Pacific*, Institute for international Economics, Washington D.C. November, 1996, 33-61.

Yang, Y. (1996), 'China: CAAC Expands Air Links to 9 Countries', *China Daily*, April 10, 1996.

Zhang, A. (1998), 'Industrial Reform and Air Transport Development in China', *Journal of Air Transport Management*, Vol. 4, No. 3, 155-164.

Glossary

Air Service Agreement
> An agreement, typically negotiated between two national governments, granting specified aviation rights to airlines from the countries involved.

Aviation Rights

First Freedom Rights
> The right to fly over a foreign country without landing.

Second Freedom Rights
> The right to land at specified point in a foreign country for the purposes of refueling and maintenance, but not to pick up or disembark traffic (passengers, cargo, or mail).

Third Freedom Rights
> The right to pick up traffic in home country and carry it to a foreign country.

Fourth Freedom Rights
> The right to pick up traffic in a foreign country and carry it to home country.

Fifth Freedom Rights (beyond rights)
> The right to pick up traffic in a foreign country and carry it to a third country.

Sixth Freedom Rights
> The right to carry traffic between two foreign countries via home country. This is a combination of third and fourth freedoms.

Change of Gauge
> The right to change the size of its aircraft operating on a given route.

Cabotage:
> The right to carry traffic between two points within a foreign country.

Bilateral Agreement
> Formal arrangement between two governments covering trade in air services. The phrase is often used to refer to an air service agreement.

Block Time
> Total flight time, measured from when the aircraft moves from the loading point before take-off until it stops at the unloading point after the flight.

Code Sharing
> A marketing arrangement between two or more airlines allowing a connecting flight on two or more different carriers to be displayed on the CRS as a single carrier service.

Double Disapproval
> Arrangements in bilateral air service agreements whereby fares can be disallowed only if rejected by both contracting countries.

Flag Carrier
> A country's national carrier. Countries with only a government owned airline often identify the airline as the national flag carrier.

Frequent Flyer Program
> A scheme offering flights or other benefits to travellers who fly long distance and/or often. The qualification criteria can be based on the distance travelled or the number of trips taken, and are usually weighted by the class of ticket purchased.

Hub and Spoke Network
> Traffic is collected from a number of 'spoke' or feeder points and consolidated at the hub airport prior to being redistributed out of the hub to connect with flights to another destination.

Infrastructure (aviation)
> Air traffic control facilities, runways and airport terminals.

Multi-designation
> Nomination of more than one airline to operate international air services from the home country to a particular country

Open Skies
> An agreement two or more nations that leads to free trade in aviation services, usually by eliminating entry barriers, and prohibiting government regulations of routes and capacity. At present, the U.S. open skies policy does not allow cabotage in the U.S., and is still subject to foreign ownership restrictions.

Slots
> The right to land and/or take-off from an airport at a specified time.

Stage Length
> The distance flown between taking-off and landing.

Yield
> Airline revenue per unit of traffic.

Yield Management
> Manipulation of prices to obtain the most revenue from each flight.

Index

For Product Safety Concerns and Information please contact our EU
representative GPSR@taylorandfrancis.com
Taylor & Francis Verlag GmbH, Kaufingerstraße 24, 80331 München, Germany